# The History Of Conspiracy And Abuse Of Legal Procedure

## Percy Henry Winfield

# THE HISTORY OF
# CONSPIRACY AND ABUSE
# OF LEGAL PROCEDURE

BY

PERCY HENRY WINFIELD LL.D.

OF ST JOHN'S COLLEGE, CAMBRIDGE, AND THE INNER TEMPLE,
BARRISTER-AT-LAW; LECTURER IN LAW AT ST JOHN'S
AND TRINITY COLLEGES, CAMBRIDGE

CAMBRIDGE
AT THE UNIVERSITY PRESS
1921

# CAMBRIDGE STUDIES
# IN ENGLISH LEGAL HISTORY

This series of studies has been designed as an agency for furthering scientific investigation in regard to the development of the laws of England and thus for advancing the knowledge of one of the most important aspects of British and world history. At the beginning of the work of carrying out this design it is fitting that a few words should be said about the nature of the studies, their general scope, their purpose, and the functions which they should fulfil in the life of the present day.

Two kinds of studies will be included in the series: monographs and editions of texts. Dr Winfield's illuminating study, *The History of Conspiracy and Abuse of Legal Procedure*, a work which consolidates the results of years of painstaking, skilful and learned research, is published in the present volume as the first of the monographs. This study may be taken as an indication of the general character of the monographs which are to follow. It is intended that most of the monographs shall be studies, based on original researches in manuscript and printed materials, of some special period or of some special topic; but at the same time it is hoped that certain of the studies will trace, on more general lines, broader aspects of legal evolution. Some of the monographs will embody, in appendices, select texts which explain or illustrate certain of the subject-matters dealt with by the authors. The second group of studies will consist of editions of legal-historical texts which have not been published hitherto, or which have not as yet been published in a form consonant with modern critical standards. In each one of this second group of volumes there will be explanatory notes and an introduction of some length dealing with the nature of the texts and their significance in the development of the law. While the studies thus embrace two kinds or groups of publications—monographs and editions of texts—it is not thought to be necessary or even desirable to mark off the two kinds one from the other and to characterize each one of them by a distinctive title as a separate series. Both of the groups are of the nature of studies; and they will both be published as one series under the general heading of *Cambridge Studies in English Legal History*. No undertaking can be given in advance as to the time of publication of the successive volumes in the series; but it is hoped that two volumes may be published in the course of every year.

While the separate volumes will deal with particular subject-matters, the general scope of the series as a whole will be as broad and extensive as the history of English law itself. The point of view which has been adopted in planning the series is that English law has a place in world history and not merely in insular history. The whole course of the development of historical science during the last hundred years has prepared the way for the taking of this world view-point in respect to the origin, growth, and diffusion of English law. The 18th century produced historical works of high merit and permanent value; and individual thinkers of the time, such as Leibnitz, Vico, Turgot, Herder, and Burke, made bold and fruitful contributions towards the philosophic interpretation of history as the life of humanity, ever evolving and progressing throughout the centuries by processes of growth, decay and revival, every age linked to every other. But there were several causes which impeded the growth of history as a science, chief among them being the failure of the *Aufklärung* to grasp the historical significance of religion and the middle ages, the lack of the critical faculty in dealing with the testimony and value of authorities, the almost entire absence of teaching, and the restrictions which were placed on access to historical materials and on liberty to publish results. The 19th century—the " age of the Second Renaissance," as Mr Gooch so appositely describes it in his *History and Historians in the Nineteenth Century*—brought about a sweeping change in all the conditions essential to the growth of historical science. Liberty of thought and expression, the judicial attitude of mind, and insight into the different ages of the past led to the growth of history as an independent science which gives light and guidance to all the other social sciences. In divers ways Niebuhr led the way in the placing of history upon this scientific basis; and many other historians gained inspiration from his methods and writings. In all civilized countries the new science took root and flourished. The result has been that all ages of history, all peoples, all aspects of life have been subjected to an exacting critical examination. The survey of the historian now embraces the world; and he can trace, in many of its fundamental outlines and in considerable wealth of detail, the evolution of civilization throughout all the ages.

This general progress in historical studies during the 19th and 20th centuries has included law within its scope. The legal systems of the world—in antiquity, in the middle ages and in modern times—have all been subjected to the examination of scholars trained in scientific methods of research. These studies are still in progress. Much still remains to be done; and the doing of it will take generations. But already it is possible to see certain of the main lines and characteristics of universal legal history. It is slowly coming to the consciousness of scholars that a continuous process of evolution throughout the centuries connects the laws of antiquity with those of medieval and modern times.

The scientific study of the laws of the Babylonians, Egyptians, Hebrews, Greeks, Romans and other peoples of antiquity has been facilitated by the recent discovery of codes and other legal sources; and already a vast literature deals with the laws of those ancient communities. Hitherto these studies have been concerned for the most part with the development and characteristics of the separate systems and with a comparison of the several systems one with another. The continuity in ancient legal history has not as yet received the attention it deserves. But scholars have already perceived that the historical relations of the several ancient peoples led, by processes of conquest and the diffusion of civilization, to the spread of laws and to the incorporation of their elements in other systems. Ihering, the great Romanist, held the view that, if we would search for the origins of Roman law, we must go back to Babylon; and we have learned, since Ihering wrote the *Vorgesichte der Indoeuropäer*, that the Baby-

lonian Code of Hammurabi remained in force even through the
Persian, Greek and Parthian conquests and that it survived to
influence Syro-Roman law and the later Mahommedan law in
Mesopotamia. These and many other results of recent researches
shew the way to the future study of the ancient law from the
point of view of evolution and continuity. Only by such methods
of study shall we understand the nature of the ancient foundations of medieval and modern law in the several parts of the
world which owe their civilization to Eastern as well as to
Western peoples. The passing of the world from ancient to
medieval times meant indeed no break in legal tradition, for
the legal systems of the middle ages were based in large measure
on the evolution in antiquity. Chief among the ingredients of
western European law in the middle ages were Germanic and
Roman elements derived from the age of antiquity: but there
were also embodied in medieval laws Hellenic and other strains
which came out of the ancient world and which were in origin
neither Germanic nor Roman. The transformation of these
ancient elements and the introduction of newer features by the
processes of political, ecclesiastical, economic, and social growth
laid in the medieval age the foundations of the modern systems
of law in the western European countries and in the communities throughout the world which have derived their
civilization from Europe.

For the last century trained legal historians—Eichhorn, Savigny,
Ihering, Mitteis, Brunner, Gierke, Karlowa, Esmein, Viollet,
Brissaud, Pertile, Hinojosa, and many others—have been en-
gaged in telling parts of this long story of the law's evolution
throughout the ages. The historians of English law have made
their own contribution to the story. The study of English legal
history during the last half-century, characterized by the work
of the great masters like Maitland and Ames, is indeed one of
the important aspects of the vaster movement in historical,
more particularly in legal-historical studies, which has marked
the last hundred years. The literature of English legal history
produced by this small but eminent group of scholars shews
not only familiarity with the researches of legal historians in
other countries, but also a grasp of the place of English law in

world history. The lessons which they have taught should not be forgotten by the present generation. The present is an age when the vision of men, scholars no less than statesmen and traders, is directed not solely to individual countries; it is directed in ever-increasing degree to the world at large. This same vision should inspire and guide the work of those who are charged with the task of investigating the history of the English law. That vision is no less than this: that English law is a world-system, a system related in many ways throughout its evolution to other bodies of law and extended in the course of centuries far beyond the confines of England to many other regions. Many of its roots go back to the Germanic customs of the Continent and the North in the age of antiquity; while others reach to the Norman law and through Norman law to the *Lex Salica*. Fundamentally Germanic in its origins and in its earlier development, the English law owes something also to Roman and Canon legal influences in the middle ages; while, through the growth and spread of those systems or by other processes of evolution, it may also owe more than we now suspect to Greek and other bodies of ancient and medieval law. The well-known origin of certain elements of English and of European maritime law in the ancient sea customs of the Greeks points the way to other researches of a similar kind. Nor even in modern times has English law been free from the subtle influences of foreign law and of foreign juridical thought: factors such as these have counted in legal growth far more than is oft-times imagined.

But these historical links between English law and the legal world outside England have not all been due to the process of importation. Exportation has also played a rôle of profound significance. The spread of English law beyond the confines of the homeland began in the age before the Norman Conquest; and before the middle ages were past it had established itself in Wales and in parts of Ireland and Scotland, and it may have left its influence upon the legal institutions of the King's lost provinces in France. In modern times it has spread to America, the dominions, the colonies, and India. In the course of this long process of diffusion throughout the world the English law has met in its new environments not only native customs, but the laws and customs of civilized peoples. In the middle ages as well as in modern times it has met Celtic laws; in the period of modern imperial expansion it has met bodies of continental-colonial law, such as the French, Spanish and Dutch, compounded in part of Germanic and Roman elements; while in India and elsewhere it has met the Hindu and Mahommedan laws of the East. The growth of English law in the environment of these other systems forms one of the most important aspects of English legal history in its setting of world history. Nor should we forget that even in countries which have never been under British sovereignty English legal institutions and English modes of juridical thought have left an abiding impress.

It is this conception of the place of English law in world history which has dictated the scope of the present series of studies. It is hoped that by means of monographs and editions of texts various aspects of this development extending through the ages and reaching to many parts of the world may be brought into clearer light. Questions of legal origins and of the historical links between the English and the other legal systems of the world will receive due attention. Likewise within the scope of the series are the relations between legal and institutional growth and the relations between legal growth and the political, religious, economic and social aspects of development. While emphasis will be laid on the growth of medieval and modern common law and equity, attention will also be directed to ecclesiastical, maritime and local law. It is also planned to include in the series studies in the evolution of English law within some of its environments outside England, for example, in Ireland, in the United States, in Canada, in Australia, and in India. In brief, any aspect of the world history of English law will be an appropriate subject for study; and it may find its place in the series.

If now the question be asked as to the fundamental aim of the writers of monographs and the editors of texts who contribute to the series, the answer must be that their purpose can only be the purpose which inspires all historical research. That purpose is expressed in the words of one of the epistles of Hieronymus: "to know and to teach those things which are true."

Selden adopted these words as his own: and to Selden, as to the other English legal historians of his time, the knowing and the teaching of the truth of the past did not mean the "studious affectation of bare and sterile antiquity, which is nothing else but to be exceeding busy about nothing," it meant, on the contrary, "regard of the fruitful and precious part of [the past], which gives necessary light to the present in matters of state, law, history." The canon of Hieronymus has also had currency for Selden's successors in our own time; and they distinguish, as he did, between the sterile and the fruitful parts of the past. It was zeal in the discovery of the fruitful parts of historic truth which animated the vast labours of Maitland and gave character to his histories of the law as forces in the thought and life of the present day. It is this same eager quest for truth which has endowed the work of other masters in English legal history with creative and fruitful qualities.

The search for truth, which is to animate these researches in the history of the laws of England, needs no ἀπολογία. The quest for truth in any field of enquiry needs no defence. Nor, in the present state of historical studies, is it necessary to enter into an elaborate explanation of the importance of a knowledge of the successive stages of evolution lying at the basis of the laws administered by the English courts and by the courts of the many jurisdictions which have derived the fundamentals of their jurisprudence from England. Let only this be said. The history of English law as a world-system is an integral part of the cultural history of mankind; and as such it has an importance difficult to overestimate. It not only forms a contribution of far-reaching scope to the study of comparative legal development, it also serves to throw light on many aspects of the political, ecclesiastical, economic, and social evolution of Western civilization. Apart from this broader significance, English legal history is intimately interwoven in the whole historical development of the English empire of the middle ages and of the British empire of modern times; and that imperial history of English law is today one of the main links which bind together the several parts of the British Commonwealth, while it serves, at the same time, as a common bond of unity between that Commonwealth

and the United States of America. Furthermore, in England
and in each one of the several jurisdictions which trace the main
sources of their jurisprudence to England, the history of the
English laws serves as a guide to the legal profession, the courts,
and all other agencies of legal administration. It likewise provides
necessary enlightenment to all who are concerned, in one way
or another, with the shaping of the form and content of the law
to meet the ever-changing needs of society. These, then, are
certain of the true functions which the world history of the laws
of England fulfils. These functions are as important today as
they were yesterday. They will be as important tomorrow as they
are today.

By its function in the processes of law-administration and
law-making English legal history serves immediate and practical
ends. Judges, legislators and administrators cannot, by a stroke
of the pen or by a fiat of jurisprudential thought, cut the laws
of their communities loose from the past. This has not happened in countries which, like France and Germany, have
codified large portions of their law: it cannot happen in countries,
like England and America, which base their jurisprudence in
large measure on judicial precedents. Nor does present-day
juridical thought in England and America seek to break with
the past and to allow the historical study of law to fall into
decay. The juristic thought of today properly emphasizes the
growing importance of concentrating the efforts of all the factors
in legal administration and legal amendment upon the problem
of the ends which the law should be made to serve in our own
day and generation. In essence those ends are no less than the
embodiment of political, economic and social justice in legal
justice; and they are ends vital to progress. One of the bene-
ficent fruits of this and of other lines of present-day juridical
thought is that legal tradition is now seen in its true perspective
as the actual outcome of the past, but not as the fetter which
enslaves the present and the future. Out of the thought of the
present day one of the true and useful functions of legal history
as the embodiment of legal tradition is thus emerging into
clearer light. That functional use of legal history is the study
of legal traditions, in their course of development and in the

light of the conditions which produced them and gave them continuity, in order that they may be used with intelligence by the courts or that they may be modified, or even abolished, by the law-making powers. This is not a new thought; it is an idea long held by legal historians of broad vision everywhere. It is, for example, the thought which underlies a large part of Mr Justice Holmes' masterly address on "The Path of the Law," delivered in 1897. "The rational study of law," he declares, "is still to a large extent the study of history. History must be a part of the study, because without it we cannot know the precise scope of rules which it is our business to know. It is a part of the rational study, because it is the first step towards an enlightened scepticism, that is, towards a deliberate reconsideration of the worth of those rules."

It is hoped, then, that the *Cambridge Studies in English Legal History*, by making some contribution to the knowledge of the history of English law as a world-wide and not merely as an insular system, may be an agency in the fulfilment of the several functions of legal history. Fortunate it is that there are already in progress other series of publications of texts and of essays which have as their purpose the encouragement of the study and the advancement of the knowledge of English legal history. The series inaugurated by the publication of the present volume will not conflict with the valuable work of the Selden Society nor with that of other societies and scholars. On the contrary, the aim is to supplement the work that is being done by other agencies.

Any success which this series of *Cambridge Studies in English Legal History* may have in making its own special contribution to learning must be due to the scholarly labours of the writers of monographs and the editors of texts. From scholars who value the studies to which this series is devoted and who envisage the useful functions which such studies should serve may there come, therefore, both guidance and co-operation. Only by these means can the high standard set by Dr Winfield in this first volume of the series be maintained.

H. D. H.

18. iv. 1921

# AUTHOR'S PREFACE

THIS book was begun ten years ago as a piece of research on the history of the law of conspiracy. The scope of it widened to the history of abuse of legal procedure in general. Absence during the war almost completely interrupted its progress, and when work was resumed on it, it seemed better to state the modern law of abuse of legal procedure as well as its history. After completion of the manuscript, circumstances beyond my control made it necessary to detach the historical from the modern part and to publish each of these separately instead of as one book. This process of detachment was not altogether easy, and was found unworkable in the last two chapters; apart from them, the matter in this book is purely historical. The modern part will shortly appear under the title, *The Present Law of Abuse of Legal Procedure*, but will not be included as one of the volumes in *Cambridge Studies in English Legal History*, because that series is confined in its scope to the history of the law as distinct from the statement of its present principles. The historical evolution in the present work, however, leads naturally to the modern law set out in *The Present Law of Abuse of Legal Procedure*.

The history of perjury is fairly well known, and there is already in existence a good monograph by Mr Oswald on contempt of court. These topics are therefore omitted.

The library class-marks for some of the MSS. consulted may possibly have been altered during the last ten years. For convenience sake, use has been made occasionally of the 1878 English edition of Bracton, but with the caution which is notoriously essential.

Perhaps it is not irrelevant to add that if the printed *Registrum Brevium* could be annotated with all the variant writs, which we know from MS. Registra to have been tried at one time or another, a wonderful addition would be made to the history of English legal procedure, and incidentally to the history of

English substantive law; for behind those intricate games of procedural chess in the Year Books which seem so tedious to the modern eye, the judges of England were creating the Common Law,—the κτῆμα εἰς ἀεί which has outlived the sneers of Swift and the hatred of Bentham.

It is a pleasure to express my very sincere thanks to my friend, Professor Hazeltine, for his valuable suggestions and kindly encouragement at every turn, and, in particular, for bringing to my notice Mr Bryan's book on the law of conspiracy, published in the United States in 1909. I am also indebted to the past and present editors of the *Law Quarterly Review*—Sir Frederick Pollock, and Mr A. E. Randall—for their kind inclusion in the *Review* of portions of the work at a time when the likelihood of its completion seemed remote; and to the staff of the Cambridge University Press, for the care which they have bestowed on the work.

P. H. W.

18. iv. 1921

# CONTENTS

# CONTENTS

# INDEX OF STATUTES

# INDEX OF YEAR BOOKS

# INDEX OF CASES

xxvi INDEX OF CASES

# CHAPTER I

## THE EARLY HISTORY OF ABUSE OF PROCEDURE, AND ESPECIALLY OF CONSPIRACY

### THE EARLY MEANING OF CONSPIRACY

§ 1. The early meaning of conspiracy must be examined at the outset, as constant reference to it will be necessary.

An authoritative definition of conspirators is given in *Statutes of the Realm* (ed. 1810, I. 145):

Conspirators be they that do confeder or bind themselves by Oath, Covenant, or other Alliance, that every of them shall aid and [bear[1]] the other falsly and maliciously to indite [or cause to indite[2]] or falsly to move or maintain Pleas; and also such as cause Children within Age to appeal Men of Felony, whereby they are imprisoned and sore grieved; and such as retain Men in the Country with Liveries or Fees for to maintain their malicious Enterprises[3]; and this extendeth as well to the Takers as to the Givers; and Stewards and Bailiffs of great Lords, which by their seignory, office or power, undertake [to bear or maintain Quarrels Pleas or Debates, that concern other Parties[4]] than such as touch the Estate of their Lords or themselves. This Ordinance and final Definition of Conspirators was made and[5] accorded by the King and his Council [in his Parliament the thirty-third year of his Reign[6]]. And it was further ordained, that justices assigned to the hearing and determining of Felonies and Trespasses[7] should have the Transcript hereof*.

The title of this piece of legislation according to the "Margin of the Inrollment," is "Ordinacio de Conspiratoribus." It is dated "De Parl. 33 Edward I in Octab. B Marie." In the

---

[1] *Sustain the enterprize of*
[2] *or cause to be indicted, or falsely to acquit people*
[3] *and to drown the truth.*
[4] *to maintain or support Pleas or Quarrels for Parties, other*
[5] *finally*          [6] *in this Parliament etc.*
[7] *in the several Counties of England*
\* The shape of the brackets and the notes corresponding to the brackets are reproduced exactly. *St. of the Realm*, I. Introd. xliii explains that italicized notes indicate suggested corrections in translation justified by the original language of a statute, but not authorized by printed or MS. translation.

## 2    THE EARLY MEANING OF CONSPIRACY

printed copies of the Statutes it is styled "Diffinitio de Conspiratoribus. A Definition of Conspirators"; and these copies
annex to this definition another one of champertors: "Campi
Participes sunt qui per se vel per alios placita movent vel
movere faciant; et ea suis sumptibus prosequuntur, ad campi
partem, vel pro parte lucri habenda."

The definition of conspirators also appears in *Rot. Parl.* I. 183
as "Ordinatio de Conspiratoribus." No comment is made upon
it, the date is the same[1], and the text is substantially the same
except for the omission of the sentence relating to those who
instigate infants to make false appeals.

This loosely strung description presents conspiracy in an
unusual form to the eye of a modern lawyer. Ancient conspirators are those who combine, and so far they resemble
their present descendants. But combine to do what? In effect
to abuse legal procedure. This is not quite an exact paraphrase
of the Ordinance, for it does not allow for the vague phrase
"such as retain Men in the Country with Liveries or Fees for
to maintain their malicious Enterprises." But mediaeval judges,
as will be seen later, practically confined their interpretation of
the Ordinance to abuse of legal procedure[2], and without some
knowledge of the early law relating to this it is impossible to
understand the history of conspiracy.

§ 2. A word may be added here as to the meaning of conspiracy before the Ordinance of Conspirators. Its technical
signification, if any, seems to have been much the same as after
33 Ed. I. Thus, in 29 Ed. I, de Helmeswell and de Maldone
were attached "de placito conspirationis" because "per con-
spiracionem et confederacionem" maliciously made between
them they had procured citation of the complainant before the
Bishop of Lincoln's Court "de transgressionibus"[3]. In the
same year, John de Den impleaded for conspiracy five jurors
who, after they had given a verdict for him in an assize between
him and W. de Tudenham, had unsuccessfully claimed 10 marks
from him as a reward. They then procured from de Tudenham

---

[1] Transl. ed. of the Statutes by George Ferrers about 1541 gives the
date 27 Ed. I (f. cxxv).

[2] For a suggested explanation, see J. W. Bryan, *Development of the
English Law of Conspiracy*, p. 12, n. 10.     [3] *Abb. Plac.* 295.

a certificate which would enable him to change their verdict for one in de Tudenham's favour. John got nothing by his writ, because he could have recovered by attaint or in some other way[1]. In 25 Ed. I, a plea of conspiracy was brought apparently against a servant and his master; the servant's defence was that he had merely assisted his master in an assize and that this was lawful[2]. The sense of abuse of legal procedure is not, however, always so easy to trace. In 22 Ed. I, a parson, who at the request of some of his parishioners had given them legal advice, contended that the writ of conspiracy was a judicial writ or granted in a special case[3], and was not appropriate for trying a charge of abduction which parents had brought against him (presumably because his advice related to the marriage of their daughter)[4]. The fact that the parents brought a writ of conspiracy at all shews the vagueness of the term before its definition in 33 Ed. I, but even here the idea that the parson's conduct was an improper meddling in a legal dispute, if not in actual litigation, may have been the ground on which the writ was procured.

§ 3. Conspiracy does not seem to have been used in this period to indicate illegal combinations of other kinds; but that such combinations were known appears from a case in Bracton's *Note Book* which has an echo in the bitter trade disputes of our own time. In Stafford, several men had sworn, and made others swear, that they would make no suit to the mills of William Wymer, and had proclaimed in Stafford market-place that if any one did make such suit they would seize his cattle to the use of the King, and thrust him into prison. William sought redress for this, and though the accused escaped on a technical point, he got a writ to the sheriff of Stafford protecting such as wished to make suit to the mills[5]. Again, in 1225, the Abbot

---

[1] *Abb. Plac.* 295.      [2] *Ibid.* 237.

[3] "breve de conspiracione est breve de judic[ibus] vel quasi in speciali casu concessum." In the printed Register of writs, the writ of conspiracy appears under the original, not the judicial, writs (f. 134). But the meaning of these terms was not settled at this date (*post*, pp. 38–39), nor were the contents of the Register itself. The case merely ends with the statement that the complainants got leave to abandon the writ.

[4] *Abb. Plac.* 291.

[5] Case 479 (A.D. 1230). It is indexed "Conspiracy" probably for lack of any other term. Cf. a similar use for purposes of translation in *Placita Anglo-Normannica*, 12.

of Lilleshall complained that the bailiffs of Shrewsbury did him many injuries against his liberty, and had issued a proclamation forbidding sale of merchandise to the Abbot or his men under a penalty of 10s.[1]

## ABUSE OF LEGAL PROCEDURE GENERALLY

### (1) IN ANGLO-SAXON TIMES

§ 4.  The Laws of Edgar provide that he who shall accuse another wrongfully, so that he either in money or property be the worse, shall, on disproof of the charge by the accused, be liable in his tongue, unless he make compensation with his "wer"[2]. The Secular Laws of Cnut contain a nearly similar provision[3]. Leges Henrici Primi[4], besides repeating Edgar's and Cnut's penalties, inflict loss of tongue upon one who falsely accuses his lord before a justice; while lying denial of a judgment debt due to the lord involves a punishment varying with the delinquent's birth[5]. But the Anglo-Saxon ruler was faced by a dilemma which was to trouble the judges of England for ten centuries. In his eagerness to crush calumny he might stifle honest attempts to vindicate the law. Hence, while the doomsman who gives a false doom pays the King 120s., one who swears that he knew not aught more just goes quit[6]. Perhaps the early sanctity of an oath made this a more efficient compromise of the difficulty than it appears to be.

### (2) AFTER THE CONQUEST

§ 5.  In so far as abuse of procedure took the form of a false accusation of what would now be called crime, a distinction must be drawn between appeals and indictments.

---

[1] *Select Pleas of the Crown*, S. S. 1. pl. 178. Here again, the case is indexed "conspiracy," though the word does not appear in it.

[2] III Edgar 4. Liebermann, *Gesetze der Angelsachsen*, vol. 1. Thorpe, *Anc. Laws and Inst. of England*, 1. 286–7 (where ref. is Edgar II, 4). So too Quad. Lieb. *ibid.*

[3] II Cnut 16. Lieb. *ibid.* 320–1. Thorpe, 384–5. So Quad. Lieb. *ibid.*

[4] A.D. 1114–1118 acc. to Brunner, *A–A Essays*, II. 17.

[5] LIX, 13, 14. Lieb. *Ibid.* 579. Thorpe, 557–8.

[6] Cnut (Secular) 15. Thorpe, 1. 384–5. A judge was liable to a similar penalty, and was similarly protected. *Ibid.* 266–7. Cf. *Laws of William the Conqueror*, 1. 13. *Ibid.* 472–3.

## *Appeals*

§ 6. A *wite* of 60s. was payable to the King by an appellor who was beaten in the battle which tested his appeal of felony[1]. Amercements for false appeals were common enough. The records of the Exchequer and Curia Regis afford examples. In 14 Hen. II, Reimundus de Baldac owes 20 marks to the King "pro appellatione Walteri probatoris de falsonaria"[2], and three years later, Joslenus de Hocton is amerced 20s. for unwarrantably charging Osbert Luvel with the death of another[3]. So too, "Emma Concubina presbiteri de Nethford debet dimidiam marcam pro falso appello"[4]. In 10 Rich. I, a half mark "pro falso appello" is noted[5]. A case in the time of John indicates that in addition a civil remedy may have existed for malicious appeals. An appeal of robbery was found to be due to spite and hate, and the appellee appears subsequently to have brought an action against the appellor. But the nature of the action is not specified, nor is its result[6]. Bracton tells us that a vanquished appellor is to be committed to gaol for punishment as a "calumniator," but he is to lose neither life nor limb, although according to the law he is liable to retaliation[7]; but if he retracts on the field, not only must he go to prison[8], but both he and his sureties for the prosecution are to be amerced, for here he has not done what he obliged himself to do, while in the former case the defeat may be no fault of his, and though he is to be sent to gaol, yet mercy is sometimes shewn to him because he fights in defence of the peace[9]. So says Bracton, and a generation later, amercement followed a failure to prosecute the appeal only if such failure were due to negligence, and not if it were through death[10]. The law cannot be said to have erred in

---

[1] P. and M. II. 539.    [2] Madox, *Hist. Exch.* I. 429.
[3] *Ibid.* 558.    [4] *Ibid.* 556.
[5] *Rot. Cur. Reg.* (ed. Palgrave), I. 173, 179.
[6] *Select Civil Pleas* (*temp.* John), pl. 181.
[7] Bracton (ed. Twiss), II. 404–5. For examples of imprisonment and amercement see Bracton's *Note Book*, pl. 1084, 1664 (A.D. 1225).
[8] Cf. *Pleas of Crown for Gloucester* (A.D. 1221), No. 309, where appellor was imprisoned and made fine for withdrawal from appeal.
[9] Bract. II. 444–5, 460–1. Cf. Bracton's *Note Book*, 1460, for a case (A.D. 1220) where this excuse prevailed. Britton (ed. Nichols), I. xxiii. 9, practically repeats Bracton. Cf. *Fleta*, lib. I. cap. 34, sect. 32.
[10] *Fleta*, I. 27. 15.

harshness towards appellors[1], but it needed strengthening in appeals of a vicarious character. Men of straw were instigated to bring false appeals. If they lost the ensuing battle, they could compensate neither the King nor the appellee, and the fear of imprisonment would be discounted by the chance of winning. 13 Ed. I (St. West. II) c. 12, A.D. 1285 (often referred to as "Quia multi per malitiam"), was designed to prevent this. Its terms which were the subject of some judicial and juristic comment are thus translated[2]:

Forasmuch as many, through Malice intending to grieve other, do procure false appeals to be made of Homicides and other Felonies by Appellors, having nothing to satisfy the King for their false Appeal, nor to the Parties affected for their Damages, It is ordained, That when any, being appealed of Felony surmised upon him, doth acquit himself in the King's Court in due Manner, either at the Suit of the Appellor, or of our Lord the King, the justices, before whom the Appeal shall be heard and determined, shall punish the Appellor by a year's imprisonment, and the Appellors shall nevertheless restore to the Parties appealed their Damages, according to the Discretion of the Justices, having respect to the Imprisonment or Arrestment that the Party appealed hath sustained by reason of such Appeals, and to the Infamy that they have incurred by the Imprisonment or otherwise, and shall nevertheless make a grievous Fine unto the King. And if peradventure such Appellor be not able to recompense the Damages, it shall be inquired by whose Abetment or Malice the Appeal was commenced, if the Party appealed desire it; and if it be found by the same Inquest, that any Man is Abettor through Malice, at the suit of the Party appealed he shall be distrained by a judicial writ to come before the Justices: and if he be lawfully convict of such malicious Abetment, he shall be punished by Imprisonment and Restitution of Damages, as before is said of the Appellor. And from henceforth in Appeal of the Death of a Man there shall no Essoin lie for the Appellor, in whatsoever Court the Appeal shall hap to be determined.

§ 7. We find shortly after this enactment an inquiry directed concerning sheriffs, their clerks and officers who have falsely and maliciously made provers appeal innocent people, or hindered them from appealing the guilty, and such as are guilty of this offence are to be imprisoned during the King's

---

[1] Cf. P. and M. II. 539 sqq.      [2] *St. of the Realm*, I. 81.

pleasure[1]. It is possible that this special class of cases may have prompted the framers of the statute; and the pardon granted to provers (accomplices who confessed their own felony and appealed their confederates) if they substantiated their appeals[2] throws further light on the motives which led a man to play the legal catspaw.

§ 8. We have elaborate comments on the statute by Stanford[3], Coke[4], and Hawkins[5], but considering the early period at which appeals became practically obsolete, they must (at least in Hawkins' time) have been pieces of legal antiquarianism. Reported cases on the statute after the close of the Year Book period are not easy to find. It does not appear to have been entirely adequate. The unreliable *Mirrour* considered it reprehensible from the false appellor's point of view, first, because the pecuniary penalty under it is cumulative instead of being alternative to corporal punishment, secondly because it gives jurisdiction over abettors without an original writ[6]. On the other hand, the author of *Fleta* was apprehensive that it would diminish pleas of the Crown, and terrify those who wished to institute a proper appeal, and he hints that between the timid appellor and the corrupt jury the rogue might escape prosecution altogether[7]. But there is evidence that the statute in its working favoured the false appellor rather than the guilty appellee. If the false appellor were already in prison he was beyond its reach, and sheriffs and gaolers egged on prisoners who were in their custody to become approvers, and to appeal wealthy and reputable persons of some felony which would lead to their imprisonment and ransom. As such payment did not benefit the King, he interfered by an Ordinance of 1311 which forbade the imprisonment of persons so accused if they could find bail for their appearance at the next Gaol Delivery to

---

[1] Britton, I. xxii. 5. *Fleta*, I. 20 (De Capitulis Coronae et Itineris), 109, probably refers to the Statute: "Item qui habuerint robbatores imprisonatos, & eos fecerunt appellare fideles & innocentes causa lucri, & quandoque impedierint ne culpabiles appellarent, & per quorum procurationem talia facta fuerint."

[2] *Ibid.* I. xxv. 9.

[3] Sir W. Stanford, *Les Plees del Coron.* lib. III. cap. 11.

[4] 2 Inst. 382.     [5] 2 P.C. ch. 23, sect. 137 sqq.

[6] Ed. W. J. Whittaker, S. S. vol. VII. 193.     [7] I. 34. 48.

answer the charge[1]. 1 Ed. III st. 1. c. 7[2] refers to the evil
again, and requires the judges to inquire and determine such
plaints whether at the suit of the party or of the King. But it
was not till 14 Ed. III st. 1. c. 10[3] made the sheriff's deputy
keepers of a prison punishable with death if they compelled
their prisoners to appeal another that the root of the abuse
was struck.

§ 9. At a later date, the procedure under 13 Ed. I c. 12 was,
at any rate in one particular set of circumstances, thought to
be more efficient than the other remedies against conspirators.
In 1402, the Commons complain to the King of conspirators
who made a practice of maliciously indicting in Middlesex
residents in other counties who are outlawed for treason and
felony on these indictments before they have any knowledge of
them; and they ask that on acquittal of the accused the conspirators may be convicted by the same inquest which acquits
the accused. The reply is that the statutes and Common Law
in this case are to be kept and protected, and that on attaint
by process of law the conspirators must render to the aggrieved
party damages and restitution having regard to his imprisonment and ill fame, and that they make fine and ransom to the
King[4]. But at times neither statute nor Common Law satisfied
the appellee[5].

§ 10. The purview of 13 Ed. I c. 12 goes much further than
the preamble. It has been said that it "is a typical piece of
mediaeval legislation. It desires to punish malicious appeals;
it actually punishes every appeal that ends in an acquittal"[6].
Read narrowly, it certainly does look as if the appellor himself
were subject to the grievous penalties laid down, irrespective
of the goodness or badness of his motives, provided only the
appellee were acquitted; while the abettors must have shewn

[1] *St. of Realm*, 1. 165–6, S. S. vol. XVI. Introd. ciii.
[2] *Ibid.* 253–4.        [3] *Ibid.* 284.
[4] *Rot. Parl.* III. 505 a. Perhaps Art. sup. Cart. 28 Ed. I c. 10 which provided punishment for conspirators was found to be too slow, as it involved
the possible bringing of a plaint of conspiracy at some later date than that
at which the accused was acquitted. The procedure under 13 Ed. I c. 12
is summary.
[5] *Rot. Parl.* III. 445 a (1399). The Council undertakes to do justice on
a false appeal of treason.        [6] P. and M. II. 539.

"malice" to make themselves liable. But whether there was a wholesale confusion of the just with the unjust in the operation of the statute is not clear. One point is free from doubt; damages were not recoverable by the accused if, prior to the appeal, he had been indicted of the same felony, for such indictment, though it terminated in his acquittal, implied a good cause for the subsequent appeal[1]. The Year Books illustrate this, with respect to the abettors[2], though the inquiry against them was not to be stopped if the indictment were formally defective (e.g., in not shewing the day, date, or place of indictment, or the judge before whom it was taken)[3]; and with respect to the appellor himself, as early as 1367, when an acquitted appellee vainly prayed for damages against a widow who had appealed him of the death of her husband[4]. Such a defence was not available to him if the appeal preceded the indictment, or if he were indicted as principal and appealed as accessory, or *vice versa*. Apart from this, was he allowed any general plea of good faith in bringing the appeal? Stanford admits that the letter of the statute may be against this wider interpretation, but seeks to justify it by authorities which do not support his reference[5]. Coke states that *malitia* refers only to procurers and abettors[6]. Hawkins, about a century later, argues that it is unimaginable that the framers of the statute should have intended to imprison for a year and to fine an appellor who had reasonable evidence for commencing an appeal; but he owns that the reports and books of entries shew that damages seem to have been awarded as a matter of course against the appellor, malice or no malice,

[1] Stanf. P.C. 168. 2 Hawk. P.C. ch. 23, sect. 28.
[2] 14 Hen. VII, f. 2 where the reason is put by FINEUX C.J.C.P. 22 Lib. Ass. pl. 39. Pasch. 17 Ed. II, f. 534 indicates (without expressly deciding) that no inquiry will be made of abettors in such circumstances. In Hil. 33 Hen. VI, f. 2, the whole Court agreed with *obiter dictum* of DANBY J. to the same effect.
[3] Trin. 26 Hen. VIII, f. 8, *per* FITZ-JAMES C.J.K.B., and the rest of the Court.
[4] 40 Ed. III, f. 42. Same case in 40 Lib. Ass. pl. 18, which, however, omits the reasons for the decision.
[5] P.C. 168 citing Fitz. *Abr. Corone*, 178; 22 Lib. Ass. pl. 39 (which merely shews that abettors are not liable if there be a previous indictment); and Mich. 40 Ed. III, f. 42 (same rule as to appellor).
[6] 2 Inst. 384.

if the appellee were acquitted[1]. In a case of Richard II's time, a plaintiff was fined £5 for admitting his appeal to be false, and it is said, "the law is such, if a man knows his appeal is false, he shall go to prison and be fined," from which it might be inferred that good faith would have excused him; but there is nothing to shew that this case was upon 13 Ed. I c. 12[2].

§ 11. The "other Felonies" mentioned in the statute included rape which was made a felony by another part of the statute, and, according to the weight of authority, all crimes subsequently made felonies by the legislature[3].

§ 12. The appellee has no remedy unless "he doth acquit himself in the King's Court in due Manner." These words were "so material that all the weight of this statute lies upon them"[4]; and it was by a strict construction of them that the judges sought to prevent the statute from scaring just accusers. They might have attained this object more directly by an analysis of "malice," but the difficulties of probing motives perhaps made them prefer the more technical course. Thus, while an acquittal in law, just as much as an acquittal in fact, sufficed to give the appellee his remedy, yet the only conspicuous instance of the former was that in which acquittal of the principal also freed an accessory, or a principal in the second degree, who had been appealed with him[5]. On the other hand, there were many apparent acquittals in law which gave the appellee no damages because they were no real test of his innocence, e.g., alleging that the appellant was a bastard, had an elder brother, or was never legally married[6]. So too, if the verdict were that the appellee killed in self-defence or by misadventure, because he must still buy his pardon[7]; or if a plea in bar or a demurrer

---

[1] 2 P.C. ch. 23, sect. 138. The references to the books of entries (e.g. Rastall 56, *Booke of Entries* 52) support this. The references to the reports are too slovenly to verify.      [2] Pasch. 11 Rich. II (Bellewe, *Appeal*).

[3] Stanf. P.C. 168. Coke, 2 Inst. 384. Cf. 2 Hawk. P.C. ch. 23, sect. 138.

[4] Stanf. P.C. 169.

[5] Stanf. P.C. 168. Coke, 2 Inst. 385. 2 Hawk. P.C. ch. 23, sect. 141 where the reason is given. Stanford's reference to 33 Hen. VI, f. 2 is not convincing, that case being one of conspiracy. Copleston and Stowell's Case. 2 Inst. 385.      [6] Stanf. P.C. 169.

[7] *Ibid.* 2 Hawk. P.C. ch. 23, sect. 140. But 22 Lib. Ass. pl. 77, which is cited by Stanford and Hawkins in support of this is on conspiracy, not false appeals, though an analogous point arose there. Coke takes it to be

were successful[1], or if the acquittal were on an insufficient original writ, for these last three cases left the defendant liable to another prosecution[2]; so too where the appellor was barely nonsuited[3], though in this case as in many others, where he was not liable for damages under the statute, he might have to make a fine[4]; but if the appellor were nonsuited *and* the appellee were acquitted, the latter got his damages and inquiry[5]. An erroneous acquittal was held to be useless in Y.B. Pasch. 9 Hen. V, f. 2, but the accounts of the case are inconsistent, and in so far as error in procedure was salved by appearance, there seems to be no principle in its favour[6].

§ 13. It was settled that though justices of *nisi prius* could assess the damages referred to in the statute, and make inquiries directed by it as to the sufficiency of the appellor and as to the abettors, yet they had no power to give judgment for the damages; for the statute applied only to justices before whom the whole appeal was determinable, and not to those of *nisi prius* who had no cognizance of the appeal before trial, and no original power to try it[7]. This was probably not the serious limitation on the efficacy of the statute which it appears to be, since the commission of assize (which would enable them to give judgment for the damages) was no doubt issued as at the present day in combination with that of *nisi prius* to the same persons.

§ 14. It was held not long after the passing of the statute an authority on the absence of malice (2 Inst. 384); but the case as printed does not bear this out.

[1] Stanf. P.C. 169.　　　　　[2] 2 Hawk. P.C. ch. 23, sect. 140.

[3] Br. *Abr. Appelle*, 151. Fitz. *Cor.* 102 leaves it open whether the nonsuit there were a bare one.　　　　　[4] *Ibid.* 159.

[5] 41 Lib. Ass. pl. 24. 2 Hawk. P.C. ch. 23, sect. 142. Coke, 2 Inst. 385.

[6] Stanf. P.C. 169. Br. *Abr. Restitution*, 8. Fitz. *Abr. Corone*, 68. 2 Hawk. P.C. ch. 27, sect. 107. The abridgments of the case are not consistent with the report in the Year Book. Fitz. *Abr. Corone*, 444, refers to a case Pasch. 19 Ed. III (year not included in printed Y.B.) in which it was said that an insufficient indictment or appeal prevents an acquitted appellee from recovering damages. This case does not appear in Y.B. in Rolls Series. Trin. 26 Hen. VIII, f. 3, shews that appellee who had been acquitted on an appeal, and against whom there had been an indictment for the same felony, was entitled to an inquiry of damages and abettors, though he produced a defective copy of the indictment. But this, of course, does not indicate that the indictment itself was defective.

[7] Stanf. P.C. 169–70. Coke, 2 Inst. 386. 2 Hawk. P.C. ch. 23, sect. 141.

that no inquiry of abettors could be made on behalf of a monk or wife, because the monk could not sue without his abbot, nor the wife without her husband[1]. In Coke's commentary on the statute there is the more general proposition that they have no remedy under it[2], but the authority[3] on which this is based is impugned in the case of the wife by Hawkins, and at any rate if husband and wife were acquitted on an appeal made against them jointly, they could have a joint judgment for the damage done to the wife[4].

§ 15. If no damages were recovered against the appellor, no inquiry was to be made as to abettors, unless the appellor could pay part only[5]. Thus, in 1389, 500 marks damages were assessed against a woman who had sued a false appeal. She had only 20 marks to satisfy them, and Thomas Metham and John Frere who had abetted her were imprisoned and condemned to pay 440 and 40 marks respectively to make up the deficit[6].

§ 16. If the jury fixed the damages at too low a figure, the appellee could have an original writ of abetment and count for greater damages, since the verdict on this point was not on the merits of the case[7]. We have scanty authority on what justified abetment of an appeal. The persons most likely to have a sound excuse would be the injured party's kin. But even here the law vacillated. In 1292, a defendant to a writ of abetment pleaded that he was brother of the man for whose death another had brought a false appeal, and that the statute did not apply to him, because he could still bring an appeal on his own account against the plaintiff in this writ. METINGHAM J. however, forced him to answer whether he had abetted through malice, which seems to shew that mere kinship was not a defence[8]. Again, in the Eyre of Kent, 6 and 7 Ed. II[9], a woman brought

---

[1] Hil. 13 Ed. II, f. 403 (SPIGURNEL J.).     [2] Coke, 2 Inst. 386.

[3] Fitz. *Abr. Corone*, 276, where the rule as to the monk is alleged to extend to the wife.

[4] 2 Hawk. P.C. ch. 23, sect. 144. There is evidence in earlier times that the judgments should be separate. Hil. Rich. II (Bellewe, *Baron and femme*, p. 62).

[5] Stanf. P.C. 170. Coke, 2 Inst. 386. 2 Hawk. P.C. ch. 23, sect. 145.

[6] *Rot. Parl.* III. 260 a.

[7] Stanf. P.C. 171. Coke, 2 Inst. 387. 2 Hawk. P.C. ch. 23, sect. 142.

[8] 20 and 21 Ed. I (Rolls Series), 310–12.     [9] S. S. vol. XXIV. 126.

a false appeal for the death of her husband against John of T. who was found not guilty. His counsel claimed damages under the statute, and, the woman being unable to pay these, the jury named three abettors, one of whom was the deceased's brother. BRABAZON J. seemed to be of opinion that his relationship was no excuse, but the reporter adds a note that he had heard it laid down by BEREFORD and ORMESBY JJ. that neither the brother of the man slain nor any of his blood could be abettors since it was their natural duty to prosecute the slayer. Coke represents a case of 6 Ed. III as deciding that the heir or other near of kin may abet the wife in the appeal, and that the relatives of the deceased are not within the statute, because they are bound to avenge his death[1]; and in 6 and 7 Ed. VI, MOUNTAGUE C.J. emitted an *obiter dictum* approving this case[2]. The law obviously ought to have accepted blood relationship as evidence only of an abettor's good faith, but this was urged at a period when the whole law of appeals had become atrophied[3].

§ 17. Whether the appellee could avail himself of the writ of conspiracy, and what, if any, connection 13 Ed. I c. 12 had with malicious indictments are questions which can be better considered when conspiracy itself has been examined.

It may be added that boroughs occasionally answered the manufacturer of false appeals according to their particular customs. In the 15th century, a false appellor in Winchelsea was attached and his goods were at the King's will; in Lydd, he made a fine to the King or was imprisoned, and had to compensate the appellee[4].

### Indictments

§ 18. *Abuse of indictments before the Statute of Conspirators.* Accusation by presentment or indictment[5] grew up under Henry II, rapidly became popular, and thrust aside the appeal and its barbarous methods of trial. The Statute of

---

[1] 2 Inst. 384. The report in Trin. 6 Ed. III, f. 33 is of a case on champerty, and HERLE J. merely says *obiter* that he had seen the party in a writ of abetment avow the abetment because he was next in blood to the appellor.

[2] *Partridge* v. *Strange.* Plowden, Pt. I at p. 88.

[3] 2 Hawk. P.C. ch. 23, sect. 140.

[4] *Borough Customs*, vol. I, S. S. vol. XVIII. 87.

[5] The terms were not quite identical. P. and M. II. 652, n. 4.

Conspirators of uncertain date (but probably about 21 Ed. I) was designed to check malicious indictments. But long before this, false presentments had been punished. Amercements "pro stulta presentacione," "pro falsa presentacione," are frequent in *Rotuli Curiae Regis*[1]. There are pretty nearly as many amercements for concealment, as for accusation of wrongdoers; and when we find on the same page a list of nine people bracketed for amercement at half a mark each side by side with another batch of six amerced for concealment[2], we have but one of many proofs that the law required a nice discernment between officiousness and lethargy in the discharge of one's public duties. On the Gloucestershire Plea Roll for 1221, there appear ten cases[3] of amercement for concealment, six for false presentment[4], and some of the former are so numerous[5] that these "unprofessional policemen" certainly needed awakening to their duties by the King's justices. Corruption may have had something to do with their silence[6], but it is more likely to have been due to dislike of performing an unpaid and thankless office[7]. The records of the minor courts tell the same tale. It is said that in the Fair Court of St Ives there is a fine of jurors for concealing offenders, and a few years later they are amerced in the same Court for falsely presenting that Hugh Cut receives harlots in his house[8]. There are hints that jurors could escape the expensive risks attached to their functions by a timely outlay of money. Yorkshire "judices[9] et juratores" of Henry I's time bargained for future exemption from their duties for £100[10].

§ 19. Bracton[11] points out the danger of accepting lying

---

[1] E.g. I. 181–2; apparently 10 Rich. I.   [2] *Ibid.* 182.

[3] Pl. 51, 121, 160, 180, 211, 263, 311, 338, 385, 432.

[4] Pl. 15, 55, 133, 181, 217, 239.

[5] Concealment of eleven *loquelae* by one set of jurors. Pl. 338. Cf. pl. 385, 432.   [6] Cf. *Fleta*, I. 27. 15.

[7] *Glouc. Plea Roll*, Introd. xxxiii. There had been no Eyre for five years, and that may have tended to make them more apathetic. *Ibid.* xx.

[8] *Select Cases in the Law Merchant*, vol. I. S. S. vol. XXIII. pp. 18, 84 (A.D. 1287 and 1302). Technically, a court could probably not "fine" anybody. P. and M. II. 517.

[9] The equivalent of "doomsmen." P. and M. I. 548.

[10] Pipe Roll, Hen. I, p. 34, cited S. S. vol. XXIV., Introd. xxxix, note 1.

[11] II. 452–3 sqq.

rumours where persons are indicted upon common fame. The source of suspicion should be good and grave persons, not malevolent slanderers. It is not to be said, "Jesus crucifigitur et Barabas liberatur." Again it may be that a lord is indicting his tenant of some crime to have his land, or that one neighbour indicts another for hatred. Our law knows the story of Naboth's vineyard. There were jurors corrupt enough to confederate in accusing the innocent, and it is directed that they be ransomed at the King's pleasure and that their oath never again be admitted. Sheriffs were sometimes as bad, for they bribed persons to indict falsely and packed panels to make this easier[1].

§ 20. It was not merely in criminal litigation that the courts made an unsuccessful claimant pay. Amercements "pro falso clamore" followed loss of a civil case almost as a matter of course[2].

"Then again every default in appearance brought an amercement on the defaulter and his pledges. Every mistake in pleading...brought an amercement on the pleader if the mistake was to be retrieved. A litigant who hoped to get to the end of his suit without an amercement must have been a sanguine man; for he was playing a game of forfeits"[3].

### The writ de odio et atia

§ 21. This writ was of common occurrence in early times, though its very name has long ceased to be more than a memory. It can conveniently be treated under the headings of (1) Its nature and origin. (2) Its scope. (3) Its decay.

§ 22. *Nature and origin.* The form of the writ is given by Bracton, and runs thus:

Rex vic. salutem. Praecipimus tibi, quod per probos et legales homines de comitatu tuo diligenter inquiras, utrum A de N captus & detentus in prisona nostra, de tali loco de morte B under rectatus & appellatus est, rectatus sit vel appellatus de morte illa odio et

---

[1] Britton, I. xxii. 19 and note (*d*). The sheriff of Northampton in 30 Ed. I organized a "company of the pouch" for this purpose.
[2] Bracton's *Note Book*, Index "Amercements." The Great Roll of the Pipe for Rich. I (ed. Hunter) may be opened almost at random on the chance of finding a payment of this sort. Cf. *Rot. Cur. Regis*, I. 174, 176, to take two examples only. Bigelow, *Plac. Ang.-Norm.* 226 (Men of Thanet "in misericordia pro falso clamore").
[3] P. and M. II. 519.

atya, vel eo quod inde culpabilis sit: & si odio & atya, quo odio & qua atia, vel quis inde culpabilis sit, & inquisitionem quam inde feceris &c.[1]

The gist of this is that the sheriff is directed to inquire by an inquest, whether *A* be appealed of *B*'s death by hate and spite, or because *A* is guilty. If it were found to be hate and spite, *B* could get released by a further writ enjoining the sheriff to put him in the keeping of twelve sureties[2].

To what then does the writ *de odio et atia* owe its origin? Would a modern lawyer think of it as analogous to the writ of *habeas corpus* or to the action for malicious prosecution? Is its purpose to get a man out of gaol pending trial, or to get rid of a lying charge against him? Neither apparently. Not the first, because most of the early cases do not so much as refer to imprisonment—much less complain of it; nor the second, because it was used as a plea, not as an action, and its main object was to escape the hated trial by battle. Whatever popularity this may have had at first with the upper classes, it was detested by the traders and the community in general; and in the end it was discountenanced by their betters and their ruler. Henry II dare not kill it outright, but he could starve it by offering his subjects a more rational form of proof—the sworn inquest; and one of the agents in spreading the inquest was the writ *de odio et atia*.

The mode in which it worked has been already traced for us. In the 12th century, the only mode of accusing a felon was the appeal, and the normal mode of trying him was by battle. The appellee could flatly deny the charge, but beyond that he could not go. No special plea was open to him. This was changed with the introduction of the inquest procedure. It had to be bought from the King, but it was worth the purchase, in order to get a trial by the verdict of the neighbours instead of the senseless battle. Moreover, the time had come when the appellee could meet the appeal with *exceptiones*, or special pleas, one of

---

[1] III. f. 123. Cf. Reg. Brev. f. 133. The writ is common enough in MS. Registra, e.g. Camb. Univ. Lib. Ii. vi. 28 (early 14th century); Inner Temple Lib. 504 (4), 511. 4, 511. 9 (all 14th century); Bodleian, Rawlinson C. 612 B, 454, 464.

[2] Bract. III. f. 123. Reg. Brev. 133. It got later the name of *tradas in ballium*.

which was that he had been appealed by spite and hate. To test this, or any other *exceptio*, he could buy the inquest procedure. If the inquest found against him, he could still deny the charge and have trial by battle; if the finding were in his favour, the appeal was quashed, and the appellee could get the writ which directed the sheriff to release him from prison. But soon the King insisted that every one appealed of felony should be arraigned at his suit, even if the appeal had failed. Then the only result of successfully pleading spite and hate to an appeal was the replevy of the appellee until the next coming of the justices in eyre[1].

The writ has been attributed to Henry II[2], and it was common enough early in the time of John[3].

The general plea to an appeal of felony, e.g. homicide, was "venit et defendit omnem feloniam & pacem domini regis infractam, & quicquid est contra pacem domini regis, & omnia quae versus ipsum proponuntur"[4]. The special plea of hatred and spite could be dovetailed into this, as where Juliana de Clive appeals Robert of rape, and Robert defends all, and says that she appeals him by hatred and spite, and the jury find him not guilty[5]. But spite and hatred may stand alone as the only plea[6]. Sometimes the details of them are added[7].

What is wanted is, in the great majority of cases, trial by jury, but, exceptionally, after the general denial and the allegation of spite, there is a request for battle[8]. The ordinary appellee,

---

[1] P. and M. II. 587–589. Cf. Mayer, *Geschworenengericht und Inquisitions-prozess* (Munich, 1916), 141–149. In the Eyre of Kent, 6 and 7 Ed. II, he was to appear on the first day of the sittings, or his mainpernors would be answerable. S. S. vol. XXIV. p. 7.

[2] McKechnie, *Magna Charta*, 420–421. Is this traceable to Glanville, lib. 14, ch. 3, who, in speaking of homicide, says "in hoc placito non solet accusatus per plegios dimitti, nisi ex Regie placito"? If so, the evidence is weak.

[3] *Select Civil Pleas* (temp. John), S. S. vol. III. pl. 181. *Rot. Cur. Reg.* II. pp. 265 (A.D. 1199), 278. *Select Pleas of the Crown*, S. S. vol. I. pl. 25, 78, 86, 87, 88, 91, 92, 94, 95, 104 (ranging from A.D. 1201 to 1211).

[4] Bract. f. 138 b.

[5] *Pleas of Crown for Gloucester* (A.D. 1221), pl. 76. Bract. *N. B.* pl. 1548. *Select Pl. of Cr.* S. S. vol. I. pl. 84, 86, 87, 94, 203.

[6] Bract. *N. B.* pl. 1697.

[7] *Ibid.* pl. 396. *Select Pl. of Cr.* S. S. vol. I. pl. 84 (? A.D. 1201). Three causes are particularized for the spite. So too pl. 87, 203.

[8] *Select Pl. of Cr., ubi sup.* pl. 202.

however, had no stomach for this. In many cases, there is no special plea of spite, but a general denial of liability, an offer of money for an inquest to say whether the accused be guilty or not, and a finding by the jury of not guilty, with a rider that the charge was made by hatred and spite[1]. This marks a further step in the development of the jury system. It is the stage wherein the whole question of guilty or not guilty, and not merely particular pleas are decided by the jury—the stage at which the accused comes before the justices and puts himself on the verdict of 12 jurors for good and ill[2]. When that point was reached, the writ de odio et atia was doomed to become obsolete. If the jury could take account of the question it raised as part of the general issue there was no need to plead spite and hatred specially.

There is abundant evidence to shew that the writ in its origin was not designed primarily to procure release of an accused person until his trial began[3]. In all the cases cited we hear no complaint of imprisonment, and in one of them, although the appellee's demand for an inquest is provisionally successful, he is actually ordered to remain in custody till the day fixed for his appearance[4]. Moreover, the sums paid for the writ were so great in amount that it cannot be supposed that they were paid merely to avoid imprisonment[5]. It is true that one consequence of a successful plea of hate and spite was usually the liberation of the accused until the eyre of the justices or further proceedings against him by the Crown[6], but that was not necessarily the only motive that prompted an application for the writ. For we know that the same consequence of provisional freedom followed if the accused were of good fame[7]. Not but what the prospect of being at large must have influenced the accused to some extent. Vile and malicious accusations were quite frequent

---

[1] Pl. of Cr. for Gloucester, pl. 436, 314.   [2] Ibid. pl. 384.
[3] Bract. N. B. pl. 1548, 134. Select Pl. of Cr. S. S. vol. 1. pl. 25, 78, 81, 84, 86, 87, 88, 91, 94, 95, 202, 203.
[4] Sel. Pl. of Cr., ubi sup. pl. 104 (A.D. 1211).
[5] "Der Beklagte, welcher sich auf das Breve de odio et atia beruft, bretet für dasselbe Summen an von so hohem Betrage, dass man nicht annehmen kann, sie seien bloss zur Vermeidung der Haft bezahlt worden." Brunner, Die Entstehung der Schwurgerichte (Berlin, 1872), 472.
[6] Britton, Liv. 1. c. xxv. sect. 9. Bract. III. f. 121.   [7] Britton, ubi sup.

enough to plunge many a man into prison; gaol deliveries were often few and far between, and there he might have languished if there had been no writ *de odio* by which he could ultimately get replevied till the next visit of the justices. Bracton draws a picture of the writ being granted by a compassionate King in answer to the tearful entreaties of the parents and friends of an innocent person who has long been in prison. But John was not the kind of monarch likely to be influenced by appeals to his pity which were not also appeals to his purse, and, as has been indicated, the chief motive in getting the writ was a preference for trial by jury to trial by battle.

§ 23. *Scope of the writ.* It was certainly not limited to cases of homicide, as Blackstone states[1], and Coke[2] and Hawkins[3] imply. The *Mirrour* gives as one item in its list of legal abuses that the writ could only be obtained in this crime[4], but quite apart from the inherent unreliability of this book, there is positive proof that it is wrong here. Britton makes the writ applicable to any felony[5], and between 1200–1225 it appears in appeals of robbery, receipt of outlaws, wounding, arson and felonious assault, as well as homicide; in fact the cases on robbery are far more numerous than those on homicide[6].

At first the writ was confined to appeals because they were the only mode of accusation of a felony. But when indictments became popular the writ spread to them[7]. Thus, while the writ given by Bracton makes mention of appellees only, the writ in the printed Register does not specify the mode of the malicious accusation, and in its conclusion includes by implication both appellees and persons indicted[8]. But it was quite possible for the defence of hatred and spite to be set up to an indictment without any application for the writ. In 1221, two men were indicted, and it was said of one of them that the flesh of a stolen cow was found in his outhouse. He replied that it was

[1] III. 128–129.   [2] 2 Inst. 42.   [3] 1 P.C. ch. 29, sect. 4.
[4] Ed. Whittaker, S. S. vol. VII (Bk. v. ch. 1, Abuse No. 59).
[5] Liv. I. ch. xxv. sect. 9.
[6] *Select Civil Pleas*, S. S. vol. III. pl. 181. *Select Pl. of Cr.* S. S. vol. I. pl. 25, 78, 84, 86, 87, 88, 91, 94, 95, 104, 202, 203. Bract. *N. B.* pl. 134.
[7] Britton, *ubi sup.* The *Mirrour* reckons this as an abuse. S. S. vol. VII. Abuse No. 60.
[8] Reg. Brev. 133.

put there to spite him and to disinherit him of some land which he held of one Warren, whose wife had put the flesh there, and then sent for the King's serjeant and shewn him how and where to take the accused. He was acquitted of the charge, and Warren was committed to gaol[1].

The writ has been identified with one referred to in Magna Carta, 1215, c. 36: "Nichil detur vel capiatur de cetero pro brevi inquisicionis de vita vel membris, sed gratis concedatur et non negetur." At any rate, this provision which was intended to make issue of the writ, which it mentions, free, was taken by the framers of the St. West. II (13 Ed. I) c. 29 (A.D. 1285) to be that *de odio et atia*. It enacts that a writ of trespass *ad audiendum et terminandum*[2] shall not in future be granted before any justices except those of either bench and those in eyre, unless it be for a heinous trespass, where a speedy remedy is required and the King thinks that it should be granted. Nor from henceforth shall a writ to hear and determine appeals be granted before justices assigned, unless in a special case and for a cause certain, when the King commandeth. But lest the parties appealed or indicted be kept long in prison, they shall have a writ *de odio et atia* "like as it is declared in Magna Carta and other statutes." Here the primary purpose of the writ seems to have been to get a release from imprisonment pending trial, but it is a mistake to regard it as in any way connected with the writ of *habeas corpus*[3].

Not long after Magna Carta of 1215, we find a case in which one mark is offered for a verdict as to whether the appeal be by spite or hate[4]. How is this to be reconciled with c. 36 of the Charter which requires the writ to be issued "freely"? It is said that "freely" still made it necessary always to pay for the writ, but, if that be so, what was the use of inserting the word in the Charter at all? Nor can c. 36 be interpreted

[1] *Select Pl. of Cr.* S. S. vol. I. pl. 170.
[2] A commission for hearing and determining any outrage or misdemeanour. Cf. Reg. Brev. f. 123.
[3] McKechnie, 417 sqq. Another view of c. 36 marks it as the dividing line between the period in which the appeal to the jury on the general issue of not guilty was merely a privilege for sale by the Crown, and the period in which it became a right. Brunner, *Die Entstehung der Schwurgerichte*, 473.
[4] Bract. *N. B.* pl. 134 (A.D. 1222).

as meaning that there should be a mere drop in the price paid. We have indeed cases before Magna Carta where as much as ten marks were offered for the inquest[1], but usually a bargain was struck at much less than that—three or two marks, or even one[2]. Perhaps the case of 1222 was an evasion of the law, for in the year previous there are two instances in which nothing was offered for testing the defence of hatred and spite by a jury[3], and the same applies to a case of 1226[4].

We shall find in the course of this book, that most of the methods devised to check abuse of legal procedure were themselves abused. The writ *de odio et atia* was no exception to this. In Edward I's reign, persons indicted of murder got into the habit of procuring inquests favourable to them by the sheriff and the writ *de odio*. These inquests were packed with their relatives and friends. The accused were thus replevied till the coming of the justices in eyre before whom they were found guilty. The St. West. I (3 Ed. I) c. 11 stopped this by requiring at least two of the members of such an inquest to be knights, and none of the inquest to be akin to the accused, or otherwise open to suspicion[5].

§ 24. *Decay of the writ.* When the appellee got the right to submit the whole question of his guilt or innocence to the jury, and not merely special pleas, and when gaol deliveries became more frequent, the ground was cut from under the writ, and it fell into obsolescence[6]. Hale adds as another reason, the trouble of getting and enforcing it, for there must be a writ to inquire *de vita et membris*, then the taking of an inquisition, and finally a bailing by 12 persons[7].

The theory held by some high authorities that it was abolished in 1278 by the Statute of Gloucester (6 Ed. I) c. 9 cannot be accepted[8]. That Statute dealt with a matter entirely different.

[1] *Rot. Cur. Reg.* II. p. 265 (1 John).
[2] *Select Pl. of Cr.* S. S. vol. I. pl. 78, 84, 88, 91, 94 (one mark); 86, 95, 104 (two marks); 81 (three marks).
[3] *Pl. of Cr. for Gloucester* (A.D. 1221), pl. 76, 434.
[4] Bract. *N. B.* pl. 1697.      [5] *St. of Realm,* I. 29.
[6] P. and M. II. 589.      [7] 2 P.C. 148.
[8] Foster, *Crown Cases,* 285. Stephen H.C.L. I. 242, III. 37. Coke says that the writ was taken away by 28 Ed. III and revived by 42 Ed. III c. 1, and that the Stat. of Gloucester restrained it. 2 Inst. 42, 315.

It provided that no writ should be granted to inquire whether a man killed another by misfortune, in self-defence, or non-feloniously in any other way, but that he was to be imprisoned till the coming of the justices, and to put himself on the country for good and ill. If self-defence or accident were proved, the King might pardon him, if it so pleased him.

What had happened before this, was that persons charged with homicide had made a practice of getting a royal writ ordering the sheriffs and coroners to take an inquest as to whether the death occurred by felony or misadventure, and if the latter were found the accused was pardoned[1]. This was forbidden by the Statute. It cannot have been aimed at the writ *de odio et atia*, for the St. West. II (13 Ed. I) c. 29 mentions it as a remedy, and examples of the writ occur as late as 1314–1315[2]. And long after this, writers like Coke and Hale regarded it as still alive, though not active[3].

## THE STATUTE OF CONSPIRATORS

§ 25. The Statute of Conspirators must occupy the remaining sections of this chapter.

As translated in *Statutes of the Realm*, the Statutum de Conspiratoribus runs[4]:

Where it is contained in our Statute that none of our Court shall take any Plea to Champerty by Craft nor by Engine; and [that no[5]] Pleaders, Apprentices, attornies, Stewards of Great Men, Bailiffs [nor any[6]] other of the Realm [shall take for Maintenance or the like Bargain, any manner of Suit or Plea against other[7]] whereby all the Realm is much grieved, and both Rich and Poor troubled in divers manners; It is provided by a common Accord, That all such as from henceforth shall be attainted of such Emprises, Suits or Bargains, and such as consent thereunto, shall have Imprisonment of Three years, and shall make Fine at the King's Pleasure. Given at Berwick upon Tweed the Twentieth year of the Reign of King Edward[8].

[1] P. and M. I. 587–589, 480–481.
[2] *Rot. Parl.* I. 323. *Eyre of Kent*, S. S. vol. XXIV. p. 7.
[3] P. and M. *ubi sup.*
[4] Brackets and notes are reproduced. Their rationale is explained *St. of Realm*, Introd. xliii.      [5] *Now.*      [6] and
[7] do take Pleas to Champertie, and by other Crafts all manner of Pleas against all manner of Men.      [8] Son of King Henry.

Our Lord the King at the information of Gilbert Rowbery Clerk of his Council, hath commanded, that whosoever will complain himself of Conspirators[1], Inventors and Maintainers of false Quarrels [and Partakers thereof[2]] and Brokers of Debates, that [Gilbert Thornton shall cause them to be attached by his writ, that they be before our Sovereign Lord the King, to answer unto the Plaintiffs by this Writ following:[3]] Rex Vic. salutem; Precipimus tibi quod si A de B fecerit te securum de clamore suo prosequendo, tunc pone per vad & salvos pleg G de C q sit coram nobis a die Sce Trinitatis in xv dies, ubicumque tunc fuerimus in Angl, ad respondendum praefato A de placito conspiracionis & transgressionis secundum ordinacionem nostram nuper inde provisam, sicut idem A racionabiliter monstrare poterit quod ei inde respondere debeat. Et habeas ibi nomina plegiorum & hoc breve. T. G. de Thornton etc.[4]

This is printed in *Statutes of the Realm*[5] after the enactments of Ed. II and among those of uncertain date. The Statute Law Revision Act, 1887, repealed the portion from "Our Lord the King" to the end; time has buried alive the rest, and left part of the headstone a blank. In attempting to fill this, we cannot be wiser than the Commissioners charged with editing the Statutes, but it is at least possible to get some hint of the date from other evidence which they have supplied, and the point is of some importance in discussing the question whether the writ of conspiracy existed previous to this enactment. They state that in all the English editions, as also in the printed copies where both text and translation are inserted, this has been printed as one Statute of 33 Ed. I[6] under the title "the Statute of Champerty"[7]; that in the oldest printed copies by Pynson and Berthelet the first part is given as a separate instrument intituled "Statutum de Champertie" and dated at Berwick, 11 Ed. I, that these old printed copies also contain

---

[1] Sustainers of false suits.    [2] That they may thereout have a share.

[3] *Persons so grieved and complaining, shall come to the Chief Justices of our Lord the King, and shall have a writ of them, under their seals to attach such offenders to answer to the parties grieved, so complaining before the aforesaid justices; and the writ following shall be made for them.*

[4] Et si quis super hujusmodi ad sectam conquerentium factam convictus fuerit, habeat prisonam quousque lesis satisfecerit et versus dominum Regem graviter redimatur. *Tottell.*

[5] I. 216.    [6] Pulton (ed. 1670) gives it a definite month—Sept. 1305.

[7] In an edition of Stat. by George Ferrers about 1541, the title is "a statute of conspyratours" (f. clxxxviii).

an instrument intituled "Statutum de Conspiratoribus" as of
33 Ed. I in which the Statute of Champerty is again erroneously
printed with some verbal variations and dated 20 Ed. I, and the
provision and the writ against conspirators is subjoined; that in
Tottell's printed copy, 1556, the two statutes are given as
separate articles, that as to champerty being dated 11 Ed. I,
that as to conspirators undated[1]. The Statute (assuming it to
be one and not two pieces of legislation) concerns itself in its
first part chiefly with champertors, in its second part chiefly
with conspirators and maintainers. The evidence in *Statutes of
the Realm* points to the date of Part I as 11 Ed. I or 20 Ed. I.
External confirmation of either date seems to be lacking. The
preamble refers to a statute prohibiting champerty on the part
of members of the King's court and maintenance on the part
of anybody else. Three such statutes (exclusive of this one)
passed in Edward I's reign—3 Ed. I c. 25 (West. I)[2] which
directs the punishment of royal officers who maintain suits in
the King's courts in order to share the subject of the suit;

[1] MS. in Camb. Univ. Lib. Mm. v. 19 is referred to by the Commissioners as giving the first part of the Statute with a marginal "quere
xxxiii." The MS. is said to be 14th century and on examination proved to
be in only roughly chronological order. It does not contain Part II of the
Statute. Without being guilty of the presumption of putting forward
evidence which the Record Commissioners may have thought comparatively
worthless, the results of an examination of the following MSS. of Statutes
in the Bodleian Library may be noted:

Rawlinson, C. 612 b ("Statutum de Conspiratoribus" practically the same
as in *St. of the Realm*); Rawlinson, C. 666 ("Diffinitio Conspiratorum"
which is like Part II of the St. of Conspirators in *St. of the Realm*, and is
preceded by "Statutum de Chamnptours" which is like Part I of the St.
of Conspirators but is expressed to be made "lan du regne le roi E quart";
and is followed by "Statutum de Conspiratoribus," 33 Ed. I, which is really
the "Ordinacio de Conspiratoribus" of that year); Rawlinson, C. 454
("Statutum de Conspiratoribus" which is Part II of the printed Statute
omitting all reference to Thornton, and "Statutum de Champart" which is
Part I of the same); Rawlinson, C. 459 ("Statutum de campi parte" like
Part I of the printed St. of Conspirators); Bodley 940 ("Statutum de
Champtie" as in preceding MS., but omitting dating clause); Douce 98
("Statutum de Conspiratoribus"—Parts I and II of the printed Statute
but no mention of Thornton); Tanner 450 ("Statutum de Conspiratoribus"
gives Part I as in printed edition and immediately after adds the writ of
Part II without any preface as to Rowbery or Thornton). These MSS. are
not mentioned in App. C to vol. 1 of *St. of Realm*. Their approximate
periods will be found *post*, pp. 33 sqq.

[2] *St. of Realm*, I. 33.

13 Ed. I c. 49 (West. II)[1] which repeats the prohibition and threat of punishment in fuller terms, directly mentions champerty, and applies to the seller and buyer of the subject of litigation; and 28 Ed. I c. 11 (Articuli sup. Cart.)[2] which forbids any officer or any other to take upon him the business that is in suit in order to have part of the thing in plea, on pain of forfeiting its value. Giving of such things is also prohibited and any one is allowed to sue under the statute on behalf of the King. The preamble is that

the King hath heretofore ordained by Statute that none of his Ministers shall take no Plea for Maintenance [al. "to Champertie"] by which Statute other officers [al. others than officers] were not bounden before this time.

On these materials it is useless to speculate at any length as to which (if any) of these three statutes Part I of the Statute of Conspirators refers, or whether it preceded or followed the third of them. Preambles were not constructed with much exactitude, and the doubtful reading of parts of 28 Ed. I c. 11 and the Statute of Conspirators adds to the uncertainty. Perhaps the definite severity of the punishment in Part I of the latter statute indicates that it was later than 3 Ed. I c. 25 and 13 Ed. I c. 49 both which apparently leave the penalty to the judge's discretion; and so far 20 Ed. I seems a more probable date than 11 Ed. I for Part I. There is some colour for this view in a petition to Parliament in 1290[3].

§ 26. As to Part II of the Statute of Conspirators, two officers of the King are mentioned in it—Gilbert Rowbery and Gilbert Thornton[4], the former as Clerk of the Council on whose information the King directs the remedy, the latter as the person

---

[1] St. of Realm, I. 95.          [2] Ibid. 139.

[3] Rot. Parl. I. 58 b–59 a. An Abbot claimed an advowson from H, who procured a corrupt judgment by promising this advowson to one of the judges who tried the case. He also conveyed 15 acres to John of S. Helens (who had been removed in the same eyre for conspiracy) to get the jurors to speak falsely against the Abbot. The Abbot asks the King to inspect the charters of the realm and make some remedy for him. The King "rogabit," and cannot act otherwise than according to the law of the land. This is a case of champerty, and if Part I of the St. of Consp. had already passed, one would expect some reference to it.

[4] Tottell's variant reading does not mention Thornton. St. of Realm, I. 216, note 5.

to whom complaints may be made to secure the issue of the writ which constitutes the remedy. Gilbert de Thornton was King's attorney 8–14 Ed. I (A.D. 1280–6). It is uncertain whether this office were then anything more than a special appointment to act for the King in a particular proceeding. He was made C.J.K.B., 18 Ed. I (1289), and there is evidence of his acting as late as August 1295, 23 Ed. I[1]. It is not an unreasonable inference that the writ mentioned in Part II was to issue from de Thornton as a judge, and this places the date of that part between 18 Ed. I and 23 Ed. I. Gilbert de Rowbery (or Roubery) was a man of some importance in the courts before his promotion to the King's Bench in 23 Ed. I (1295)[2]. It is likely that he ceased to be Clerk of the Council before or on this promotion, and this, combined with the deduction as to de Thornton, suggests that Part II of the Statute was not after 23 Ed. I. So much for the evidence inherent in Part II. The first piece of extraneous evidence shews that it was not later than 28 Ed. I c. 10 (Art. sup. Cart.), for that recites that the King has provided a writ out of the Chancery against conspirators[3].

§ 27. A so-called "*De Conspiratoribus Ordinatio*," 21 Ed. I (1293) must next be considered. The text is:

De illis qui conqueri voluerint de Conspiratoribus in patria placita maliciose moveri procurantibus, ut contumelie braciatoribus placita illa et contumelias ut campipartem vel aliquod aliud commodum inde habeant maliciose manutenentibus et sustinentibus, veniant de cetero coram justic' ad placita Domini Regis assignatis, et ibi inveniant securitatem de Querela sua prosequend'. Et mandetur Vic' per Breve Capitalis justic' et sub sigillo suo, quod attachientur quod sint coram Rege ad certum diem: Et fiat ibi celeris justicia. Et illi qui de hoc convicti fuerint puniantur graviter, juxta discretionem justiciariorum praedictorum, per prisonam et redemptionem: Aut expectent tales Querentes Iter Justic' in partibus suis si voluerint, Et ibidem sequantur etc.[4]

This is not identical with Part II of the Statute of Con-

---

[1] Foss, *Judges of England*, III. 162.
[2] Foss, III. 293. He is several times mentioned jointly with de Thornton as delivering a record to the latter. *Rot. Parl.* I. 29 (A.D. 1290), I. 81, 82 (1292), I. 113 (1293).
[3] *St. of Realm*, I. 139.          [4] *Rot. Parl.* I. 96 a.

spirators, but it bears such a strong family resemblance to it, that there must have been some connection between them, and it is to be found in the terms of the writ which are set forth in the Statute, but omitted in the Ordinance, and indicate that the Statute was not later than 21 Ed. I and probably passed in that year[1]. It may be that the Ordinance was later mistaken for a Statute[2], and there is some significance in the fact that the Statute does not appear on the Roll[3]. Coke speaks of Part II as an Ordinance and the writ given in it as being allowed by authority of Parliament. The Ordinance, according to him, was enacted at the Parliament holden 21 Ed. I,

which ordinance you may read in *Vet. Magna Charta*. But there it is set down to be made 33 Ed. I which errour there, and the mistaking by Richard Tottell the printer, in quoting 33 Ed. I to this branch (as if the makers of this act had been imbued with a propheticall spirit) would in the next impression be amended[4].

That there was urgent need for strengthening the law against conspirators shortly before De Conspiratoribus Ordinatio is shewn by a complaint of many citizens of London to Parliament that justice will never be done to plaintiffs owing to the conspiracies and machinations of the City Clerks and Officers, and their corrupt favouring of wrong doers[5].

[1] A petition of 1293 against champerty recites 3 Ed. I c. 25 and requests its enforcement. Had Part I of the Statute of Conspirators passed previously, it would probably have been recited. *Rot. Parl.* 1. 92 b.

[2] Cf. Bryan, 15–17; and see P. and M. 1. 181 for the difficulty of distinguishing ordinance and statute in Bracton's time.

[3] Its source in *St. of the Realm* is a Harleian MS.

[4] 2 Inst. 561 sqq. No independent authority, apart from those already cited, has been found to confirm Coke's implication that the two parts of the Statute were made at different dates. His view as to the date of Part II was adopted by Lord Holt in *Savile v. Roberts* (Mich. 10 Will. III) 1 Ld. Raym. 374, and by Reeves, *Hist. of Eng. Law*, 11. 239. Jenks, *Short Hist. of Eng. Law*, 143–4, says the writ of conspiracy was based on 28 Ed. I st. iii. c. 10 (Art. sup. Cart.) and the ordinance, 33 Ed. I st. ii; but 28 Ed. I c. 10 indicates that the writ is older (*ante* 26). Wright, *Crim. Consp.* 18, refers to "the first Ordinance of Conspirators" (this is the St. of Consp. Pts. I and II); "the second Ordinance of Conspirators (28 Ed. I c. 10)" (*ante* 26); and "the third Ordinance of Conspirators (33 Ed. I)" (*ante* 1).

[5] *Rot. Parl.* 1. 48 a, A.D. 1290. *Preceptum est* by the council of the auditors of complaints in the City that those suspected of machinations, conspiracies and procurations be removed from their offices, until inquisition and complaint be ended.

§ 28.  The result is:

(1)   There is some likelihood that Part I of the Statute of Conspirators was made law in 20 Ed. I rather than 11 Ed. I, and that it cannot be proved beyond reasonable doubt that it was not made 21 Ed. I.

(2)   The date of Part II is likely to have been 21 Ed. I.

The year 33 Edward I was assigned to the Statute by Tottell and others[1] perhaps through confusion of the "Ordinacio de Conspiratoribus" of that year which defines conspirators[2] with the "De Conspiratoribus Ordinatio" of 21 Edward I[3].

---

[1] E.g. 1 Hawk. P.C. ch. 72, sect. 1.
[2] *Ante* 1.                                                                [3] *Ante* 26.

# CHAPTER II

## THE WRIT OF CONSPIRACY

### ORIGIN OF THE WRIT

§ 1. Did a writ of conspiracy[1] exist at Common Law, or was it due only to the Statute of Conspirators? Later commentators on the Statute thought that there was a writ at Common Law[2]. Coke states that the ordinance was but an affirmance of the Common Law, and that the writ was maintainable both in criminal and civil cases[3]. But the authorities[4] he quotes do not support this, and from similar remarks of his in another part of the *Institutes*[5], it is clear that his real source is an imaginative passage in *Mirrour of Justices* which includes among "homicides in will" those who appeal or indict an innocent man of a mortal crime and fail to prove their charges, and alleges that such were formerly punishable with death, but that Henry I mitigated this to corporal punishment[6]. The *Mirrour* elsewhere enumerates among abuses of the Common Law the issue of this writ without inserting in it the substance of the plaint, and one might argue from this to the existence of the writ at Common Law, on the assumption that though a writer might misstate the law, he would hardly manufacture it first and then criticize his product; but the author of the *Mirrour* was unfortunately capable of doing both[7].

§ 2. We have judicial as well as juristic *dicta* that the writ existed at Common Law. FAIRFAX J. in 11 Henry VII says

---

[1] Strictly, one can scarcely speak of "the" writ, for writs of conspiracy in the written and printed Registers differ in important details from that in Part II of the St. of Conspirators.

[2] Stanf. P.C. 172, 2 Hawk. P.C. ch. 23, sect. 138.

[3] 2 Inst. 561.   [4] The Register, Fitz. *N. B.*

[5] 2 Inst. 383.

[6] Ed. S. S. vol. VII. iv. 16. 136. Cf. P. and M. II. 539, n. 7. The *Mirrour* was probably written between 1285–90. S. S. vol. VII. Introd. xxiv. Brunner, *A–A Essays*, II. 38.

[7] IV. 16, sect. 40. Thus he states that leases are not allowed beyond 40 years (which was not the law) and that it is an abuse that this should be so. S. S. vol. VII. pp. 75, 164 and Introd. xxxvii.

that at Common Law it did not lie except upon an indictment for felony, but that it had been extended by statute to trespass[1]. CLENCH J. in *Shotbolt's Case* said that a conspiracy grounded upon an indictment of felony must be against two at least, for the action is founded upon the Common Law[2]. Four judges in *Smith* v. *Cranshaw* are reported to have gone further than this. In the course of a resolution, they say that false accusations and conspiracies concerning the life of a man at the Common Law were an offence and injury to the party, though no indictment were preferred, that the Statute made on this point only affirmed the Common Law, and that the definition of conspirators in 33 Ed. I gives no remedy, but refers this to the Common Law, "whereby it appears that the Statute conceives this to be wrong and punishable by Common Law, otherwise it had given a remedy"[3].

§ 3. The difficulty of considering the truth of this view is naturally increased by the uncertainty of the date of Part II of the Statute of Conspirators, but assuming that it was 21 Ed. I, nothing has been traced of a writ of conspiracy before that date. Glanvill says nothing of it. Bracton is equally silent in his *Note Book* and *De Legibus Angliae*. Indeed, in the latter, a writ of inlawry is given in circumstances to which the writ of conspiracy if it had then existed would also have been applicable. *A*'s neighbours, coveting his land, maliciously cause him to be indicted of robbery when he is abroad, and the County Court in ignorance of the cause of his absence outlaws him. The writ sets out these facts, and directs *A*'s inlawry. Surely, if the writ of conspiracy had been invented, Bracton would elsewhere have noted it, as one of *A*'s remedies on his acquittal of the charge of robbery[4]. The *Mirrour*, it is true, mentions the writ in a passage which has already been dismissed as untrustworthy[5]; and in the chapter on the view of frankpledge states that all hundredors are to inquire once a year of all manner of

---

[1] Trin. 11 Hen. VII, f. 25. Serjeant Keeble was under the same impression *arguendo*. So too Mich. 5 Ed. IV, f. 126; but the report leaves it open whether the allegation were judicial or forensic. No decision is reported.

[2] 28 and 29 Eliz., B.R. Godbolt, 76.

[3] 1 Car. I, B.R. W. Jones, 93. 2 Rolle, 258.

[4] II. 362–3.                    [5] *Ante* 29.

conspirators[1], but this merely refers to the criminal remedy; and so, no doubt, does Britton when he speaks of an inquiry to be directed concerning "alliaunces" between neighbours to the hindrance of justice, and as to those who procure themselves to be put upon inquests and juries; such offenders are to be ransomed at the King's pleasure, and their oath is never again to be admitted[2]. In *Goldington* v. *Bassingburn*[3], BEREFORD C.J. said that the St. West. II "gives a writ in a general way for a plea of conspiracy, etc. But the King, being advised that this Statute was too general, ordained another which names the cases of conspiracy; and this he has done in this writ" (*sc.* in this action). The parts of the Statute relevant to abuse of procedure are cc. 12, 36, and 49. None of them mentions conspiracy, and one only (c. 12) refers to a writ—which compels malicious abettors of appeals to come before the justices[4]. It may be that this is the writ to which BEREFORD refers. There seems to be no doubt that the subsequent Statute which he says "names the cases of conspiracy" is either the Statute of Conspirators, 21 Ed. I, or Ordinacio de Conspiratoribus, 33 Ed. I[5]. In a second report of the case, BEREFORD says, "This writ is not founded on law, but is provided to punish falsehoods and wicked deeds," and the learned editor takes this to mean that the writ is not given by the Common Law[6].

§ 4. There are eight MSS. of Registrum Brevium in Cambridge University Library attributed to the 13th century. Six of these contain no writ of conspiracy[7]. In one of the two remaining MSS.[8] there is one such writ, but it is that annexed to the Statute of Conspirators, and like it includes the words "secundum ordinationem nostram"; in the other MS.[9] we have six writs of

---

[1] Book I, ch. 17   [2] I. xxii. sect. 9.

[3] (1310), *Y. B. Trin. 3 Ed. II*, ed. S. S. 194.   [4] *Ante* 6.   [5] *Ante* 1.

[6] *Y. B. Trin.* 3 *Ed. II* (ed. S. S.) 196 and n. 1.

[7] Hh. VI. 5; Ii. VI. 13 (Register only 14 pages); Mm. I. 27 (*temp.* Ed. I); Add. 3584 F (*circ.* 1300); Kk. v. 33 (1236–1267. See Maitland, *Coll. Pap.* II. 142); Ee. I. 1 (earliest years of Ed. I; probably includes none of his statutes. Mait. *ibid.* 156). Maitland's warning as to settling the date of any Register needs emphasis, *op. cit.* 116.   [8] Add. 3022 D (?1294).

[9] Add. 3469 E. It is probably early 14th century rather than 13th. A writ of champerty founded on Art. sup. Cart. 28 Ed. I c. 11 is added immediately after the writs on conspiracy. It is nearly identical with the writ of champerty in the printed Register, f. 183.

conspiracy. The first is remarkable. The facts which raise it may
be thus paraphrased. *A* and *B*, "conspiratione inter eos praehabita," and "subdole machinantes" get *C* who is under age
to make a recognizance in the form of a statute merchant constituting an acknowledgment of indebtedness to *A*, their object
being to use this for the purpose of swindling him of his lands
on his coming of age. *C* procures a writ of *certiorari*, which
sets out these facts stating them to be "contra legem et consuetudinem"; it orders those before whom the recognizance
was made to certify its time and tenor to the King[1]. It is
doubtful whether this should be classified as a writ of conspiracy
at all. The fact that it has no duplicate among the writs of
conspiracy in the printed Register, and only one in the other MSS.
examined[2] might lead to the inference that it was a product of
the Chancery, which did not stand for long the fire of the law
courts[3]. In *Goldington* v. *Bassingburn*[4], however, we get a writ
of conspiracy on much the same facts, and though the writ was
abated because the words "and have there the names of the
pledges and this writ" were omitted, yet there was no allegation
that it was inappropriate to the circumstances; a second writ of
conspiracy seems to have been purchased after the abatement
of the first, and no notice was taken of the argument that a
writ of deceit would have been proper, and the plaintiff won
his case. The argument, however, appears to have prevailed
at a later date, for in the printed Register there is a writ of
deceit so closely akin to it that it would probably have passed
muster under that heading[5]. The writ there is a *pone*, but the
type of grievance for which it is framed as a remedy is the
same. By it, several persons are directed to shew why "conspiratione inter eos...praehabita," they "callide praegravare
machinantes" *X* went before the Mayor of Southampton, and
there swore that one of them (*A*) was *X*, and *A*, under this

[1] In the Bodleian Library, MS. Rawlinson, C. 310 has a writ (No. 1 under
conspiracy) practically identical.
[2] 21 in C. U. Library, 24 in Bodleian, 3 at Inner Temple. Those at the
British Museum I have not had an opportunity of consulting. There are
many. Maitland, *Coll. Pap.* II. 116.
[3] Other writs had the same fate. Mait. *ibid.* 122.
[4] (1310), *Y. B. Trin.* 3 *Ed. II*, ed. S. S. 195–8. It is probably the case to
which Reeves refers, *Hist. Eng. Law*, II. 328. [5] f. 115.

pretence, entered into a recognizance in the form of a statute merchant acknowledging a debt to *K*. Thereon, the defendants afterwards procured false and malicious proceedings against *X* "contra formam ordinationis in hujusmodi casu provisae." This well illustrates deceit[1] in its earliest legal form—cozening a court in some way[2]. It was a wrong strongly resembling conspiracy, and more will be said of it later. Here it is enough to note the fluidity of some writs before the phrases in them had crystallized as terms of art. The absence of any definition of conspiracy before 33 Ed. I would justify experiments with the writ, and the Ordinance of that date gives a description generous enough to admit the cases now under discussion. The writ in the MS. concludes "contra legem et consuetudinem," that in the printed Register substitutes "contra formam ordinationis"; in *Goldington* v. *Bassingburn*[3], it runs "against the form of the ordinance by the common counsel of the King's realm in this case made"; but "lex" was used too vaguely at the period of the first writ to imply in it any necessary reference to some enactment[4].

The second writ in this MS. is for false indictment "de latrocinio" and other trespasses, and is much the same as No. 1[5] in conspiracy in the printed Register; the wrong is alleged to have been committed "contra formam ordinationis per nos et consilium nostrum in hoc casu provisae"[6].

The third writ is against persons who by conspiracy have falsely and maliciously procured the accusation, imprisonment, and maltreatment of another for breaking a seal attached

[1] There was a writ of *audita querela* which might have covered this case. F.N.B. 102 H. Cf. *ibid*. 99 I "And there are divers other writs of disceit in the form of a writ of *audita querela*."
[2] Cf. P. and M. II. 534–6. The writ has been traced to John's time. *Select Civil Pleas*, pl. 3 (1201).　　　　[3] S. S. vol. XX. p. 198.
[4] P. and M. II. 175. "The whole mass of legal rules enforced by the English temporal courts can be indicated by such phrases as ...*lex et consuetudo*." Bracton in at least one passage contrasts the two. *Ibid*.
[5] I have numbered these writs for convenient reference.
[6] Practically similar writs are included in Bodleian MSS. under conspiracy—No. 1 in Bodleian 940 (probably *temp*. Ed. I), and No. 2 in Rawlinson C. 310 (14th century. It winds up "contra formam ordinationis per nos & filium nostrum in hoc casu provisae"). The ordinance referred to is no doubt "De Conspiratoribus Ordinatio," *ante* 26.

"cuidam pixide" and carrying away four pounds "pollardorum," and there is apparently no conclusion similar to that in the second writ[1]. The fourth is a writ of *pone* on the following facts. *R* made a recognizance in the form of a statute merchant acknowledging a debt of £45 to *A*, was imprisoned thereon, and died in prison. Seisin of his lands and tenements was adjudged to *A*. The defendants falsely and maliciously procured a charter in *A*'s name, alleging that some one else was seised of the lands after *A*'s death. They are summoned to shew cause why they did this "contra formam ordinationis." The word "conspiracy" is not mentioned, and it is difficult to see how the case could fall within either the definition of Ordinacio de Conspiratoribus[2], or De Conspiratoribus Ordinatio[3], assuming that these were at that time law. If the writ were ever adopted, it is not included in the printed Register under conspiracy[4]. The fifth writ is one of conspiracy with the usual ending[5], and so is the sixth[6].

§ 5. The MSS. of Registrum Brevium in the Bodleian Library also afford no evidence that the writ of conspiracy existed at Common Law. Of 24 examined, no such writ was discoverable in 15 which range over the late 13th century, the 14th and even the early 15th[7]. It may seem surprising that 14th and 15th century Registra should not contain writs of conspiracy,

---

[1] The last words are "ad dampnum ipsius T etc." But it is quite possible that the usual conclusion is implied in "etc." and this is confirmed by the same writ in Bodleian MS. Rawlinson, C. 310 which has the conclusion implied (Writ No. 3).  [2] *Ante* 1.  [3] *Ante* 26.

[4] Bodleian MS. Rawlinson, C. 310 has a writ (No. 4) practically identical.

[5] A blank in the MS. makes part of the false indictment uncertain. But it seems to have corresponded with that in a writ in MS. Add. 3505 G (C. U. Lib.) where false and malicious procurement of an indictment for the receipt of a homicide is alleged.

[6] Inserted among the writs of trespass in the next folio but one.

[7] Rawlinson, C. 331 (Edwardian); 507 (only a few folios); 292 (Ed. I or II); 612 B (ditto); 666 (probably early Ed. III); 168 (15th century); 665 (possibly Ed. II; there is a writ of champerty based on articles made by Edward "nuper Rex Angl."); 692 (Rich. II); Douce 137 (13th century, after 1272); 98 (Ed. I or II); 139 (perhaps early 14th century); Bodley 559 (Ed. I or II); Add. C 188 ("teste" clause in writ of right has date Jan. 22nd, 22 Ed. [I]); Laud Misc. 596 (early 15th century); Tanner 400 (early 14th century, part of MS. is missing). In approximating the dates of these MSS., some help has been derived in many of them from the fact that copies of the Statutes in similar handwriting were bound up with them.

particularly when it is pretty clear from other MSS. of the like dates that Registrum Brevium so far as this head was concerned was settled before the end of Edward III's reign. But the MSS. of the Register vary greatly in size and completeness, and even where two of them are nearly contemporaneous, one may consist of but a few folios, while the other may be five or ten times as large. The nine MSS. examined which do include writs of conspiracy are remarkably instructive both of the fluctuations through which they passed before the printed Register is reached, and of the intensely organic growth of the Register itself. We begin with three MSS. each containing two writs of conspiracy. The first of these is probably of Edward I's reign[1], and the first writ in it has already been classified[2]. The second has no duplicate in the printed Register, and shades off into deceit. It alleges that the defendants "de uno mes [uagio] etc. exheredare & aliis modis inquietare subdole machinantes eundem [the plaintiff]" procured his indictment and imprisonment for robbery, and while he was in prison caused him to be impleaded of this messuage without his knowledge, and thus judgment went against him by default, until he "inde fuerat deliberatus." It has the common form ending "contra formam ordinationis"[3]. The second Register is probably early 14th century[4], and its first writ is like that in the printed Register[5], while the second merely consists of variants of this. The third Register is 14th century[6], and its first writ resembles that in the first Register[7]; the second is like No. 4 in the printed Register[8]. A MS. probably of Edward III's reign[9] has five writs,

[1] Bodley 940.

[2] *Ante* 33, n. 6. It has the usual reference at its end to the ordinance which is expressed to be made "per nos et consilium nostrum."

[3] Cf. Palgrave, *King's Council*, 71–75, for a petition to Parliament raising a somewhat similar question (4 Hen. IV).

[4] Tanner 450. The writ of champerty implies that Ed. I was still living ("Cum inter caeteros articulos quod ad emendationem status populi de regno nostro...*duximus* concedend," etc.). In it are also "capitula narrationum" in Norman-French. The note on conspiracy is LXV.

[5] f. 134. It states acquittal of the plaintiff before "Johnē de Stannde & sociis suis," justices of gaol delivery. This judge is untraceable in Foss.

[6] Rawlinson, C. 464.

[7] Bodley 940. But it concludes "contra formam ordinationis per nos & filium nostrum in hujusmodi casu provisae."     [8] f. 134.

[9] Rawlinson, C. 310. A list of dates of the different kings of England is

but there is some internal indication (as indeed might be expected) that they issued from the *officina brevium* at different dates. The first has been previously noted[1]. So have the second[2], third[3] and fourth[4]. Some writs of trespass follow, then three on champerty, and then a fifth on conspiracy not reproduced in the printed Register[5]. It is directed against conspirators who have maliciously procured the disseisin of the plaintiff from a common of pasture, and appears to be an early experiment[6]. Two more 14th century Registers have six writs apiece[7], which are identical with the first six in the printed Register, and are followed by the note, also to be found there, that the writ does not lie against indictors[8]. Our next Register, probably of the earlier years of Ed. III, is like these two, but has a seventh writ where the indictment complained of was for the receipt of one charged with divers felonies and trespasses[9]. Finally we have the nine writs of the printed Register complete with notes in a MS. probably of the latter part of Ed. III's reign[10] and in another of the earlier years of Richard II[11].

§ 6. There are three MSS. Registra in the Inner Temple Library, all assigned to the 14th century. One of them has no writ of conspiracy, and we gather from it that whoever may have been the parent of the mythical Common Law writ of conspiracy, Walter of Merton of Henry III's Chancery was not;

inserted in similar writing on the front of the folio with which the Register begins. It winds up with a note of Ed. III's coronation (his death is added but apparently by a different hand).

[1] *Ante* 32, n. 1.    [2] *Ante* 33, n. 6.    [3] *Ante* 34, n. 1.
[4] *Ibid.* n. 4.    [5] f. 134.
[6] It refers to the ordinance [of conspiracy] as having been made "per nos et consilium nostrum."
[7] Rawlinson, C. 454 (The Statutes in similar handwriting by which the Register is preceded seem to shew that it is after 1350); and 667.
[8] f. 134.
[9] Rawlinson, C. 459. The "Teste" clause in the writ of right gives the date Feb. 14th in the fourth year of Edward. And the Statutes in the same volume which precede "extenta manoris" end with "Statutum de anno quinto" the commencement of which refers to Edward III.
[10] Rawlinson, C. 897.
[11] Bodley 941; a large Register. The "Teste" clause in the writ of right has the date July 12th in 4 Rich. II. In neither of these MSS. are the marginal notes so full as in the printed Register, and both omit the query appended to the note which follows the seventh writ which runs "quare tamen, quare le secunde brief que sensuit est fayt en tiel cas et cetera."

for it does not appear among a list of writs attributed to him[1]. The second represents the writs and notes complete as in the printed Register, except that No. 9 is missing[2]. The third is also similar, but No. 2 and No. 9 are not included[3], and an unusual writ begins the list[4]. Th. de S. had succeeded to a prebend formerly held by *J*. *A*, *B* and *C* conspired to defraud Th. de S. of his prebend by forging an instrument which alleged that *A* had a title in it prior to that of *J*. This looks like any modern case of conspiracy and is detached from the customary mediaeval meaning of abuse of legal procedure, though it is very likely to lead to it.

§ 7. Registrum Brevium in its printed form yields no more proof of the existence of a Common Law writ of conspiracy than do the MSS. The nine writs of conspiracy given there all express or imply (as do the Bodleian and Inner Temple MSS.) the conclusion "contra formam ordinationis in hujusmodi casu provisae"[5].

The writ was certainly in existence as early as 22 Ed. I, but the case which shews this is no answer to the question of its Common Law or statutory origin[6]. There is nothing in it contrary to the view that it is based on the Statutum de Conspiratoribus, Part II, to which we have assigned the conjectural date of 21 Ed. I.

The conclusion then seems likely that no writ of conspiracy existed at Common Law[7].

### CLASSIFICATION OF THE WRIT IN THE REGISTER

§ 8. The writ under the Statute of Conspirators[8] differs from those in the printed Register. As the nine writs there conform for the purpose of this comparison to one type, the first only need be quoted:

Rex vicecomiti L salutem. Si A fecerit te securum etc. tunc pone etc. B and C quod sint coram nobis etc. ostensuri quare conspiratione

---

[1] 511.9 (VII. f. 89). See the prefatory remark at f. 119 *b* ("Sequitur nunc," etc.).　　[2] 511.4. Writs of conspiracy are at f. 75.
[3] 504 (4). Conspiracy begins f. 95.
[4] It is in a different hand from the rest.
[5] Reg. Brev. f. 134.　　　[6] *Abb. Plac.* 291. *Ante* 3.
[7] Wright, *Crim. Conspir.* 15 is to the same effect.　　[8] *Ante* 23.

inter eos apud N. praehabita, praefatum A de quodam jumento furtive apud N capto & abducto indictari, & ipsum ea occasione capi, & in prisona nostra War, quousque in curia nostra coram dilectis & fidelibus nostris R and S justitiariis ad gaolam nostram de War deliberand'. assign, secundum legem & consuetudinem regni nostri inde acquietatus fuisset, detineri falso & maliciose procurarunt, ad grave damnum ipsius A & contra formam ordinationis in hujus-modi casu provisae Et habeas ibi nomina etc.  T. etc.[1]

This writ differs from that under the Statute (1) in being more explicit, for it gives details of the alleged conspiracy; and (2) in being levelled against two defendants, while the statutory writ mentions but one.  Both these differences will be discussed later[2].  The statutory writ is not incorporated in the printed Register, though it is doubtless the parent of the writs there, and leaves traceable resemblances in its offspring.  The MS. Registra have in historical progression a steadily increasing number of writs which all, with the exceptions already noted, conform to the type in the printed Register[3].

§ 9.  Whether these writs are to be classified as original or judicial is a question to which our law replies differently at different stages of the meaning of those terms.  In 22 Ed. I, it is argued that the writ is "breve de judic[ibus] vel quasi in speciali casu concessum" as compared with the writ for ab-ducting a woman which is a Common Law writ formed in the Chancery[4].  The distinction here taken corresponds nearly with Maitland's: "The original writ issues out of the Chancery, the judicial issues out of a Court of Law; we can say no more"[5]. In this case the Court expressed no opinion either way on the soundness of the argument.  On the other hand, Art. sup. Cart. 28 Ed. I c. 10[6] refers to the writs of conspiracy as "briefs de chancellarie"; and Y. B. 32 and 33 Ed. I[7] implies that such writs were issued by the Chancery very soon after the Statute of Conspirators, for it is noted that such writs are now for-bidden in the Chancery, though the writ in this particular case

[1] f. 134.       [2] Post 59.
[3] Ante 31 sqq.       [4] Abb. Plac. 291. Ante 3.
[5] Coll. Pap. II. 124.  The St. of Consp. it will be remembered mentions GILBERT DE THORNTON C.J.K.B. as the person from whom the writ is to issue.  Ante 23, 25.
[6] St. of Realm, I. 139.       [7] Ed. Horwood in Rolls Series, p. 463.

was allowed because it had been purchased before the pro-hibition[1]. It might be inferred from this either that the Chancery had been issuing writs of conspiracy in competition with those issued by the Courts under the Statute of Conspirators, or that writs of conspiracy should be classed as "original." But either inference is unsafe at a period when "original" and "judicial" are not used exactly. According to Bracton[2], original writs are formed "super certis casibus de cursu et de communi consilio totius regni concessa et approbata," and are unchange-able without the consent of the makers, while judicial writs arise from original, and vary according to the pleas of the litigants. A puzzling third class—"magistralia"[3]—is added; and nothing is said to shew that all three classes may not have had to pass the *officina brevium*; in fact, the author of Fleta expressly states that they must, and speaks of "brevia judicialia in Can-cellaria"[4]. By the time that we reach the printed Register[5], writs of conspiracy are original in the familiar sense that they begin litigation as opposed to judicial writs which are issued in the course of litigation[6].

## SCOPE OF THE WRIT OF CONSPIRACY

### 1. *Its application to false appeals*

§ 10. Before considering generally the scope of the writ, the question of its application to appeals had better be discussed, for it is easily detachable from the rest of the topic, and the law of appeals soon became etiolated by the growth of the indictment above it.

Stern and definite punishment was fixed for those who brought or abetted false appeals by 13 Ed. I c. 12[7]. It is asserted that even before this, the writ of conspiracy lay against them. Thus, MS. Registra Brevium state in their notes on

---

[1] Ed. Horwood in Rolls Series, p. 463.     [2] VI. 260–3.

[3] P. and M. I. 194, n. I suggests an explanation. Coke makes them a species of original writs (Co. *Litt.* 73 *b*). Theloall suggests alternatively that they are writs on the case (*Le Digest des Briefs Originals*, 1687).

[4] Lib. II. cap. 13, sect. 14. *Ibid.* sect. 8. Cf. P. and M. I. 197, n. 3.

[5] Maitland knew of no edition earlier than 1531. *Coll. Pap.* II. 124.

[6] As a general classification, even this is not exact, for some writs figure under both heads. Maitland, *loc. cit.*     [7] *Ante* 6.

conspiracy that by this statute a man shall not have a writ thereof for any appeal which shall be terminated before justices of record, and that the judicial writ conferred by the statute against abettors is in lieu of conspiracy[1]; and the printed Register is to the same effect[2]; but it queries the statement in a marginal note on the ground that there is no express prohibition of the writ of conspiracy by 13 Ed. I c. 12[3], and in the text on the ground that the next writ but one (No. 9 in the series) was made to meet the case of those who procured false appeals against another. These doubts and writ No. 9 are lacking in the MS. Registers. Again, Stanford thought that the writ of conspiracy applied even before 13 Ed. I c. 12 to procurers of false appeals, and that the statute gave a speedier remedy to the appellee than the writ[4], and Coke reproduces this in more general terms[5]. Hawkins says that by the Common Law a defendant may recover damages for a false and malicious appeal by writ of conspiracy against the appellant[6]. But these opinions are based on the assumption that a writ existed at Common Law, which is probably wrong, and the point of its application to appeals could not, it is submitted, have been raised before the Statute of Conspirators Part II (21 Ed. I).

Is there any evidence that it was raised or settled after that date? The Statute of Conspirators itself gives us no direct information. It speaks of "Conspirators" (without defining them), "Inventors and Maintainers of false Quarrels, [and Partakers thereof] and Brokers of Debates" as the persons who are amenable to the writ of conspiracy[7]. It seems that "Quarrels" (*querelae*) did not include appeals[8], and it is unknown whether "Conspirators" there included false appellors. The definition of conspirators in Ordinacio de Conspiratoribus (33 Ed. I) is not much more explicit[9]; but within it are those who confederate

---

[1] MSS. C. U. Lib. Ff. I. 32 (f. 140, 14th century); Gg. v. 19 (15th century); Ff. v. 5 (*temp.* Rich. II); Ll. iv. 17 (*temp.* Ed. I). So too Bodleian MSS. Rawlinson, C. 897 and Bodley, 941; and Inner Temple MSS. 511, 4 and 504 (4).          [2] f. 134. So too F.N.B. 114 F.
[3] Given as c. 9 in Rastall's ed. 1531, and as c. 14 in Yetsweirt's ed. 1595.
[4] P.C. 167.          [5] 2 Inst. 384.          [6] 2 P.C. ch. 23, sect. 138.
[7] *Ante* 23.          [8] P. and M. II. 571–2.
[9] MS. Ll. iv. 17 in C. U. Lib. (*temp.* Ed. I) makes the definition of 33 Ed. I comprise those who combine "pur destruer occidere ou inditer

"falsly to move or maintain Pleas," and appeals may well be
implied in "Pleas"[1]. After 33 Ed. I, a writ of conspiracy would
lie against two at least, and therefore only against two or more
false appellors or procurers of appeals. No attempt is recorded
to apply it between 21 Ed. I and 33 Ed. I to one false appellor[2].
Such authority as we have after the later date deals with the
writ as applying to joint false procurers, not to false appellors,
with one dubious exception[3]. Before proceeding to discuss this
authority, it may be asked why the person falsely appealed
should have wanted the writ of conspiracy at all, when 13 Ed. I
c. 12 provided a seemingly efficient remedy against false
appellors and procurers. At first sight, there is no conspicuous
difference between the sanctions under the writ[4] and 13 Ed. I
c. 12[5]. Indeed in one class of cases, the latter seems to have
been regarded as superior[6]. But Stanford points out as possible
advantages of the writ of conspiracy that perhaps the damages
assessed by the inquest taken by the parties in conspiracy
would be more beneficial than those assessed by the inquest of
office under 13 Ed. I c. 12, and that the former inquest could
be challenged and attainted for a false verdict; again process
by *capias* and *exigent* which applied in conspiracy was not
possible under the statute, so that if the abettor were not dis-
trainable, the appellee would have no remedy; lastly, the
damages payable by the abettors under the statute were payable
on the appellor's account (since he would be incapable of
satisfying them himself) and not on their own, and thus the

ou faire appeller ou inditer ascun home," and states that the writ of conspiracy lies in such cases; but its rendering of the Ordinance in this and
other parts is untrustworthy. *Natura Brevium* (ed. Tottell, 1576) reproduces
this, as well as a remark in the MS. that the St. West. II c. 12 substituted
the judicial writ there mentioned for the writ of conspiracy in so far as the
latter applied to false appeals. Both MS. and book impliedly confine the
writ to the acquitted person in a false appeal or indictment.

[1] Used to mean both civil and criminal proceedings. Glanv. Bk. I, ch. 1.
Cf. Bract. III. 76, 266; IV. 32 (civil cases).

[2] The writ in St. of Consp. Pt. 2 (21 Ed. I) mentions only one defendant.

[3] *Per* SCROPE C.J.K.B. in Mich. 13 Ed. II, *post* 42.

[4] Plaintiff to recover damages, and defendants to be taken. The villainous
judgment was limited to conviction at the suit of the King. Stanf. P.C. 175.

[5] *Ante* 6.

[6] *Rot. Parl.* III. 505 a. *Ante* 8.

writ of conspiracy would be useful to enable the appellor to recover these independent damages against the abettors[1].

§ 11. Assuming these to be the reasons why appellees desired the writ of conspiracy, there is little doubt that it was ultimately held that they could have it. The simplest case is where the appellee is acquitted by verdict apart from any complication arising from a previous indictment, or a nonsuit on the appeal. Fitzherbert states positively that the appellee shall not have a writ of conspiracy, because by 13 Ed. I c. 12 it shall be inquired of abettors, and if they be found, he shall have a writ of *scire facias* against them out of the same court where he is acquitted to render him damages[2]. But this is criticized by Stanford, who concedes that there would be some sense in the alleged rule so far as it would prevent the appellee from getting damages twice over (first by the statute and then by the writ of conspiracy), but objects to the unreasonableness of converting this into the assertion that no writ of conspiracy lies on a false appeal[3]. The note in the Register already quoted[4] is also adverse to Fitzherbert, and writs Nos. 3, 4 and 9 in it seem applicable to the acquitted appellee[5].

§ 12. We have next to consider the case of nonsuit of the appellor. In Mich. 13 Ed. II, SCROPE[6] said that the statute (sc. of Conspirators) gives conspiracy where one man causes another to be indicted, and not where he makes an appeal[7]. Here, the plaintiff in a writ of conspiracy counted that the defendant and another had procured *C* to sue a false appeal against the plaintiff, and that *C* was nonsuited on the appeal. It was argued that this action sounded in abetment, and that

---

[1] P.C. 172. This last argument on Stanford's own shewing is not convincing. For he cites (171 *b*) Fitz. *Abr. Acc. sur lestat.* 28 (Mich. 3 Ed. II; not in the printed Y.B.) to shew that an original writ of abetment for greater damages than those assessed in the appeal was held good.

[2] F.N.B. 114 F.               [3] P.C. 172.               [4] *Ante* 40.

[5] Fitzherbert confines No. 9 to the special case of acquittal by verdict after nonsuit of the appellor. Such acquittal would be on arraignment of the appeal by the King. *Post* 47.

[6] Probably HENRY LE SCROPE C.J.K.B., June 15, 1317–Sept. 1323. The case is in Fitz. *Abr. Consp.* 25, not in the printed Y.B.

[7] The report is ambiguous: "lou il fait appele" may be an ellipsis for "lou il fait autre estre appele." In that case SCROPE'S opinion is that the St. of Consp. does not apply to those who abet false appeals.

the appropriate writ was that of abetment[1] not of conspiracy. Herle, the other counsel tried to prompt the memory of the Court as to another case in which a writ of conspiracy was successfully brought against abettors. But nothing was decided, and a series of subsequent cases proceeds on the assumption that the writ did lie, subject to qualifications against the procurers of false appeals. Thus in Pasch. 17 Ed. II, f. 544, a writ of conspiracy was brought against $B$[2] for falsely procuring the plaintiff to be appealed by $T$ who was nonsuited; no decision is reported, but from neither bench nor bar is there a hint that the writ was abateable merely because it was totally inapplicable to false appeals. One of the main arguments was that as the appellor was only nonsuited there was no proof that the appeal was false[3], but SCROPE[4] pointed out that as there was no previous indictment, this shewed the innocence of the appellee and the falsity of the appeal. In Mich. 17 Ed. II, f. 509, where there had also been a nonsuit of the appellor, and inquiry of the Sheriff and Coroners shewed that no previous indictment had been arraigned, Hervy argued that this was not acquittal because the appellee could be attainted of the same thing; but again no decision appears, and in later law this view does not seem to have been adopted[5]. It was argued also that the writ of abetment, not of conspiracy, was the proper remedy, but the Court expressed no opinion on this. In Hil. 5 Ed. III, the writ was adjudged good where an appellor was nonsuited, and the appellee had been acquitted at the suit of the King[6]. Several MS. Registers[7] note that the writ was abated by the King's Bench at Nottingham[8] before G. LE SCROPE in the tenth year[9] because it was brought in a case where an appellor had been non-

---

[1] Under 13 Ed. I c. 12.

[2] According to Fitz. *Abr. Consp.* 26, there were several who procured the appeal.     [3] Shardelowe.

[4] *Ante* 42, n. 6.     [5] Stanf. P.C. 148.

[6] Fitz. *Abr. Consp.* 22. Not in the printed Y.B.

[7] E.g. Camb. Univ. Lib. Ff. 1. 32 f. 140; Ff. v. 5; Gg. v. 19. Bodleian; Rawlinson, C. 897.

[8] Northampton in MS. 504 (4) Inner Temple Library.

[9] Apparently of Ed. III. GEOFFREY LE SCROPE was appointed C.J.K.B. in 2 Ed. III, and perhaps resumed his office about 11 Ed. III. I am indebted to Mr Hilary Jenkinson, of the Public Record Office, for verification of the initial "G."

suited, and alleged that the appellee "acquietatus fuisset," thus giving rise to the inference of law that he had been acquitted by a jury, whereas the record stated merely "quietus recessit." This note is reproduced in the printed Register[1]. But a writ was pretty soon framed which avoided this procedural mistake[2]. It appears as No. 7 in the printed Register, and is included in the MS. Registers cited[3]. In 18 and 19 Ed. III[4], John Beauflour brought a writ of conspiracy against several for conspiring to cause him to be appealed by one Isabel of the death of her husband. Isabel was nonsuited, and John was then arraigned at the King's suit and acquitted[5]. Nothing was decided, but again no objection was raised on the score that the writ was inapplicable to false appeals. In 19 Ed. III[6], the facts were similar except that after the appellor's nonsuit, a writ was issued to the Sheriff and Coroners to certify whether they had any indictment against the appellee. They had none, and he passed quit. In his writ of conspiracy, he used the common form phrase "acquietatus fuit," and it was objected that he had never been acquitted. But WILLOUGHBY J. did not accede to this.

§ 13. So far, the cases considered have been those in which no indictment preceded the appeal. Of the next two cases, Mich. 21 Hen. VI, f. 28 raises the question whether the writ of conspiracy would lie for one who had been indicted and appealed of the same offence, and acquitted on the indictment; while in Hil. 33 Hen. VI, f. 7 it was mooted whether he could have it if he were acquitted on the appeal, but not on the indictment. In the first case, Henry Brokesby sued a writ of conspiracy against several for conspiring to indict him of the death of J. P. The defence was that when Brokesby was

---

[1] f. 134 b. "G. LE SCROPE" of the MSS. appears in Rastall's ed. 1531 as "syr E. 1," and in Yetsweirt's ed. 1595 as "syr G. L."

[2] Y.B. 19 Ed. III (Rolls Series), 346 shews that in at least one case after 10 Ed. III "acquietatus fuit" was as good as "quietus recessit."

[3] No. 6 in Ff. 1. 32, Ff. v. 5, and Gg. v. 19.

[4] Y.B. (Rolls Series), 566–8.

[5] Plaintiff alleged in his pleading that the defendant's acts were "contrary to the Ordinances in such case provided." The learned editor notes that these were 28 Ed. I c. 10 and 33 Ed. I (Ordin. de Consp.). It is submitted that De Consp. Ord. 21 Ed. I (ante 26) might be added.

[6] Y.B. (Rolls Series), 346.

arraigned upon the indictment, J. P.'s wife came before the justices before whom Brokesby was arraigned, and delivered to the Sheriff within a year of J. P.'s death a writ of appeal of his death[1]. The Sheriff notified and read this to the justices, who nevertheless arraigned Brokesby upon the indictment, and he was acquitted. Could it be said that this was an acquittal sufficient to support the writ of conspiracy? NEWTON C.J.C.P. said:

I know well that it is usual on our circuit, if one be indicted of the death of a man to arraign him within the year if we have full notice and knowledge that he will be convicted[2]; for if he be arraigned and convicted, no wrong or error is done; and the law in such cases is that he shall suffer death for death, but the justices cannot know if the dead man have a wife or any heirs. And if he have a wife or heirs, if he who is indicted be convicted, the wife or heirs have [achieved] their object; for all they want is his death, i.e. execution; if then one be arraigned within the year, this arraignment is lawful, and though he be acquitted, he shall not be acquitted at the suit of the wife or heir[3], for then he would put his life twice in jeopardy, and rather than this the wife and heir shall lose their action[4], and this in favour of life; so it seems that he was lawfully arraigned, and consequently lawfully acquitted.

A good deal of discussion ensued, much of it being directed to the question whether the justices had had proper notice of the appeal. In the meantime, Brokesby died and the other defendants waived the plea and pleaded not guilty. NEWTON C.J. and PASTON J. thought that the notice was insufficient, as the Sheriff had broken the seal before it was handed to them, and it was but an escrow, and that therefore they did well to arraign

[1] "And no such appeal shall be abated for default of fresh suit, if the party shall sue within the year and the day after the deed done." St. of Gloucester 6 Ed. I c. 9.

[2] PASTON J. thought that in strict law the Judges should not delay judgment for the benefit of a possible appellor, though they might do so as a matter of practice. This the Court admitted.

[3] Later, 3 Hen. VII c. 1 expressly preserved this right, while it abolished the mischievous judicial practice established in 1482 of not allowing a man indicted of homicide to be arraigned within a year for the same felony at the King's suit. Stephen H.C.L. I. 248.

[4] The report is puzzling here. It makes NEWTON save the wife's or heir's right to bring the appeal, and in the next breath take it away—a rather violent twist of the St. of Gloucester (n. 1 *supra*). The versions in Fitz. *Abr. Consp.* 6, and Br. *Abr. Consp.* omit the quotation.

Brokesby on the indictment[1]. According to another report[2], PASTON (as well as NEWTON) was of opinion that there had been a proper acquittal, and that the writ of conspiracy would lie.

In Hil. 33 Hen. VI, f. 1 (also reported in Mich. 34 Hen. VI, f. 9), DANBY J.[3] said *obiter* that if a man be indicted and then appealed, and acquitted on the appeal, he shall never have conspiracy nor recover any damages, for no inquiry of abettors is possible; and the whole Court conceded this, PRISOT C.J.C.P. adding as a reason that the plaintiff was acquitted on the appeal, not on the indictment. DANVERS J. then said that if the appellant had been nonsuited, the appellee would have had conspiracy. PRISOT said this was true, because the appellee was arraigned afresh at the King's suit, that is, on the appeal, not on the indictment. DANVERS J. added that it had been adjudged that the appellee should have conspiracy where the appellant was nonsuited before declaration[4].

The principles underlying the restrictions on the right to bring a writ of conspiracy against procurers of false appeals which appear in the cases are not easy to disinter from the graveyard of mediaeval procedure in which they are buried, unless something be said of the procedure itself.

And first, it must be noted that to appeal any one of a crime implied a far more serious probability of his guilt than to indict him of it[5]. For while the rumours upon which many early indictments were founded were often discovered to be unsubstantial[6], an appellor, if he were honest, had definite reasons for instituting his accusation, and the penalties to which he was liable if his appeal failed were a constant reminder to him not to undertake it lightly[7]. As an appeal raised a strong presumption of guilt, even if the appellor were nonsuited, the appellee was not allowed to go quit, but was arraigned upon

---

[1] Br. *Abr. ubi sup.* It is added that if they had had sufficient notice, they ought not so to have arraigned him.

[2] Fitz. *Abr. Consp.* 6. So too F.N.B. 115 H.

[3] So the report in 33 Hen. VI, f. 1, and Fitz. *Abr. Consp.* 4. In 34 Hen. VI, f. 9, this is put in the mouth of Billing, one of the counsel.

[4] So both reports. Fitz. *Abr. Consp.* 4 makes DANVERS J. say that he shall not have conspiracy; but F.N.B. 114 E seems to tally with the reports.

[5] Stanf. P.C. 147.

[6] Bract. II. 452–3. Cited by Stanf. P.C. 97.        [7] Stanf. P.C. 147.

the declaration[1] in the appeal at the suit of the King[2]. The reason for this was as old as Bracton, and it still obtained in Stanford's time[3]. As the King did not fight and had no champion but the country, the trial of the appeal was by the country, not by battle[4]. But no such strong presumption of guilt was raised nor consequently on nonsuit was there any arraignment at the suit of the King where the appellor had not appeared and declared, for it was quite possible for the writ of appeal to have been procured in the appellor's name by some person of whom he knew nothing, and this possibility could not be eliminated till the appellor had appeared and declared[5]. Assuming that he had not done so[6], and that he had been nonsuited, the King, it is true, made no arraignment of the appellee; but the law did not even then regard the accusation as entirely rebutted, for the practice was that the Court inquired of the Coroner if there were any indictment against the accused[7], and only if there were none did he go quit[8]. Now suppose that an appeal were preceded by an indictment, and that the appellor as before were nonsuited after declaration. The rule still holds that the appellee is to be arraigned at the suit of the King; for the presumption of his guilt stands, and stands so firmly that this arraignment is on the appeal, and not on the indictment[9].

This outline of procedure on appeals goes far towards making the cases intelligible. The result of them is that those who

[1] Appeals could be commenced by writ or bill; in the former case, they had to be followed by the declaration which specified the cause of the appeal. Stanf. P.C. 64. 2 Hawk. P.C. ch. 23.

[2] There was no such arraignment where the appellee was acquitted on the appeal, or where an approver admitted his appeal to be false. Stanf. P.C. 148. 2 Hawk. P.C. ch. 25, sect. 10.

[3] Bract. II. 446–9; "quia adhuc subesse possit felonia quamvis appellatus appellum declinaverit." Stanf. P.C. 147. Cf. Britton, I. xxiii. 10.

[4] Bract. II. 448–9.

[5] Stanf. P.C. 147–8; cited and adopted by Hale, *Hist. Pl. Cor.* II. 149*, 150*. Cf. 2 Hawk. P.C. ch. 25, sect. 9 where it is added that the writ of appeal by itself contained no certainty of the facts.

[6] Pasch. 17 Ed. II, f. 544.

[7] The absence of a declaration made this necessary since all details of the charge were in consequence unspecified. Stanf. P.C. 148. 2 Hawk. P.C. *ubi sup.*

[8] Stanf. P.C. 148. Y.B. *ubi sup.*

[9] Stated as common practice ("le ley est use de faire issint") in Pasch. 4 Ed. IV, f. 10. Cited Stanf. P.C. 148.

procured appeals could be made liable in the writ of conspiracy at the suit of the appellee:

(1) Possibly if the appellee were acquitted by verdict, but this is doubtful[1].

(2) If the appellor were nonsuited[2] in his appeal, and the appellee were arraigned and acquitted at the suit of the King[3].

(3) If the appellor were nonsuited before appearance and declaration in his appeal, and there were no indictment against the appellee[4].

In (2) the nonsuit of the appellor combined with the appellee's acquittal at the suit of the King, in (3) the nonsuit of the appellor coupled with the absence of any indictment of the appellee, dissipated the charge against the appellee and made it likely that the appeal had been made with an improper motive. The writs appropriate to (2) and (3) are given by Fitzherbert[5]. They do not differ materially, except that in (2) the plaintiff alleges "acquietatus fuisset," which indicates acquittal by verdict at the King's suit; while in (3) the phrase changes to "quietus recessit," and thus evades any possible objection that might be raised against the use of "acquietatus" on the score that that word must be limited to acquittal by verdict. In (3), as already stated, there would be no verdict (unless presumably the Sheriff and Coroners found that on nonsuit of the appellor, there was nevertheless an indictment against the appellee, in which case he might be acquitted by verdict on that)[6]. Earlier in the

---

[1] *Ante* 42.  　　　　　　　[2] *Semble* after declaration.

[3] Hil. 5 Ed. III, Fitz. *Abr. Consp.* 22. Cf. *Y. B.* 18 *and* 19 *Ed. III* (Rolls Series), 566.

[4] *Semble*, Pasch. 17 Ed. II, f. 544. 19 Ed. III (Rolls Series), 346. The latter case does not state whether the nonsuit were before appearance and declaration. Hil. 33 Hen. VI, f. 1, and Mich. 34 Hen. VI, f. 9, per DANVERS J., "It has certainly been adjudged that he [the accessory—à fortiori the principal] shall have conspiracy where the appellant was nonsuited before declaration." *Contra* Fitz. *Abr. Consp.* 4 "he shall not have conspiracy"; but the context shews that this is a slip.

[5] F.N.B. 114 F, G.

[6] The first of the two writs in Fitzherbert is for procurement of a false *indictment* where one would have expected appeal. The hypothesis inserted in brackets in the text might explain this, but the omission of any reference in the writ to the false appeal would still be remarkable. Other conceivable explanations are the textual emendation of "indictari" into "appellari"

history of the writ, "acquietatus" had a looser meaning, and passed or would have passed as correct in at least two cases where there was no verdict[1]. But in 10 Ed. III, as we have seen, the writ was abated on the ground that "acquietatus fuisset" implied acquittal by verdict, and the words were therefore out of place on nonsuit of the appellor[2]. And this seems to have led to the framing of two alternative writs which appear in the printed Register[3], and correspond in general with those given by Fitzherbert. They are No. 7 and No. 9. The former runs:

[Rex vicecomiti etc. Si A fecerit te etc. tunc pone etc. B and C quod suit coram nobis etc.] "ostensuri quare conspiratione etc. ipsum S per R de morte I patris sui appellari, & ipsum, etc. in prisona nostra, etc. quousque idem A etc. per considerationem curiae nostrae inde quietus recessit detineri, etc. Et ipsum in prisona Marescalciae nostrae coram nobis quousque etc."

This covers the same ground as Fitzherbert's second writ. No. 9 substantially resembles No. 7 except that the words "secundem legem & consuetudionem regni nostri inde acquietatus fuisset" are substituted for "per considerationem...recessit," and thus make the writ roughly equivalent to the first given by Fitzherbert.

(4)   If the appellee were indicted and then appealed, and the appellor were nonsuited; and it was immaterial whether the nonsuit were after or before declaration. For, in the former case, the appellee would have been arraigned and acquitted at the suit of the King[4], in

---

(which is arbitrary), or application of the writ to any false procurer of an indictment, and limitation of Fitzherbert's second writ to any false appellor (which does great violence to the preceding paragraph in Fitzherbert's text). Stanf. P.C. 174 says that "quietus recessit" is used when a writ of conspiracy is brought on acquittal in appeal at the suit of the King after nonsuit of the party.

[1]  Y.B. 19 Ed. III (Rolls Series), 346, ante 48. Mich. 17 Ed. II, f. 509, where HERVY J. admitted the argument that where there is a nonsuit of the appellor and no preceding indictment, the writ of conspiracy should say of the appellee "acquietatus est," not "deliberatus est." No decision is reported.

[2]  Ante 43–44.           [3]  ff. 134–5.

[4]  Per DANVERS and PRISOT JJ. Hil. 33 Hen. VI, f. 1. Mich. 34 Hen. VI, f. 9.

the latter on the preceding indictment[1], and once
again any doubts as to his innocence would be dis-
pelled, and there would be evidence of abuse of the
appeal.

On the other hand, if the accused were first indicted, and
then appealed, and acquitted on the appeal, he could recover
nothing by the writ of conspiracy[2]. This seems inconsistent.
Why should the writ be inapplicable when the appellee is
actually acquitted[3], and applicable when the appellor is merely
nonsuited? The problem puzzled Stanford. His reason for
the difference—and he alleges that Fitzherbert gave it[4]—is that
the appeal could not be deemed to be founded on malice in the
former case, because there was an indictment. But he points
out that this would apply just as well in the latter case. A
possible explanation is the following. It has been pointed out
that if there were a nonsuit, the appellee was arraigned afresh
at the King's suit; and that the trial was by the country, not
by battle. If he were acquitted as against the King, it would
therefore be an acquittal by verdict which would at the same
time dispose of the suspicion raised by the indictment, for any
proceedings on the latter would be barred by plea of *autrefois
acquit*. Hence, there is a complete vindication of the appellee's
innocence. But where he has been acquitted of the appeal, on
the arraignment at the suit of the appellor, his acquittal may
have been by battle, and not by the country, and while it
disposes of the presumption of his guilt arising from the appeal,

[1] F.N.B. 114 E. Cf. *dictum* of DANVERS J. that it had been adjudged that
the appellee should have conspiracy where appellant was nonsuited before
declaration. *Ante* 46: also Hil. 21 Hen. VI, f. 28 where NEWTON C.J.C.P.
asked MARKHAM (counsel) whether, if the appellor were nonsuited after a
year and a day, an arraignment previously made on an indictment would
be good, and the action of conspiracy lie, adding his own opinion that it
would. "Ad quod non fuit responsum."

[2] *Per totam curiam* Hil. 33 Hen. VI, f. 1; nor could he recover under
13 Ed. I c. 12, *ante* 9.

[3] Stanf. P.C. 172 states that "Appel [an obvious mistake for "conspiracy"]
gist a cest jour, auxibien in acquital sur appel, come il faut in acquitall sur
enditement." But this statement must be limited by the context to acquittal
on nonsuit in an appeal where there is no indictment.

[4] In the editions which I have consulted F.N.B. 114 B merely states that
the reason is "because he is acquit upon the appeal, and not upon the
indictment, etc."

it leaves untouched the presumption raised by the indictment, for which of course battle was not the appropriate mode of trial, and to which *autrefois acquit* could not be pleaded. Thus a stain is still upon his reputation which makes the appeal a just one. But the authority which supports this explanation is not free from doubt. Stanford himself states the rule that *autrefois acquit* cannot be pleaded by an appellee acquitted in battle to an indictment[1]. But he queries it on the ground that Bracton held the contrary[2]. Fitzherbert's Abridgement gives a note in Hil. 12 Ed. II (Corone 375) which is in favour of the rule, but it is not clear whether it reproduces anything more than an *obiter dictum*.

## SCOPE OF THE WRIT

### 2. *Its application in general*

§ 14. The writ, we have seen, was created by the Statute of Conspirators of the probable date, 21 Ed. I, which made it applicable to "Conspirators, Inventors and Maintainers of false Quarrels [and Partakers thereof,] and Brokers of Debates"[3]; and the law did not define "Conspirators" till 33 Ed. I. The cases in which the word is used between these dates are scanty. That of John, the parson of Sulthorn, has already been mentioned[4]. One of his defences to a writ of conspiracy brought against him apparently for having given legal advice to some of his parishioners was that it was lawful for anybody to assist or advise his friends in litigation in the King's Court. The complainants got leave to withdraw, and John went quit, but on which of his defences does not appear[5].

It is conceivable that he might have been, if not a "conspirator," at least an "inventor and maintainer" of a false "quarrel," or a "broker of debates." Seven years later, the writ was held to cover the malicious procurement of one, de Welleby, to be cited before the Archdeacon to the Bishop of

[1] P.C. 106.

[2] II. 416–7. Hale, *Hist. Pl. Cor.* (ed. 1736) II. 249 repeats Stanford's statement and doubt.

[3] *Ante* 23.　　　　　　　　　[4] *Ante* 3.

[5] *Abb. Plac.* 291.

Lincoln for trespass[1]. On the other hand, John de Den, in the same year sued the writ unsuccessfully against jurors who had procured a certificate which enabled them to give a false verdict against him, the argument being that he could have recovered by attaint or in some other way[2].

§ 15. The definition of 33 Ed. I includes:

(1) Those who combine falsely and maliciously to indict or cause others to be indicted.

(2) Those who combine falsely to move or maintain pleas.

(3) Those who cause infants to appeal men of felony.

(4) Those who retain men in the country with liveries or fees to maintain their malicious enterprises.

(5) Stewards and bailiffs of lords who by virtue of their office undertake maintenance of pleas concerning other persons[3].

Such authority as we have on the writ of conspiracy after 33 Ed. I is in fact confined to the first and second of these heads[4], and by far the greater bulk of it illustrates the first. If advantage were ever taken of the third, fourth and fifth heads by applying the writ to them, it soon became obsolete to that extent, not because the evil (at any rate in the last two cases) disappeared but, because the periodic disorder of the kingdom made stronger measures necessary. Of livery, maintenance, and champerty more will be said hereafter; it need only be premised here that they were the changes upon which lawlessness was rung throughout our history till strong central government was established.

§ 16. *Criminal accusations.* An analysis of the cases relating to the writ in the Year Books[5], and the Abridgements of

---

[1] *Abb. Plac.* 295 (29 Ed. I). Coke, 2 Inst. 561 sqq. states (as *Abb. Plac.* does not) that this was "an action by original writ of conspiracy," and gives the terms of the writ.

[2] *Abb. Plac. ibid. ante* 2. There is a plea of conspiracy in *Abb. Plac.* 237 (25 Ed. I); but the ambiguity of "placitum" makes it uncertain whether the case involved a writ of conspiracy, or were criminal.     [3] *Ante* 1.

[4] Cf. Ruston's argument in *Goldington* v. *Bassingburn* (3 Ed. II, S.S. 193) that the writ is given by Statute in two cases—champertous pleas, and imprisonment on a false indictment. BEREFORD C.J. did not assent to this.

[5] Including those edited by the Selden Society or in the Rolls Series, and also the reprint of Bellewe in 1869. The indexes of 17th century editions of Y.BB. are bad. Ashe's *Promptuary* is more reliable.

Brooke and Fitzherbert[1], gives a rough guide to the circumstances in which its aid was most often sought. Of 52 such
cases, no less than 35 are raised upon the alleged procurement
or making of false criminal accusations. Seven only of these
accusations were by appeal, the other 28 by indictment. There
were eight cases in which the object of the conspiracy was abuse
of procedure, but not of criminal procedure; one case which
is not abuse of procedure at all; and eight in which the reports
do not state the object. This proportion of the cases on malicious
criminal to malicious civil proceedings, is pretty well reproduced in the writs of the printed Register[2], where eight out of
the nine writs are against those who have procured false appeals[3]
or indictments[4].

§ 17. Where the procurement is of a false indictment, it is
usually indictment of felony, and this in later times is reflected
in commentaries on the definition of conspiracy, which "in a
more special meaning is understood to be a confederacy between
two or more falsely to indict another, or to procure him to be
indicted of felony"[5] or "is a consultation and agreement
between two or more to appeal or indict an innocent falsely
and maliciously of felony"[6]; and this is supported by a weighty
opinion that the writ in cases other than these is founded on
deceit or trespass rather than conspiracy[7]. But even in the
early history of the writ, there are signs that it could be sued
against defendants who procured a false indictment of mere
trespass, and not of felony. One such case at least is reported
even before the definition of 33 Ed. I[8], and in Pasch. 3 Ed. III,
f. 19[9], SCROPE[10] met the argument that the writ is given only

---

[1] Who obviously had access to MSS. not always identical with those upon
which the Y.BB. were based.        [2] f. 134.        [3] Nos. 2, 3, 7, 9.
    [4] Nos. 1, 4, 6, 8.        [5] *Termes de la Ley* (ed. 1641).
    [6] 3 Inst. 143. Cf. 2 Inst. 561 sqq. "the writ of conspiracy was maintain-
able both in cases criminal concerning life, and civil"; and Bl. III. 125. In
a Bodleian MS. of Reg. Brev. (Tanner 450, early 14th century) there is a
note that the writ can be made if a man be indicted of larceny or of a thing
for which he ought to be "reynt" at least, if convicted. "Reynt" is apparently
past participle of "raembre" and means "ransomed" (Godefroy).
    [7] F.N.B. 116 A sqq.        [8] *Ante* 51–52.
    [9] 3 Lib. Ass. pl. 13 (bill of conspiracy maintained in K.B. for one indicted
of common trespass and acquitted) is probably the same case.
    [10] Probably C.J.K.B.

where the plaintiff has been indicted of felony "whereof, if he were attainted, he would lose life and limb," by the reply that the plaintiff was just as much endangered by imprisonment in the case of indictment of trespass as of felony, and that the Court was not advised to abate the writ merely because the peril was not as great in the one case as in the other[1]. In Mich. 7 Hen. IV, f. 31, W. Gervais recovered £40 damages in an action of conspiracy, and when he prayed judgment, it was objected that the writ does not lie on indictment of trespass, "quod fuit negatum."

Against this authority there is the view of PRISOT C.J.C.P. in Trin. 31 Hen. VI, f. 15, that no action of conspiracy lies for trespass, but FORTESCUE C.J.K.B. without dissenting from this regarded the alleged facts upon which the false charge had been made as constituting a felony[2]; the dictum was therefore unnecessary to the decision[3]. In Registrum Brevium[4] writ No. 6 on conspiracy is for false procurement of the indictment of A of certain trespasses in the park of W. de N., and this is paralleled in several MS. Registra[5]. This writ has the common form ending "contra formam ordinationis" implied in "etc.," but Fitzherbert considers that this and other writs of conspiracy for false indictment of trespass and divers other writs of conspiracy are grounded upon deceit and trespass, and are properly actions of trespass upon the case[6].

---

[1] He winds up with the *dictum* (which anticipates by nearly 400 years the famous saying of LORD HOLT C.J. in *Ashby* v. *White*), "for the law sees that in every case where a man is damaged, he has a remedy without regard to the quantity of damage."

[2] Plaintiff had been indicted for attacking B with force and arms and beating and wounding him, and at the same time feloniously stealing 4s. from his purse.

[3] So was that of FAIRFAX J. in Trin. 11 Hen. VII, f. 25 (*ante* 30). LORD HOLT C.J. in *Savile* v. *Roberts* (10 Will. III, B.R.) 1 Lord Raym. 374, seemed to think that the Court had been of opinion in *Henley* v. *Burstall* (21 Car. II, B.R.) Raym. 180; 1 Ventr. 23, 25; 2 Keble 494, that no action would lie for falsely and maliciously procuring a man to be indicted of trespass; and he disapproved of that opinion. But, as reported, the decision is only that an action on the case will lie for maliciously indicting the plaintiff of a scandalous trespass. All reports of the case are condensed, but they are unanimous as to the result.      [4] f. 134.

[5] E.g. Camb. Univ. Lib. Ii. IV. 42; Ff. 1. 32; Gg. V. 19. Bodleian, Rawlinson, C. 454, 459, 667, 897. Inner Temple, 504 (4); 511, 4.

[6] F.N.B. 116 C, F, A. It is somewhat misleading to say that false indictments for misdemeanour "were beyond the purview of the writ of conspiracy." Bryan, p. 27.

§ 18. *Civil proceedings*. Illustrations of the writs mentioned at the end of (§17) may be given. Quite a number of them are against land-grabbers, who would snatch with the law's hands that form of property which then epitomized wealth and power. Thus in *Goldington* v. *Bassingburn* a false judgment had been obtained on an alleged recognizance in the form of a statute merchant and, in default thereof, adjudication of lands had been secured. An attempt (whether successful or not is unmentioned) was made to apply the writ of conspiracy to defendants who had got F to personate the plaintiff in an assize of novel disseisin[1]. A more ingenious piece of fraud occurs in Pasch. 42 Ed. III, f. 14[2]. The Abbot of T, T, and J got T to bring an assize of novel disseisin in W's name, and as his attorney against the Abbot. Of this W knew nothing. At the trial, the Abbot pleaded that W was his villein. T pleaded that W was free. The assize found that he was villein. On this, W sued the Abbot, T, and J for conspiracy. The Abbot died apparently before the case was decided, and we do not know the result of a fresh writ against his successor[3]. In the same year W. J. and R are defendants to the writ because they have procured W. J., to oust the plaintiff and to enfeoff B against whom R sued *scire facias*, and had execution so that the plaintiff lost his warranty[4]. 26 Lib. Ass. pl. 72 is another case of conspiracy to get a man to bring an assize of novel disseisin against the tenants, who won their case because the claimant was the nief of J. M. The tenants then brought a bill[5] of conspiracy against those who had procured the assize, and two of them who appeared were cast in £20 damages. Again, in 38 Ed. III, the defendant conspired and procured A to bring a bill against W before the Constable because W did not wish to enfeoff him of his land[6]. Another device for making the law defeat its own ends was for a demandant in a writ of entry by

---

[1] *Ante* 32.  　　　[2] Cf. F.N.B. 116 E.
[3] Bryan represents an emphatic opinion of one of the judges (Thorpe) as a decision (p. 25 n.).
[4] 42 Ed. III, f. 1. Cf. report in Br. *Abr. Consp.* 5.
[5] *Post* 61, n. 2.
[6] Hil. 38 Ed. III, f. 3. Cf. Fitz. *Abr. Consp.* 8. There is something lacking in the facts, which makes one of the grounds of the decision not entirely intelligible.

agreement with his adversary to get the writ adjourned for a certain time, and then before that time expired to return to Court without notifying the other party and so to recover by default. His adversary sued conspiracy but failed, because the transaction being under the forms of law could not be called a false alliance, confederacy, and collusion[1]. In another case, a Vicar, a Bailiff, and another wishing to defraud R of his messuage procured J (who had enfeoffed R) to pretend in Chancery that he was an idiot, and a writ was issued to the Escheator to inquire whether J had been an idiot from birth or not. R was allowed a writ of conspiracy[2]. So was a petitioner a few years later who had been deprived of his manor by a writ of elegit collusively procured[3]. In Ed. III's reign, we have an extraordinary tale of an ejectment obtained by false conspiracy[4]. A cruder form of plotting is an allegation that A has a better right to lands than B, the tenant, and procurement of A to sue B thereon, so that B is compelled to sell other lands to meet the expenses of protecting his title[5]. Whether conspiracy were maintainable against those who combined to forge false deeds which were put in evidence, and so caused loss of a tenant's lands is not clear; Fitzherbert thought that it was[6], but this is not borne out by the Year Books, nor his own Abridgement of those cases[7], though it is true that the writ failed in each of them on technical grounds which did not touch the real issue. A case which shews the abuse of inquisitorial rather than judicial procedure before the justices was, where

---

[1] Reeves, *H. E. L.* II. 328.

[2] *Rot. Parl.* I. 320 *b* (1314–15).    [3] *Ibid.* 376 (1320).

[4] *Rot. Parl.* II. 418 *a* (*Annis incertis*). Petitioner says that Sir John Pecche shewed the petitioner's wife naked to his retainers at midnight to prove that she was not *enceinte*. Fear prevents him from pursuing his right. Reply: ad communem legem.

[5] F.N.B. 116 B. Writ No. 5 in Reg. Brev. f. 134 (Qu. whether "A" should not be "M" in lines 5 and 8 from top of f. 134 *b*?). The case is as old as the 14th century, for the writ appears in MS. Reg. Brev., Cambridge University Library, Ff. I. 32; Ff. v. 5: Bodleian, Rawlinson, C. 454, 459, 667, 897; Bodley, 941. So too C. U. Lib. Gg. v. 19 (15th century), Inner Temple, 504 (4) and 511, 4.    [6] F.N.B. 116 D.

[7] Pasch. 39 Ed. III, f. 13. Fitz. *Abr. Consp.* 9 (forgery by defendants at *nisi prius* of false release by tenant in tail), and Trin. 46 Ed. III, f. 20. Fitz. *Abr. Consp.* 17 (forgery of false deed alleging that tenant's lands were entailed to others).

the conspirators falsely presented before the justices of oyer and terminer and all manner of rights touching the King, wardship, marriage, escheat, and relief, that the tenant of a manor had given an advowson appendant to the manor to the chaplain of a chauntry; the King thereupon by his escheator seized the manor until the tenant recovered it from the Exchequer, and sued the writ of conspiracy[1].

§ 19. There are a few instances of the issue of the writ of conspiracy for miscellaneous forms of malicious legal proceedings not necessarily having as their object the acquisition of the injured person's landed property; as where some malfeasors sued a writ of trespass against T. de C., and procured the Sheriff falsely to return an inquest (without summons) of people who had neither lands nor tenements, and T. de C.'s attorney consented to this[2]; so too conspiracy to indict another because he had not arrested a felon fleeing from justice[3]. And we have at least one case in which there was no abuse of litigation at all; in Pasch. 40 Ed. III, f. 19, de Bernais and de Herlestone brought a writ of conspiracy against a man, his wife, and a third person, because they conspired to make a false letter under the seal of two of them to the Bishop to receive their clerk for institution and induction to an advowson, after these two had already granted it to the plaintiffs; the clerk was appointed accordingly, and the plaintiffs lost their presentation for that time, but sued *quare impedit* and got their nominee put in. The defendants' acts are styled "faux ententes, disceits ou conspiracies," and it is said that an action of conspiracy lay for them, though it is not clear whether this is the decision, or merely the reporter's or compiler's opinion[4]. The case well

[1] Mich. 47 Ed. III, f. 15. Fitz. *Abr. Consp.* 18. The result does not appear in the reports, but F.N.B. 116 H says of this writ as of many others, "I shall have a writ of conspiracy." This probably means that the writ was good in the eyes of the Court, for the statement would scarcely be worth while making if it merely referred to the matter of course issue of the writ by the Chancery.          [2] *Rot. Parl.* 1. 382 a (1320).

[3] F.N.B. 116 A. The writ raising this issue is No. 4 in the Register. It is one of the earliest writs of conspiracy and constantly appears in MS. Registers, e.g. C. U. Lib. Ii. vi. 28, Ii. vi. 42; Ff. I. 32; Hh. II. 11; Gg. v. 19; Ff. v. 5; in the Bodleian, Bodley, 940; Rawlinson, C. 454, 459, 464, 467, 897; in the Inner Temple, 504 (4); 511, 4.

[4] Bryan takes it to be a decision (p. 25 n.).

illustrates the lack of a complete set of pigeon-holes for early writs. So do several writs in the Register on the borderland of conspiracy, trespass, and deceit which might as easily be classified under one of these heads as another[1]. To the examples already cited[2] may be added one which sets out that the defendants by force and arms took and imprisoned the plaintiff and ill-treated him, and took 300 of his sheep till he released himself and them by making a fine with his persecutors. This, though there is no mention of conspiracy, appears under that title in a MS. (but not the printed) Register[3]; writs similar to it are however included in the printed Register under trespass[4]. In later law, these writs may know their family name well enough, but their early pedigree gives us their clan rather than their family.

§ 20. A question that was not raised in the Courts till James I's reign was whether the writ of conspiracy lay for one accused and acquitted of high treason. The two cases which we have then are not on the old writ but are actions on the case in the nature of conspiracy, into which all the vitality of the old writ was then passing. But in one of them, *Lovet* v. *Fawkner*[5], the question was indirectly important, because COKE C.J.K.B. thought that where conspiracy would not lie against two, case would not lie against one[6]. The plaintiff sued the defendant for falsely accusing him of high treason. Coke said that he never yet knew of any writ of conspiracy having been brought for a prosecution of high treason, that there was no case in law for this, and no book in law that warranted it. "It had been a hard and a strange thing if the Powder Traitors, for the prosecutions against them, might have had writs of

[1] Cf. Mich. 13 Ed. II, f. 401, where several were attached to reply to a plea of conspiracy *and trespass* for falsely and maliciously procuring W. B. to be indicted of thieving five pigs; also Rastall's *Entries* (ed. 1596), 124 where similar facts are set out in a writ of *certiorari*.
[2] *Ante* 32 sqq.     [3] C. U. Lib. Hh. II. II.
[4] "De imprisonamento quousque finem fecerit" (f. 92). "De ovibus in uno loco capto" etc. (f. 96). "De imprisonamento," and "De imprisonamento quousque concesserit reversionem" (f. 99). "De imprisonamento quousque fecit acquietantiam" (f. 102). "De homine in prisona" etc. (f. 106). "De imprisonato quousque remisisset duas pensiones" (f. 109).
[5] (Mich. 11 Jac. I, B.R.), 2 Bulst. 270. This is the best report.
[6] Report in 1 Rolle 169 *sub nom. Lovett* v. *Faukner*.

conspiracy in case of High Treason "[1]. No judgment was ever given[2]. But in *Smith* v. *Cranshaw*[3], a Court of four judges held after much debate that action on the case would lie. At a previous hearing, CREW C.J. pointed out that treason was so heinous that every man ought to reveal it, and to allow this action would be to encourage misprision of treason[4], but the Court replied that no man is bound to reveal what is not true or to accuse any of high treason maliciously, and that it was immaterial whether the accusation were of treason or felony for neither 28 Ed. I[5] nor 33 Ed. I[6] drew such a distinction[7].

## ESSENTIALS OF LIABILITY TO THE WRIT

### (1) *Combination*

§ 21. We begin with the question whether the writ lay against one defendant. That combined wrong-doing needed much more attention from the law than individual offences is axiomatic. If in our own settled state of society "numbers may annoy and coerce where one may not"[8], much more was this possible under monarchs whose government could scarcely cope with concerted oppression, and whose law in the hands of the wicked became more deadly to the innocent than to the guilty.

The records shew that down to the end of the Tudors the great majority of the writs were against two or more conspirators. But was combination essential to the wrong? The answer to this must be considered historically, and it is as well

[1] The comparison is not happy, for all the accused were convicted there. 2 St. Tr. 185.
[2] So the report in Cro. Jac. 357.
[3] (Mich. 20 Jac. I, B.R.), W. Jones, 93 (best report).
[4] Rep. in 2 Rolle 258.
[5] c. 10 (Art. sup. Cart.).
[6] Definition of Conspirators, *ante* 1.
[7] All the judges delivered their opinions *seriatim* to the same effect. Rep. in Cro. Car. 6. Another rep. is in 2 Bulst. 271. It will be recollected that there was no clear distinction between treason and felony till the St. of Treasons, 25 Ed. III st. 5, c. 2. P. and M. II. 500. Holds, III. 253. Pemberton's argument in *Skinner* v. *Gunton*, T. Raym. 176, in so far as it cites Trin. 11 Hen. VII, f. 25, as authority on treason is unsound, for the word is not mentioned there. It may be added that a conspiracy to accuse of high treason seems to have been punishable in the Star Chamber (Case cited without further reference in *Ashley's Case*, Moore at p. 817).
[8] *Per* Lord Lindley in *Quinn* v. *Leathem* [1901] A.C. at p. 538.

to clear the ground by premising that it is the writ of conspiracy with which we are here concerned, and not with criminal proceedings, where it was well settled that combination was essential to the offence; nor with the action upon the case in the nature of conspiracy, where combination was not necessary. Neglect of this distinction has occasionally obscured the solution of the question[1].

§ 22. Taking the Statute of Conspirators 21 Ed. I as a starting point, no hint is there discoverable that the writ which it creates ran only against two or more defendants. In fact, the writ itself mentions one only[2], and presumably it was good against one till 33 Ed. I. Thus the Parson of Sulthorn did not object to the writ merely because it was brought against him only[3]. But the writ whose terms are given in the Statute soon ceased to be demanded, or at least was issued with material alterations[4]. It is easy to guess why it was unsatisfactory as it stood; it needed more padding to apprise defendants of the details of the conspiracy alleged[5]. The definition of Conspirators in 33 Ed. I makes combination essential for conspiracy which consists of (1) false and malicious indictment, or (2) false moving or maintenance of pleas; but not in conspiracy which took the form of (3) causing infants to appeal men of felony, or (4) livery, or (5) maintenance by stewards and bailiffs. But, as has been pointed out[6], the writs of conspiracy do not seem to have been employed for these last three cases, and the deduction is a fair one that after 33 Ed. I such writs should run against two defendants at least. On the whole, the authorities support this view[7].

[1] E.g. Stanf. P.C. 173 where a ref. to 28 Lib. Ass. 12 (a criminal case) is used to support an opinion as to the writ; so too F.N.B. 114 D note. 1 Hawk. P.C. 72, sect. 8 cites 38 Ed. III, f. 3 (a case on the writ), to support a proposition on criminal liability.

[2] *Ante* 23.

[3] *Ante* 3.

[4] I have traced it to but one MS. Register (C. U. Lib. Add. 3022 D). All nine writs in the printed Register f. 134 are against more than one defendant.

[5] "This writ is general, not making mention of the manner of the conspiracy." Stanf. P.C. 175 D.

[6] *Ante* 52.

[7] For text-books, see Stanf. P.C. 173; F.N.B. 114 D; Bl. Comm. III. 125; Coke, 2 Inst. 562.

Thus, in Henry IV's reign[1], R. Avery brought a bill[2] of conspiracy against John Eldestony and others for conspiring to indict him in the Marshalsea. Eldestony's defence was that the Sheriff of Middlesex had sent a precept to him as bailiff of Savoy to return 12 jurors, that he had done so, and that on the order of the Court he had sworn and informed the jurors of Avery's alleged crime. The others said that they were sworn of the same inquest, and, like Eldestony, pleaded that what they did was upon their oath and by coercion of law. GASCOIGNE C.J.K.B. held that the jurors were excused, that Eldestony's plea was doubtful, but that as only one other was named in the writ and he had been found not guilty, Avery could receive nothing against Eldestony, for "one alone cannot conspire." In another case of Henry IV's reign[3], a writ of conspiracy was brought against two. The jury found one guilty and acquitted the other. THIRNING C.J.C.P. said,

your verdict is contrary to itself, for if the one be not guilty, both are not guilty, because the writ alleges that they conspired together, each with the other; but, because you are not learned in the law, be better advised of your verdict.

And then they were put in ward, and returned and said that both were guilty. In Mich. 20 Hen. VI, f. 5, three out of four defendants pleaded guilty; the fourth alleged in justification that he with the others were a presenting jury. NEWTON C.J.C.P. thought that this plea was bad, because it did not state that the three other defendants were the "others" of the presenting jury, "for one by himself cannot conspire." *Marsh v. Vaughan & Veal*[4] is more emphatically to the same effect. One conspirator was found guilty, the other not. It was moved that

---

[1] Mich. 9. Hen. IV, f. 8 *b*, and Mich. 8. Hen. IV, f. 6 (latter part of report).

[2] Equivalent to writ; in GASCOIGNE's judgment it is referred to as such. "Bill" has historically a variety of legal meanings, not by any means confined to Chancery or criminal proceedings. Tomlins' *Law Dictionary* (ed. 4, 1835); *Termes de la Ley*; Stroud's *Judicial Dictionary*. Rast. Ent. f. 124 *b* has a precedent of a bill of conspiracy; so too *Booke of Entries* (ed. 1614), f. 109 (against several in Mich. 3 Jac. I for conspiring to indict Nicholas Stockdale for killing another by witchcraft).

[3] Mich. 11 Hen. IV, f. 2.

[4] Cro. Eliz. 701 (Mich. 41 and 42 Eliz. B.R.).

the bill[1] should abate, for it ought to be against two, and one cannot conspire alone, "and of that opinion was the whole Court." Judgment was given for the defendant. A similar unanimous expression of opinion occurs *obiter* in *Subley* v. *Mott* on facts practically similar[2]; so too Coke as Chief Justice, "no writ of conspiracy lieth unless there be two conspirators"[3]; and the leading commentators[4].

§ 23. On the other hand, in Mich. 24 Ed. III, f. 34, an Abbot and his monk sued conspiracy against J. M. and others, and counted that J. M. procured the monk to be appealed of robbery. J. M. was found guilty at *nisi prius*, but sued for reversal of the ruling, and assigned as error that judgment was returned against him before attaint of any other defendant, and he alone could not conspire. SHARESHULL C.J.K.B.[5] held that the judgment was good enough since the record stated that J. M. conspired with others by conspiracy previously had, and procured the false appeal, and thus supposed the procurement to be solely in J. M. This does not seem to be any answer to the error assigned, and is queried by Stanford, who cites to the contrary Trin. 27 Ed. III, f. 80[6], where it is said that one shall not reply until his companion comes, owing to the inconvenience of acquitting the latter when the former is found not guilty[7]; and according to another report of 24 Ed. III, f. 34, both were found guilty, but one did not appear, and judgment was held to bind him who appeared and not the other[8]. In

---

[1] *Ante* 61, n. 2.

[2] (1747), 1 Wils. 210; action was case, not conspiracy.

[3] *Obiter* in *Lovet* v. *Fawkner* 2 Bulst. 270 (11—other reports 12—Jac. I, B.R.); so too in *Knight* v. *Jermin* (31 Eliz. B.R.) Cro. Eliz. 134; and in *Smith* v. *Cranshaw* (1 Car. I) W. Jones at p. 94.

[4] Stanf. P.C. 173; F.N.B. 114 D, 115 E, 116 K, L.

[5] *Sch.* and *Sh.* in the report.　　　　　　[6] Not in printed Y.B.

[7] *Contra* Mich. 41 Ed. III, pl. 40, where Belknap conceded in argument that if default be made by one defendant in conspiracy—a personal action—the other shall reply. It is not stated what the purpose of the conspirators was. If it were to indict another of trespass, the case would agree with the general rule that the writ could lie against one for false indictment of trespass (*post* 63). The three other defendants pleaded protection. Fitz. *Abr. Protection*, 101 states that there were two other defendants and that the plea of protection on behalf of one did not avail the other, though this was an action upon the case.

[8] Br. *Abr. Consp.* 21. The Abridgements of Brooke and Fitzherbert are occasionally more like collateral reports than abstracts. Coke's qualification

Pasch. 14 Hen. VI, f. 25, the plaintiff got his verdict against one defendant, but the other pleaded successfully in bar, and it was held that he could get his judgment[1] against the former, because the latter was not acquitted by verdict, and possibly they had conspired together[2]. But this case is consistent with the general rule that one conspirator cannot be convicted and the other acquitted; all that it decides is that there was no acquittal of even one of the conspirators in the circumstances[3].

§ 24. It is said that the writ would lie against one defendant if the conspiracy were to indict of trespass or other falsity, but then it is only an action upon the case upon the falsity and deceit done, because one cannot conspire with himself; and there is certainly an early case in which one of two conspirators against whom the writ was brought successfully pleaded that he was "communis advocatus" and went quit, while the other whose defence was not accepted was found guilty[4]. This was before the statutory definition of 33 Ed. I had made combination in general essential, but there are later *dicta* in favour of the rule in Trin. 11 Hen. VII, f. 25[5]; this decided that one defendant to a statutory writ of conspiracy under 8 Hen. VI c. 10 must reply without the other.

§ 25. In Mich. 22 Rich. II[6], it was debated whether one defendant to a writ of conspiracy could be attainted if the other two died pending the writ. THIRNING C.J.C.P. thought that the writ should be abated, because the survivor could not be convicted since one cannot conspire. Counsel said that he had seen a writ before Thirning and Charleton[7], where one defendant had been convicted and the plaintiff had released his suit against the other, and had judgment against him. RICKHILL J. said,

of his praise of Brooke in 10 Rep. Introd.—"sed satius petere fontes quam sectare rivulos"—would be more valuable if we knew certainly what the "fontes" were.

[1] Y.B. rep. does not give the judgment. Fitz. *Abr. Consp.* 1 does.
[2] So F.N.B. 115 E. Cf. Stanf. P.C. 173–4.
[3] In *Smith* v. *Cranshaw*, Rolle Abr. "Action sur Case (en nature dun conspiracie)," the C.J. is made to say "Conspiracy can lie against one only," but the case is ill abridged, and perhaps his *dictum* refers to action upon the case. See rep. in W. Jones, 93.
[4] *Abb. Plac.* 295 (29 Ed. I) and Coke, 2 Inst. 562.    [5] Per FAIRFAX J.
[6] Bellewe.    [7] C.J.C.P. 1388. Fitz. *Abr. Briefe*, 888.

There is a difference between the two cases; for in your case if the one be found guilty, in a manner both are convicted, though he can plead after, and a writ of conspiracy is not maintainable against one only.

Gascoigne argued that the death of one extinguished the liability of the other of two conspirators. MARKHAM J. thought that as the writ was good at its commencement, the death of the other defendants did not abate it. No decision is reported. But a century later it was held by the whole Court that the writ would not abate in such circumstances[1].

§ 26. Text-books tell us that the writ would not lie against husband and wife, though it would against husband and wife and a third party; for husband and wife are one person[2]. The authority cited for the first proposition is not, as reported, satisfactory. In Hil. 38 Ed. III, f. 3, the writ was brought against husband, wife and a third party, and it was argued that husband and wife could not conspire. The writ was abated because it did not shew by whom it was sued, and because there was mere advice, and not procurement[3]. No opinion was expressed on the main point. In 19 Ed. III[4], where a writ was brought against husband and wife and others, and exception was taken to it on the ground that a woman, and particularly a *feme covert* could not be understood in law to conspire, the writ was adjudged to be good[5].

§ 27. The writ of conspiracy, if this analysis be correct, only lay against two at least. But was that all that the law required? Was combination not only essential to conspiracy but also the gist of it? In criminal proceedings it was; but in the writ it seems fairly clear that it was not. The writ included in Statutum de Conspiratoribus, 21 Ed. I, certainly does not refer to execution of the purpose of the combination, but then it refers to no other detail either—not even to combination; but every writ in the printed Register and its MS. predecessors (with the

[1] Pasch. 18 Ed. IV, f. 1. No reasons are reported.
[2] F.N.B. 116 K. Stanf. P.C. 174.
[3] Something seems to have been omitted in the facts.
[4] Ed. Rolls Series, 346.
[5] In Pasch. 40 Ed. III, there is a mere argument that the writ will not lie against husband and wife, but no decision is reported, and the writ was against husband and wife and another.

exception of those which reproduce merely the writ given in the Statute) states with particularity the acts done in pursuance of the combination. The definition in the Ordinance of Conspirators, 33 Ed. I, might easily raise the inference that combination sufficed. But the inference cannot stand, except as to conspiracy in its criminal aspect, against the evidence of the Register, the practice as stated by Fitzherbert[1] and Coke[2], implied in Stanford[3], the Books of Entries[4], and Blackstone[5]. Lord Holt, both at the bar[6], and on the bench[7], was emphatic that something must be done in pursuance of the combination. ✗ An argument of Keble to the same effect[8] about a century earlier puts the rule on the ground that no damage is suffered, and that the complainant is not in jeopardy of his life till he is indicted[9]. Thus, though no actual decision can be vouched for the rule, it cannot be maintained that the slight evidence to the contrary in the Year Books seriously affects it[10].

§ 28. It may be added here that where the plot had been formed in one county and executed in another, there was a procedural rule that the writ should be sued in the former[11].

[1] N.B. 114 D.   [2] 3 Inst. 143.
[3] P.C. 172–5.
[4] E.g. Rastall, Browne.
[5] III. 125.
[6] *Earl of Macclesfield* v. *Starkey* (1684–5) St. Tr. x. 1330; "for I take the law to be plain, no conspiracy doth lie without some act doth follow."
[7] *Obiter* in *Savile* v. *Roberts* (10 Will. III, B.R.), 1 Ld. Raym. 374; "for an action will not lie for the greatest conspiracy imaginable, if nothing be put in execution; but if the party be damaged the action will lie."
[8] "If two confeder to indict me, and I am not indicted, I shall never have action of conspiracy." Hil. 9 Hen. VIII, f. 18 (champerty). So too Br. *Abr. Champ.* 9.
[9] Hawkins (1 P.C. 72, sect. 2) admits the first part of this reason; he urges that the law ought to be otherwise if the grand jury ignore a bill; but in that case there is something more than mere combination.
[10] *Dictum* of WADHAM J. in 19 Rich. II (Bellewe Consp.) that a man shall have a writ of conspiracy, though the defendants did nothing but the confederacy only; and *obiter dictum* of MOYLE J. in 36 Hen. VI, f. 27 (maintenance), that if two conspire, and one give money to a juror to carry out their purpose, the gift is not conspiracy, but the speaking between them is. A *dictum* of PRISOT C.J.C.P., in Mich. 35 Hen. VI, f. 14, implies no more than that there must be at least some previous communication between the defendants to constitute conspiracy.
[11] *Post* 90.

W. H. L. P.

5

ESSENTIALS OF LIABILITY TO THE WRIT

## (2) *Falsity and Malice*

§ 29. The defendants to a writ of conspiracy were not liable unless they acted falsely and maliciously. We shall look in vain in the earlier law for any minute dissection of either term. Certain acts or occurrences were a good defence, and not much discussion was spent upon their psychological bearing, whatever the rule may have been at a later period[1].

The *nexus* by which we have bound many of these defences under one title is but a loose one; yet it is partly justified by the half conscious classification of the Tudor commentators.

"The charge of conspiracy," says Stanford[2], "ought to be that he did this with others and falsely and maliciously, as in part appears by the said St. West. II c. 12, and more fully by the Stat. 33, Ed. I[3]." And it seems that before the definition of conspirators in the latter enactment, judgment might pass against a defendant because he would not reply to the alleged malice[4]. The writ in the Statute of Conspirators, 21 Ed. I, makes no mention of malice or falsity, but it is in such general terms that it may well have implied these words; and it is very early after the Statute that the writ in the modified form in which it so soon becomes familiar contains them[5]. The genuine descendants of the writ, as distinct from those moulded on deceit or trespass, invariably incorporate them.

Not one of the nine writs of conspiracy in the printed Register[6] omits them, nor does any true writ of conspiracy in

---

[1] In *Varrell* v. *Wilson* (Pasch. 36 Eliz.) Moore, 600, pl. 828, it was held a defence to conspiracy that defendant's goods had been stolen, and found in the possession of the plaintiff against whom defendant preferred a bill of indictment, and gave evidence to the jury which acquitted plaintiff; for finding the goods in plaintiff's possession was sufficient cause of suspicion. In Viner's *Abr. Consp.* (F) 26, this is cited as a case of conspiracy. The report leaves it open whether the writ was conspiracy or case.

[2] P.C. 173. Cf. 9 Rep. at p. 57 where Coke states the essentials of "confederacy."

[3] Ord. de Consp. *ante* 1.

[4] Trin. 32 Ed. I. *Abb. Plac.* 297.

[5] *de Welleby's Case.* Hil. 29 Ed. I, *Abb. Plac.* 295.

[6] f. 134. Cf. Mich. 47 Ed. III, f. 17, where the writ with which the report begins includes these words.

the MS. Registers consulted[1]. The Ordinacio de Conspiratoribus, 33 Ed. I, defines as conspirators those (*inter alios*) who each "aid and bear the other falsely and maliciously to indite, or cause to indite, or falsely to move or maintain pleas"[2].

Probably no importance attaches to the absence of "maliciously" in the latter part of this clause. The Courts appear to have founded no distinction upon it[3].

§ 30. *Indictors.* The story of what justifies conspiracy in its old sense is the story of a long struggle to solve the legal puzzle of punishing the rogue who would kill and rob with the law's own weapons without at the same time terrifying the honest accuser or plaintiff. The King needed officials to administer his justice and from time immemorial laymen—now doomsmen, now jurors—were called upon to assist them, and again and again the King seems in danger of having his justice made the tool of the corrupt official, and the malicious layman. An oft-repeated rule is that the writ will not lie against indictors. It occurs with monotonous regularity in written and printed Registers[4], and very early in the former[5]; so too in the books of practice or comment[6]. The Year Books attest its age. In Trin. 17 Ed. II, f. 547, it was decided that indictors on the inquest could not be sued by writ of conspiracy. SCROPE[7] at first inclined to the view that if one procured himself to be put on the panel for the express purpose of indicting somebody

---

[1] E.g. (to take the earliest only) C. U. Lib. Ii. vi. 28 and 42 (early 14th century). When Bryan (p. 40) states that express reference to malice in conspiracy cases between 1307–1509 practically ceased, we must add that the writ in every such case almost certainly included "malitiose."

[2] *Ante* 1.

[3] In a bill preferred in the Star Chamber for conspiracy, the words "falso et malitiose" were essential. Per RICHARDSON J. in *Tailor* v. *Towlin* (Mich. 4 Car. I) Godbolt, 444.　　　　　[4] f. 134.

[5] C. U. Lib. Ii. vi. 42; Ll. iv. 17 (*temp.* Ed. I); Ff. i. 32; Ff. v. 5; Gg. v. 19. So too Bodleian Lib. MSS. Rawlinson, C. 454, 459, 667, 897; Bodleian, 941.

[6] Stanf. P.C. 173; F.N.B. 115 c; Reeves, II. 328. Rastall, f. 123–4 gives several pleas in bar for indictors. The indictor should put in the record of the indictment. Otherwise he would be met by the replication "nul tiel record." Y.B. Mich. 19 Hen. VI, f. 19; Br. *Abr. Consp.* 17 and Rastall's *Entries*, f. 123 a. Bryan (p. 24) correctly states the general rule that the writ did not apply against indictors, but on p. 27 proceeds on the assumption that it did.

[7] Judge C.P. Sep. 27, 1323. C.J.K.B. March 21, 1324.

the writ would lie. But to this counsel replied that when the indictor is put on the panel the law intends that he comes by the Sheriff and by distress of law, and that he does not wish to say anything except the truth on his oath. SCROPE took the broader ground in his judgment that "if the writ were granted against indictors, they would often rather refrain from indicting anybody, through fear of being oppressed." In Mich. 7 Hen. IV, f. 31, the defendants pleaded to a writ of conspiracy for indicting W. Gervais that they were impanelled for the King before the Justices of the Peace in Norfolk and that what they did was by their oath; and not a word was said against this by the other side, though they took other objections[1], and in Pasch. 4 Hen. VI, f. 23, the only objection raised to the plea that one of the defendants was an indictor was that he had not produced the record which would shew it[2]. At a later period another reason given for the exemption of indictors is "because the law intends when a man is sworn that he wishes to clear his conscience"[3]. But the doubt that troubled SCROPE was raised again in a slightly different form in Pasch. 21 Ed. III, f. 17, where a defendant pleaded that he and 11 others on oath presented the plaintiff at a leet, so that what they did, they did as indictors. The plaintiff answered that the defendants had conspired to indict long before the indictment was made. W. DE THORPE J. said that while conspirators are all the time in falsity, the defendant's oath, when he was on the inquest and sworn to speak the truth, prevented this from being conspiracy; and that it was not right to convict a man of it when he did nothing but what the law wished. But he is not reported to have dealt with the main point or to have given any decision. Nor does a later case in the same reign[4] carry us any further. There one defendant pleaded that he with other defendants was an indictor, another that he was a hundredor, and that the indictment was taken before him, and so he was like a judge

---

[1] *Ante* 54.

[2] MARTYN J. indulged in personalities at the expense of Rolf's persistent but unsuccessful arguments; "Rolf ad bien disné cest jour; car come me semble il ad mangé d'un error."

[3] Per ENGLEFIELD J. Pasch. 27 Hen. VIII, f. 2.

[4] Mich. 47 Ed. III, ff. 16–17.

in this case. It was objected to this that the defendants who
were indictors had made the conspiracy before the indictment.
Candish argued, "we must in this case maintain the ancient
judgments of our predecessors—that conspiracy cannot exist in
this case." But "all was demurred and adjourned." The
problem presented itself with an additional complication in
Mich. 20 Hen. VI, f. 5[1], where the plea was that the defendant
had been sworn with others before the Justices of the Peace
to present for the King, and informed his companions of the
felony alleged against the plaintiff. Then, before verdict, the
Justices removed him from the panel. The plaintiff replied
to this that the conspiracy took place two days before the
defendant was sworn. NEWTON C.J.C.P. drew a distinction
between the juror who gives a verdict after a conspiracy previously had, and the juror who is discharged before verdict.
After verdict given, the law implies that all that was conspired
previously was lawfully done, because his oath excuses him;
but on discharge the conspiracy shall not be deemed lawful.
Some argument and discussion ensued and Yelverton[2] (then a
Serjeant) exposed the technicality of NEWTON'S distinction by
pointing out that if the defendant could lawfully inform his
companions when he was a juror, it would be marvellous that
this should become wrongful by the act of the judge, and
PASTON J. admitted the force of this. NEWTON adhered to his
view. According to another report[3], the best opinion was that
the plea was good, and with this most commentators agree[4].
But this still leaves open the question raised by the plaintiff's
replication—that the defendant had conspired before he was.
sworn[5]. In Pasch. 5 Jac. I, the point raised in Pasch. 21 Ed. III,
f. 17, was incidentally settled in favour of indictors and their
immunity was stated in sweeping terms by POPHAM and

[1] Report continued Trin. 20 Hen. VI, f. 33.
[2] Not in Y.B. report, but in Fitz. *Abr. Consp.* 2.
[3] Br. *Abr. Consp.* 1.
[4] F.N.B. 115 D; Stanf. P.C. 173; *Contra* Tottell, Nat. Brev. "Writ de
Conspiracione." Viner, *Abr. Consp.* A (4) reproduces Br. *Abr. Consp.* 1.
[5] Stanf. P.C. 173 states that no writ of conspiracy will lie because it
cannot be intended false or malicious when the jurors do it by virtue of their
oath. The reports cited by him are not positive. 27 Lib. Ass. 12 is on a
prosecution, not a writ, of conspiracy.

COKE C.JJ., the chief Baron, the Lord Chancellor, and all the rest of the Court in the Star Chamber case of *Floyd* v. *Barker*[1]. They are said to have resolved that when a grand inquest indicts one of murder or felony, and the accused is acquitted, yet no conspiracy lies for him who is acquitted against the indictors, because they are returned by the Sheriff by process of law to make inquiry of offences upon their oath, and it is for the service of the King and the Commonwealth; and they shall not be impeached for any conspiracy or practice before the indictment, for the law will not suppose any un-indifferent, when he is sworn to serve the King. Before leaving the topic of indictors it must be noted that they were under a Statute 9 Hen. V c. 1 (made perpetual by 18 Hen. VI c. 12) liable both criminally and civilly if they were procured maliciously to indict persons of treason or felony alleged by the indictment to have been committed at a place which did not exist. Of the facts which led to the making of this law more will be said hereafter.

§ 31. *Jurors.* Thus far we have dealt with the indictor as distinct from the juror in general, but their exemption was the same, and is referred to occasionally and naturally in the same context[2]. But not always[3]; in Mich. 13 Ed. II, f. 401, the defendants say that they ought not to reply to the writ because they were sworn on the same inquest together with others, and gave their verdict according to their understanding on oath, and they claim judgment for that they were *judicatores.* Answer; they were procurers of the indictment, not *judicatores.* How the matter ended is not stated, but shortly afterwards it was held that an action in conspiracy could not, and ought not, to lie against jurors who had found one an abettor in a false appeal. Error was alleged and allowed, but on another ground[4]. Less than a century after, GASCOIGNE C.J.K.B.[5] held that their

---

[1] 12 Rep. 23. The report points Sir E. Sugden's criticism of Coke's system of turning every judgment into a string of general propositions. We are not even told what the facts were here, except that one of the defendants was a justice of the grand sessions in Anglesey.

[2] Browne, *Ent.* (1671) 130, plea of jurors put on inquest which indicted.

[3] *Ibid.* 133 (plea of defendant forced by Justices to indict and give evidence).

[4] *Abb. Plac.* 355 (Trin. 19 Ed. II).

[5] Mich. 9 Hen. IV, f. 8.

oath excused 12 men who were sworn to inquire of divers articles for the King, and who pleaded to a bill of conspiracy that what they did was upon their oath and by coercion of law. But at a later date, a jury which acquitted a felon or traitor against manifest proof might be charged in the Star Chamber[1].

§ 32. *Witnesses.* We have dealt with jurors. But what of those who informed them or the Court? Had the witness or informer as distinct from the juror a good defence to an action for conspiracy? At the outset of our history of trial by jury, the easy but plausible answer seems to be that the jurors were the witnesses. But this is true only in the sense that the jury were supposed to be pretty well acquainted with the merits of the case; "but even in the early years of the 13th century they were not, and were hardly supposed to be, eye-witnesses"[2]. Their knowledge might be made more accurate by excluding the sick, the poor, the villein, by selecting them from the neighbourhood, by the challenge, by the judge's "charge," by the statements of the party or his counsel[3], by their general duty to ascertain the facts before the trial began[4]—and yet it might be but second-hand knowledge. Was the first-hand evidence of the man who did see admitted in Court to help the jurors? There is nothing to shew that it was not, though it was probably not sworn evidence[5]. By what means or at what period the rule of making witnesses give evidence on oath in Court became universal we do not know[6], but the line between jurors and one class of witnesses appears in the practice (known in the early 13th century) of getting the evidence of a composite body of jurors and the witnesses to a deed where there was a dispute as to its genuineness; and the line becomes a fissure— perhaps a gulf—by Edward III's reign when the Year Books tell us that a person under age may be a witness, that witnesses

---

[1] *Floyd* v. *Barker*, 12 Rep. 23–24 (Pasch. 5 Jac. I). *Ante* 70.
[2] P. and M. II. 622, 628.
[3] Thayer, *Evidence*, Pt. I (1896), pp. 90, 112, 120.
[4] They had at least a fortnight for this. P. and M. II. 627. The practice is referred to by REDE J. in Mich. 20 Hen. VII, f. 11.
[5] P. and M. II. 628.
[6] Thayer, 122 et sqq.

cannot be challenged, and that they are charged differently from jurors[1].

It was for the false giving of "real" rather than "personal" evidence that the writ of conspiracy was sought in Pasch. 39 Ed. III, f. 13. One Clinton, had sued a writ of wardship against T. B. who said that he was tenant in tail under a gift of Clinton. Clinton replied that T. B. had released the lands, and at *nisi prius*, certain persons conspired to forge a false release by means of which the inquest found against T. B. The question was whether their act was conspiracy. THORPE[2] said, "And do you think that you shall have a writ of conspiracy by reason of evidence? You shall not have it," and later, "What was put in evidence is not comprised in the record. Wherefore the Court adjudges that you take nothing by your writ." In Mich. 7 Hen. VI, f. 13, conspiracy was brought against three for indicting the plaintiff. The defence was that Elis Davy one of the defendants was before the Justices "with his eye out and his tongue cut" and was sworn by them to give evidence for the King. He asked the other two defendants what he should do, and they told him to obey the Justices' order. He did so, and contended in defence that this was all the alleged conspiracy. HALS J. said that it could not be deemed the alleged conspiracy "for he has supposed in you a tortious conspiracy, and you have not, 'conu cela,' 'eins un droitrel'[3]: which thing he did by command of the Justices." But a note is added that it seems a wrongful conspiracy, because the Justices charged him to inform the inquest of those who beat, maimed and blinded him in one eye[4], and he informed the inquest of others, and so was not warranted by the Justices. This case is inconclusive. So is Mich. 35 Hen. VI, f. 14—a much fuller case which dealt rather with the informer of the jury which indicts than with the witness who testifies to the jury which tries.

[1] Thayer, 97–100 and *Y.B.* 11 *and* 12 *Ed. III*, 338, and 12 *and* 13 *Ed. III*, 4 (Rolls Series); 12 Lib. Ass. pl. 12; Fitz. *Abr. Challenge*, 9; 23 Lib. Ass. 11, there cited p. 100; cf. P. and M. II. 628–629.

[2] Either ROBERT DE THORPE C.J.C.P., June 17, 1356 for nearly 15 years, or WILLIAM DE THORPE, judge, April 23, 1342.

[3] "Droiturel" according to Godefroy means "just."

[4] "Monoculerent" presumably means this. It is an expressive compound word.

A writ of conspiracy was brought against two. It was pleaded for them that they saw the plaintiff kill J. S. and informed one of the Guardians of the Peace of this at the Sessions of the Peace at Exeter. A clerk took down in writing one of the defendant's information; and that defendant delivered it to the Guardian of the Peace, who handed it on to the grand inquest and they found a true bill. Considerable discussion, and difference of judicial opinion followed. According to DANVERS J. it was not conspiracy, for any man could inform the Justices of a felony and pray the jurors to inquire thereof, provided he did not "labour" them to indict the accused thereof. ASHTON[1] backed this view by quoting the proclamation of the justices at every Session, "Et si ascun voit venir eins, & monstr' ascun chose pur le Roy, il aura audience." PRISOT C.J.C.P. thought that the plea was bad, because it did not traverse, but merely denied a conspiracy which did not exist. The information given by the defendants was no conspiracy, for a conspiracy is a speaking among persons before a thing is done as to how it shall be done, and the words of the writ, "conspiratione inter eos praehabita," prove this. Here no such speaking was shewn. According to MOYLE J. it was conspiracy, because the defendants had shewn no interest in informing the justices, except that they had seen the deed. Had it been alleged that the deceased was the cousin or servant of the defendants, or that the common rumour of the country was that the plaintiff had killed the man, that would have given some colour to the charge[2]. Again, if this were not conspiracy nobody could ever have that action, for every defendant to it would plead that he saw the plaintiff commit the deed, and if that issue were taken against the plaintiff, then the Court would cause him to be hanged, "le quel sera inconvenient." Thus when the defendants said that they "saw," that was false by the common presumption of law, since the plaintiff was acquitted[3]. DANBY J. took the

---

[1] Unmentioned in Foss. Fitz. *Abr. Consp.* however seems to imply that he was a judge.

[2] So too DANBY J. According to Br. *Abr. Consp.* 4 "it was agreed that to say that he who was killed was his cousin or servant, or that the common fame was that the plaintiff killed him—these are good matters of plea in conspiracy." See too Rast. *Entries*, f. 124 b; Browne, *Ent.* 130.

[3] A fallacy. It was put forward by Serjeant Grevill and exposed by FINEUX C.J. in Mich. 20 Hen. VII, f. 11 (*post* 75–76).

same view, holding that the plaintiff's acquittal stopped the defendants from saying that they were present when the alleged felony was committed[1]. According to another report, the best opinion was that the special plea was bad (apparently on the ground taken by Prisot) and that the general issue should be pleaded and the matter of excuse should be put in evidence[2]. The matter was again fully debated in Mich. 20 Hen. VII, f. 11, which was an offshoot of the remarkable case *Kebell* v. *Vernon*[3] (A.D. 1502) tried on the ravishment of a woman in the Star Chamber. In the Year Book case, conspiracy was brought against E. Keble (*sic*) and several others, who pleaded that the common voice and fame was that a certain felony had been committed, and that the defendants as they were riding to a certain town, found a great multitude of people arrayed in a forcible manner, among whom was the plaintiff, and that then at the Sessions held at D. before the Justices proclamation was made that if there be any to inform the Justices, etc., that he come; that the defendants therefore came and were sworn, and shewed this matter to the justices, and then the plaintiff was indicted, etc., and that this was the alleged conspiracy. It was argued for the plaintiff that the defendants came of their own pleasure, for the defendants that great mischief would ensue if every one who gives evidence should be charged with conspiracy, for then no one would give evidence, and that would favour

---

[1] "And he wished to have said more, but he was interrupted, because all the Justices went in the Chancery."

[2] Br. *Abr. Consp.* 4. A note is added "See 37 Hen. VI, f. 3, and 22 Hen. VI, f. 35, where his [defendant's] matter is justification, he shall take this by plea, but where this is not conspiracy, administration, nor maintenance, he shall take the general issue, and shall give the matter in evidence." The cases referred to are not on conspiracy, but assuming the correctness of Brooke's statement of the law a few words may be added as to the distinction in the law of pleading here indicated. There was a considerable advantage in a special plea as contrasted with the mere plea of the general issue; it was possible for the defendant to insert in it a good deal of what would now be called evidence, and thus to apprise the jurors of his defence in a clear and permanent form instead of leaving the facts in a hazy condition in their minds, as was quite possible at a time when the evidence of witnesses apart from jurors was, if given at all, of little account and when the jurors, though they were supposed to know the facts, themselves, might have gleaned a very indefinite account of them before the trial. See Thayer, 114–120.

[3] Select Cases in the Star Chamber. S. S. vol. XVI. p. 130.

felons. GREVILL J. (then a Serjeant) contended that the defendant [Keble] gave evidence at his peril, for the law does not wish a man to give false evidence: therefore, because the plaintiff was acquitted, the evidence was false[1]; and the life of a man ought to be more specially favoured than these men who give evidence. Coningsby (then a Serjeant) argued for the defendant that everything could be pleaded in excuse of conspiracy except matters merely contrary to the issue previously tried; but that he could not say that the plaintiff in the conspiracy is guilty of felony, because he is estopped by the verdict which can never be put in issue again; here, however, the matter of the plea was not merely contrary to the issue; and TREMAILE J. and FINEUX C.J.K.B. approved this argument. REDE J. was of opinion that special matters should be pleaded for the doubts of laymen unacquainted with the law, and to put them in the judgment of the justices. He put it that the deceners[2] and reeve of a certain town are called before the Justices, and that one for the town gives evidence and informs the Justices, and the Justices command him to make a bill, and he does so, and that the person whom he accuses is acquitted and brings conspiracy; REDE thought that the defendant in such a case should plead this specially and not be driven to the general issue, and that this was not conspiracy; "for if the four men and the reeve do not come when they are called, they shall be amerced"; and he wound up, "when the defendant for the zeal of justice comes and informs the justices, and not of malice, it is right that he be discharged." FINEUX C.J.K.B. followed on the same side; his view was that the plea was an excuse, for at each sessions every man can come for the common profit, and if he come for this purpose and for the zeal that he has for justice, and not of malice, he does well enough for the common profit, which ought to excuse him,

---

[1] A harsh view, for the acquittal implies no more than that the jurors think that the witness's evidence against the accused was mistaken, not that it was a lie. See the judgment of FINEUX C.J. (*infra*).

[2] The term varied in meaning. At one time decener signified the chief man of a "dozen," later, one that is sworn to the King's peace. Deceners are also spoken of as presenting felons for theft. *Termes de la Ley* (ed. 1636).

*secus* if it were of malice; and in false imprisonment or conspiracy, the defendant shall justify, because a certain felony
was done, and the defendant had the plaintiff in suspicion, and
because he arrested him; and this excuses him because he did
lawfully, though the plaintiff was not guilty, and so here;
"wherefore he shall have the plea." According to another
report, it was conceded by the whole Court that the plea of
not guilty was inapplicable where the conspiracy was lawful
[i.e. matter of justification should be pleaded specially][1] and
the witnesses who informed the Justices seem to have established
their immunity[2] provided they came without a malicious motive;
and not long after, a decision consistent with it is reported in
Pasch. 27 Hen. VIII, f. 2, which makes the Justices order an
excuse for the production of documentary evidence and perhaps
(though this was not necessary to decide the case) for oral
testimony. One of the defendants alleged that he was steward
of the manor of Dale, and at the leet the plaintiff was presented
to him for having committed a felony. He therefore went to
the Justices at the next Sessions, and shewed them the Court
rolls containing the presentment. They ordered him to shew
the rolls to the jurors, and he did so, and the other defendant
came with him as his servant and brought these rolls. ENGLE-
FIELD J. thought that though no law forced the first defendant
to bring the rolls to the Justices, yet he did well in doing so,
and that then the command of the Justices to shew the rolls
to the jurors discharged him from any conspiracy; that if a
man be present in Court and the Justices order him, because
he has good notice of the felony, to give evidence to a jury, and
he thereby gives such evidence, he is not punishable in conspiracy; and that it is immaterial that he be not sworn to give
such evidence[3]. The case like many others in conspiracy and

---

[1] This tallies with the distinction drawn in Br. *Abr. Consp.* 4, *ante* 74, n. 2.
Had it been no conspiracy at all instead of a "lawful conspiracy," a special
plea would probably have been inapplicable, PRISOT C.J.C.P., *ante* 73.

[2] Keilwey, 81 *b*, "Et fuit sembl' per le court que les def. sont hors de case
de lestat."

[3] F.N.B. 115 E does not go as far as this—"And he who cometh into
Court, and discovereth felonies, and is sworn to give evidence to the jury,
is not chargeable in conspiracy." So too Stanf. P.C. 173, who adds the
qualification that he must not have previously conspired falsely and mali-

maintenance shews the almost inevitable uncertainty of the law in checking these wrongs. The difficulty is in understanding why the action was brought at all, for no reasonable man would think that the defendants had done wrong. On the other hand, the constant abuse of procedure in this period is shewn both by the stream of statutes and the number of cases on the topic. Even where the accusers did right in making the accusation, there is a significant tendency to speak of their act as a justifiable conspiracy rather than to admit that it is no conspiracy at all. In Tudor times, one might say that where the accused is acquitted any accusation against him is presumed to be false unless justification can be shewn, just as killing is presumed to be murder till proved to be something less[1]. The law at times seems to barricade its windows against light and air, and to leave its doors unlocked to rascals. To modern readers MOYLE J. takes an extraordinarily harsh view in the case to which reference has been made[2]. He admits that kinship, service, or common rumour may justify a man in informing the justices, and yet denies that he may do so if he merely saw the crime committed. This seems to put a premium on hearsay evidence, but it must be remembered that though the admission of witnesses was possible, yet it was not then popular[3], and that the facts of this case do not shew that the defendants were called as witnesses at the trial at all. Indeed there is no case which lays down the immunity of witnesses generally, apart from those who informed the grand jury, until *Anonymous* Pasch. 3 Ed. VI (*post* 79) and it is not clear whether this refers to civil or criminal conspiracy or is anything more than a judicial opinion as distinct from a decision[4]. And of not much more value is a resolution

ciously with others. But it must be noted that Stanford certainly, and Fitzherbert probably, refer to those who testify to the indicting as opposed to the trying jury.

[1] See FINEUX C.J. Y.B. Mich. 20 Hen. VII, f. 11; cf. ENGLEFIELD J. Pasch. 27 Hen. VIII, f. 2, "When the defendant pleads a conspiracy which is justifiable, he must conclude [in his plea] that it is the same conspiracy [as that alleged by the plaintiff]."

[2] *Ante* p. 73.    [3] Thayer, p. 130.

[4] In Browne's *Ent.* (ed. 1671) 133, the plea of a deft. in an action of conspiracy 16 Eliz. was that the Justices compelled him to bring a bill of indictment and give evidence thereon against the plaintiff, and the plaintiff was nonsuited. Cf. similar plea in Vidian, *Ent.* 145.

of the Star Chamber in *Floyd* v. *Barker* (Pasch. 5 Jac. I)[1] that
witnesses ought not to be charged in that Court, or elsewhere,
with conspiracy, when the party indicted is convicted or attaint
of murder or felony, but the almost total absence of facts in
the report leaves it open whether this were more than *obiter
dictum* and, in any event, the earlier part of the report qualifies
this by making him liable for conspiracy made out of Court
before he is sworn, since it is a private person who produces
him and not the Sheriff as in the case of jurors[2].

§ 33. *Judges*. Within limits Judges and Justices of the Peace
were probably exempt from liability under the writ of conspiracy. Probably a judge before whom an indictment was
found had no protection, unless he were a judge by commission[3]. In Mich. 12 Ed. IV, f. 18, J. Genney pleaded this
as a defence to the writ. All that the defendant seems to have
done was to read to the jury a bill of indictment which had
been delivered to him and to command them to find out
whether it were true or not. The plea seemed good to LAKEN J.
for it could not be intended that as a Justice of the Peace he
wished to do otherwise than he ought. No result is stated[4].
But a few years afterwards[5] "Catesby came to the bar and
moved that there was no difference in conspiracy between a
juror who is indicted[6] and a justice of Peace, but both shall be
excused always." Pigot opposed this by arguing that the juror's
oath salved any wrong that he had done in speaking before the
appointed time of indictment, but that Justices of the Peace
had no such excuse for "emparlance." Catesby countered this
by pointing out that justices are sworn to do their office just
as much as jurors. BRYAN C.J.C.P. pointed out that a Justice
of the Peace would need to confer, because he could neither

---

[1] 12 Rep. at p. 24, *ante* 70, n. 1.
[2] *Ante* 70.
[3] Fitz. *Abr. Consp.* 19 citing Trin. (? Mich.) 47 Ed. III, 17. There was
an attempt to put the hundredor on the same footing as a judge, and this
the Court refused to allow. For more details of case see *ante* 56–57.
[4] Br. *Abr. Consp.* 33 states an adjournment.
[5] Mich. 21 Ed. IV, f. 67.
[6] The case (though no facts are expressed) was probably on prosecution,
not action, for conspiracy, but the judges' opinions whether they decided
anything or not are of general application.

make nor hold Sessions alone, nor do anything by himself except take sureties of the Peace; that therefore he could not take necessary preliminary information alone, and that for what he did in Sessions he was excusable, but not for what he spoke outside. CHOKE J. put the case even more favourably for the defendant.

It is hard that a Justice of the Peace cannot take information outside. And if an indictment be shewn to Catesby and Pigot, Serjeants of the King, [to see] whether it be sufficient or not, they would like to converse of the matter and of the manner of the indictment in point of law.

The result is not stated[1]. The opinion of MOUNTAGUE C.J. in an anonymous case of Pasch. 3 Ed. VI[2] was that if one comes to a Justice of the Peace, and complains that J. S. is a felon and has stolen certain things, and thereon the Justice commands the complainant to prefer a bill of indictment at the next Sessions and to give evidence, and he does so, neither the Justice of the Peace, nor the complainant shall be punished in conspiracy, if the party so indicted be acquitted of the felony[3]. It was resolved in *Floyd* v. *Barker* (Pasch. 5 Jac. I)[4] that the defendant who as judge of assize had given judgment upon the verdict of death, the Sheriff who executed it, and the Justices of the Peace who executed the accused were not to be drawn in question in the Star Chamber for any conspiracy; and that even though the accused be acquitted of murder or felony, yet the judge, whether of assize, Justice of the Peace, or any other judge by commission and of record, and sworn to do justice, cannot be charged for conspiracy, for what he did openly in Court as a judge; "and the law will not admit any proof against the vehement and violent presumption of law." But if he conspired previously out of Court, this would be extrajudicial.

---

[1] F.N.B. 116 I is equally indecisive. Stanf. P.C. 173 states that the J.P. shall not be punished for conspiracy, but the only positive authority which he cites is on criminal conspiracy (27 Lib. Ass. pl. 12).

[2] Moore, 6.

[3] "Punished" makes it doubtful whether the case were one of civil or criminal conspiracy. In Vin. *Abr. Consp.* (C), 23, this is classed under actions upon the case in the nature of conspiracy, but in Moore's report (which Viner literally translates) "case" is not mentioned.

[4] 12 Rep. 23.

Due examination of causes out of Court and inquiring by testimony, *et similia* are not conspiracy for this he ought to do; but subornation of witnesses, and false and malicious prosecutions out of Court, to such[1] whom he knows will be indictors amount to unlawful conspiracy[2].

§ 34. *Officials.* There is scanty authority on the protection, if any, of officials who assisted the Court in an administrative rather than a judicial capacity. Sheriffs are referred to in the dubious case just cited (*Floyd* v. *Barker*). In Henry IV's reign, GASCOIGNE C.J.K.B. doubted whether a bailiff who had returned 12 jurors by the Sheriff's order, and had informed them of an alleged crime by the Court's order, had as such any defence to a bill of conspiracy[3]. Under Henry VIII, it seems to have been held that the Steward of a manor who shews to the Justices and (by their order) to the jurors a presentment on the Court Roll is justified by the order[4], but his immunity seems to rest rather upon the command of the Justices than his office[5]. That advice of some sort was permissible in litigation without incurring the risk of a writ of conspiracy is likely, but the limits of it are not clearly marked in the very few cases we have. Their paucity is probably due to the much more frequent use of the kindred writ of maintenance in such circumstances, and the point is fully discussed there. The Parson of Sulthorn[6] in Pasch. 22 Ed. I argued (*inter alia*) that the writ of conspiracy was inapplicable to legal help and advice given to his friends, and the plaintiffs withdrew from their suit, though it is not known whether this particular defence influenced them in doing so; and it has already been noticed that a plea of "communis advocatus" was good[7]. In *Goldington* v. *Bassingburn*, there is an opinion of BEREFORD C.J. that advice innocently given on

---

[1] *Sic.*
[2] The mere breadth of this string of resolutions lays its accuracy as a report under suspicion. *Ante* 70, n. 1.
[3] Mich. 9 Hen. IV, f. 8 (*ante* 61).
[4] Pasch. 27 Hen. VIII, f. 2 (*ante* 76).
[5] Cf. Browne's *Entries* (ed. 1671), 130, where there is a precedent of a plea that defendant had been ordered by the Justice to write out the indictment, read it over to the jury and explain it to them in English.
[6] *Abb. Plac.* 291. *Ante* p. 3.
[7] *de Welleby's case. Abb. Plac.* 295 (Hil. 29 Ed. I), *ante* 63.

request is a defence[1], and in Hil. 38 Ed. III, f. 3, where it was
alleged that husband, wife and another had conspired and procured *A* to bring a bill against *W*, ROBERT DE THORPE C.J.C.P.
said "You have not shewn in your writ by whom the bill was
sued; and also the cause of your action cannot be called conspiracy; for then every man of law will be called a conspirator";
and the writ was abated on these grounds. In *Pain* v. *Rochester
and Whitfield*, the defendants to a writ of conspiracy pleaded
that they had got a warrant for the arrest of the plaintiff on
suspicion of robbery, that the plaintiff absented himself on
notice thereof, and that a Justice after examining the matter
had committed the plaintiff to gaol, and advised the defendants
to indict him. They did so and the plaintiff was acquitted. All
the Court resolved that the plea was good because their causes
of suspicion and the plaintiff's absenting himself sufficed[2].

## ESSENTIALS OF LIABILITY TO THE WRIT

### (3) *Procurement*

§ 35. Neither in the Ordinacio de Conspiratoribus of
33 Ed. I which defines conspirators, nor in the Statutum de
Conspiratoribus of 21 Ed. I and the writ incorporated with it
is there any reference to procurement. But all the nine writs
in Registrum Brevium refer to the defendants as falsely and
maliciously procuring the wrong laid at their door[3]. Where
two conspirators got a third person to injure another by improper legal proceedings, the case seems to have been too clear
to raise any litigation; but it is doubtful whether the writ was
good if the person procured were himself one of the conspirators.
It was argued in Y.B. Pasch. 21 Ed. III, f. 17, on behalf of one
of several defendants that he was one of 12 indictors charged
to present at a leet, and that he and the rest of them had

---

[1] A.D. 1310, *Y.B. 3 Ed. II*, S. S. vol. xx. 196.
[2] Cro. Eliz. 871 (41 Eliz.) Bulst. 150, where *arguendo* it is said to be
action upon the case in the nature of conspiracy. Vin. *Abr. Consp.* classifies
it under conspiracy, but he frequently includes case under that heading.
[3] f. 134. No. 5 varies slightly the form of allegation. The MS. Registers
consulted also allege procurement. Add. 3022 D is exceptional, because it
reproduces the writ given in the Stat. de Consp. 21 Ed. I. Cf. BEREFORD
C.J. in *Goldington* v. *Bassingburn*, *Y.B. Trin. 3 Ed. II*, S. S. vol. xx. at p. 197.

thereupon indicted the plaintiff, and that even if a writ would lie, conspiracy was not the appropriate one, because one of the indictors could not procure himself; but the Court, as reported, ignored the argument. In Y.B. Hil. 42 Ed. III, f. 1[1], conspiracy was brought against W. J. and R. and another[2] for procuring W. J. to oust the plaintiff and enfeoff B. against whom R. sued *scire facias*, the plaintiff thus losing his warranty. Belknap objected to the allegation that W. J. had procured himself, and a man could not do so. *Non allocatur*, because the procurement might be taken to mean that the two procured the third to oust the tenant and to make the feoffment[3]. So too Y.B. Pasch. 42 Ed. III, f. 14, where the Abbot of *T*, *T*, and *J* were sued for conspiring to bring an assize of novel disseisin in *W*'s name against the Abbot and procuring *T* to be *W*'s attorney, and it was argued that *T* could not procure himself, and *non allocatur*. But these cases give us no answer to the question whether the writ would lie against *two* co-defendants one of whom procured the other; and on this point there is a decision in Y.B. Trin. 46 Ed. III, f. 20. Conspiracy was brought against several, alleging that one of them had forged a false deed to the effect that certain lands whereof the plaintiff was tenant were entailed to others, and he was thus put to great labour and expense to defend himself. Belknap challenged the writ because it stated that the defendants had procured one of them to forge the deed, and he could not procure himself; and for that reason the writ was abated[4]. No sound principle underlies this decision; it distinctly opens a door of escape to conspirators by a piece of procedural logic, and the writs in Registrum Brevium avoid the trap by referring to the defendants as having procured the plaintiff to be appealed or indicted without specifying who the actual appellor or indictor

---

[1] Partly reported also in Hil. 43 Ed. III, f. 10.

[2] So Br. *Abr. Consp.* 5. The Y.B. 42 Ed. III, f. 1, reads as if W. J. and R. were the only defendants. Hil. 43 Ed. III, f. 10, confirms Br. *Abr.*

[3] Br. *Abr. Consp.* 5 queries whether the writ would lie, because, though the defendants procured as above, yet if the act were not done, the action does not lie. Hil. 42 Ed. III, f. 1, seems to indicate that the warranty was lost through the procurement.

[4] So too Fitz. *Abr. Consp.* 17 and Br. *Abr. Consp.* 7. The latter adds, "mes est malement report."

was, or at most merely mentioning some person distinct from the defendants[1].

## ESSENTIALS OF LIABILITY TO THE WRIT

### (4) *Acquittal of plaintiff*

§ 36. Proof that the plaintiff in conspiracy had been acquitted of that with which he had been falsely charged was in general necessary, presumably to make good "falso" in the writ, and in the Ordinacio de Conspiratoribus, 33 Ed. I, which defines conspirators. We have already considered acquittal of a person falsely appealed[2], and it remains to discuss the same topic in connection with one falsely indicted.

Coke makes lawful acquittal of the party by the verdict of 12 men one of the elements in his definition of conspiracy[3], and, in his report of *The Poulterers' Case*[4], he notes "No writ of conspiracy lies, unless the party is indicted and lawfully acquitted; but a false conspiracy is punishable though nothing be put in execution"[5]. This qualification makes the definition more accurate[6], and it must be added that the plaintiff need not always be acquitted by a verdict in *his* favour, e.g., one accused as accessory to a crime[7]. Apart from this, Coke represents pretty closely the law of his time, and there is no lack of authority textual and judicial in his favour. Fitzherbert[8], Stanford[9], the Books of Entries[10], and Reeves[11], attest the existence of the rule both before and after Coke's time. Blackstone states that the plaintiff must obtain a copy of the record of his indictment and acquittal, but that in prosecutions for felony it was usual to deny a copy of the indictment where there was the slightest probable cause for the prosecution[12],

---

[1] As in No. 7.  [2] *Ante* 42 sqq.
[3] 3 Inst. 143.  [4] 9 Rep. 55 *b* (Mich. 8 Jac. I).
[5] This, though included in the head-note, is no part of the decision. J. F. Fraser's ed. 1826.
[6] Cf. 1 Hawk. P.C. ch. 72, sect. 2.
[7] Acquittal was not needed in action upon the case in the nature of conspiracy.  [8] N.B. 114 D.  [9] P.C. 172.
[10] "Conspiracy" in *Booke of Entries* (ed. 1614), f. 109; Browne's *Entries*, 129; Vidian's *Entries*, 145; Rastall's *Entries*, f. 123.  [11] II. 329.
[12] III. 125. In Coleridge's edition, the learned editor admits this qualification, but questions the grounds of it.

since it would greatly damage public justice, if prosecutors who had a tolerable ground of suspicion were liable to be sued whenever their indictments miscarried. Hawkins[1] reluctantly concedes the necessity of acquittal but adds a strong criticism of its principle. He argues that a new writ might well be formed for a mischief which was just as much within the Statute of Conspirators, and that if the prosecution were so palpably groundless that a grand jury ignored the bill of indictment, it was just as much a grievance as a vexatious action for which the Register did give a writ without using either *acquietatus fuisset* or *quietus recessit*[2]. But the point was, as Hawkins admits, of small practical importance in his time, when the writ of conspiracy was dying out as a mode of checking abuse of legal procedure and its vigour had passed into the action upon the case in the nature of conspiracy, which had the same scope as the old writ, and in which no acquittal of the plaintiff was essential.

Passing to decisions, the rule that acquittal was necessary was implied in Hil. 33 Hen. VI, f. 1, was agreed to *obiter* by all the Court in *Marham* v. *Pescod*[3], and was ruled in the Star Chamber in *Hurlestone* v. *Glaseour*[4]. In *Floyd* v. *Barker*[5], it was resolved that when the party indicted is convicted of felony by another jury upon "not guilty pleaded, there he never shall have a writ of conspiracy," and not long afterwards there is an opinion of CREW C.J. that conspiracy does not lie unless a man be indicted and acquitted[6]. A rule constantly appearing in books of practice is that a man shall have the writ upon an indictment before the mayor and bailiffs of any city or borough who have gaol delivery therein, if he be acquitted before them,

---

[1]  1 P.C. ch. 72, sect. 2.

[2]  No. 5 in Reg. Brev. f. 134. But the writ is really one of trespass upon the case (F.N.B. 116 B), and Hawkins' statement that an acquittal by verdict is not always necessary to maintain the writ of conspiracy must be limited to this, which he gives as an example.

[3]  Cro. Jac. 130 (4 Jac. I, B.R.).

[4]  Goulds. 51 (latter years of Elizabeth).

[5]  12 Rep. 23 (5 Jac. I, Star Chamber). It may be mere *obiter dictum*. The case is ill-reported. *Ante* 70, n. 1.

[6]  *Smith* v. *Cranshaw* (20 Jac. I, B.R.) 2 Roll. at p. 259, so too *obiter* in *Taylor's Case* (17 Jac. I, B.R.) Vin. *Abr. Actions* (Case Conspiracy. Viner's ref. to Palm. 44 is untraceable), p. 33.

for that acquittal discharges him of the felony[1]. Perhaps the
reason was that the jurisdiction of the mayor and bailiffs was
limited to prisoners in the local gaol, who had committed
offences within the town, city, or borough, and to felons taken
in the act within the same bounds. They could not try felons
indicted elsewhere and caught within their franchise except in
conjunction with the King's justices of gaol delivery. In cases
where they could act and did acquit one accused of felony,
who then proposed to sue conspiracy against his accuser, it
was as well to call the litigant's attention to the fact that it was
useless to employ a writ which stated that he had been acquitted
"in curia nostra coram...justitiariis nostris." Writ No. 4 was
designed to cover this case of acquittal in a court leet[2], and
there is nothing to shew that it did not include acquittal in
both communal and manorial courts leet.

A person who had been accused of killing and justified it in
self-defence could not have a writ of conspiracy[3], and this held
where the death had occurred by misadventure[4]; in each case
there was reasonable ground for the accusation. Acquittal in
law was not in general an acquittal which entitled the plaintiff
to bring conspiracy. Thus in *Sydenham v. Keilaway*[5], all the
judges resolved that where the party was not indicted because
the bill was ignored, no conspiracy lies; nor did it lie apparently
if the acquittal were on a void indictment, even if the accused
did not take advantage of the flaw, but pleaded not guilty and
were acquitted[6]. If one were falsely indicted of felony, and
afterwards by Act of Parliament a general pardon of all felonies
were granted, the accused could not sue conspiracy, even though
in his pleading he did not avail himself of the Act, but pleaded
not guilty and were acquitted; for his life was not in peril[7],

---

[1] F.N.B. 115 B. Reg. Brev. f. 134 reproducing almost exactly MS. in
C. U. Lib. Ll. iv. 17. Cf. Ff. i. 32; Ff. v. 5; Gg. v. 19. Tottell, *Nat. Brev.*
ed. 1576.  [2] Reg. Brev. f. 134.
[3] Fitz. *Abr. Consp.* 21 (Mich. 10 Hen. IV; not in printed Y.B.).
[4] Stanf. P.C. 173.
[5] 16 Eliz. Cited by POPHAM C.J. in Cro. Jac. 7.
[6] Per LYTTLETON J. in Trin. 9 Ed. IV, f. 12 (action of debt), Br. *Abr.*
*Consp.* 23. And see Rastall's *Entries*, Consp. 124 b. Stanf. P.C. 175 A.
[7] F.N.B. 115 G; quoted in a condensed form in Br. *Abr. Corone* 204.
So too Hil. 11 Hen. IV, f. 41, where persons indicted of felony sought to

and indeed he should not have been arraigned at all since the
Court must take cognizance of a general Act[1]. But where a
charter of pardon had been purchased and pleaded, and then
this plea had been waived and that of not guilty set up, followed
by an acquittal, the writ of conspiracy was available[2]; but
where the pardon was statutory, waiver was strictly speaking
impossible. .

Whether a successful claim by the accused of benefit of clergy
prevented him from suing conspiracy was unsettled. Finchden
as counsel in Trin. 47 Ed. III, f. 15, recollected that he had
seen a case in which it was argued that there was no acquittal
of the plaintiff who had had his clergy, but that the action was
held maintainable, though the acquittal had been by an inquest
of office. The question was raised as a side issue in a case
doubly reported in Hil. 33 Hen. VI, f. 1, and Mich. 34 Hen. VI,
f. 9. DANBY J. said that if on arraignment the accused said he
was a clerk, and prayed for a book and was afterwards found
not guilty, he should not have conspiracy, because his acquittal
was merely by an inquest of office. PRISOT C.J.C.P. thought
that he should, since no mention of the clergy would be made
in the record[3], but the report questions the soundness of
this reason, for according to books of entries mention should
be made of clergy[4]. According to another report *per optimam
opinionem*, the action would not lie[5].

The Courts did not go the length of holding that wherever
one who had been falsely accused as principal to a felony and
acquitted had an action for conspiracy, there too those accused
as accessories should have it; but they seem to have acted upon

waive the benefit of a general pardon of felonies of 5 Hen. IV in order to
get an acquittal by verdict and so ground the action of conspiracy. GAS-
COIGNE C.J.K.B. refused to allow this.

[1] Trin. 26 Hen. VIII, f. 7, and Br. *Abr. Charter de Pardon*, 1.

[2] Stanf. P.C. 173 A. If the charter were not waived, and the accused went
quit upon that, presumably he would not have been "acquitted." Perhaps
this explains the opinion of DANBY J. in Mich. 34 Hen. VI, f. 9, and the
argument of Kirketon in 42 Ed. III, at f. 15.

[3] Both opinions are taken from the later report. The earlier states that
Choke (counsel) and DANVERS J. were against PRISOT.

[4] So too Fitz. *Abr. Consp.* 4 (note).

[5] Br. *Abr. Consp.* 2.

this idea. In the case just cited, an appeal[1] of felony was brought against two—one as principal, the other as accessory—and the principal was acquitted, and the question was whether the accessory could have conspiracy. It was argued that he could not, because his life had never been in jeopardy by any jury, since the principal was acquitted. But DANBY J. said, "in this case his life was indirectly in jeopardy, for if the principal was convicted, now those of the same inquest ought to inquire if the accessory was guilty or not, or if he had appeared, etc." At the same time he admitted that the accessory would not have had the writ if the principal had died before conviction or received a charter of pardon, for *non constat* then whether the principal were guilty or not[2]. Had the appellant been nonsuited, the accessory would have had the action, for the appellee would have been arraigned afresh at the suit of the King upon the appeal[3], and the acquittal would have been by verdict[4].

Whether the verdict of acquittal passed upon the accessory or the principal, it did not affect the accessory's right to sue, but it was material to the precise form of the writ which he selected. In the first case, the writ alleged *acquietatus fuisset*, in the second, *acquietatus fuisset* of the principal and *quietus recessisset* of the accessory[5]. The two reports of the case cited above conflict as to whether the writ sued out by the accessory should mention the imprisonment of the principal as well as that of the accessory[6], but the better opinion was that it need not[7], and the writs themselves support this[8].

[1] That it was a false appeal, not an indictment appears from a dictum of DANVERS J. "If the appellant had been nonsuited in this case, the other should have had conspiracy." Hil. 33 Hen. VI, f. 2.

[2] So too Stanf. P.C. 173 A; F.N.B. 115 A, F.

[3] Per DANVERS J. and PRISOT C.J.C.P.

[4] *Ante* 48. F.N.B. 115 A.

[5] Stanf. P.C. 174 D; these writs in the printed Register are respectively Nos. 3 and 8. Judging from MS. Registra, No. 3 is earlier than No. 8, and both appear in the 14th century. The passage in Stanf. makes clear the corresponding parts of F.N.B. 115 A and H.

[6] Hil. 33 Hen. VI, f. 2, "This was held a good plea." Mich. 34 Hen. VI, f. 9, "PRISOT. The writ supposes that the said T. Swike, the present plaintiff, was imprisoned, and that is enough for him." At all events the defect was not vital, for plaintiff got his judgment.

[7] Stanf. P.C. 174 D.

[8] Reg. Brev. f. 134.

APPLICATION OF THE WRIT TO WOMEN

§ 37. It has been alleged that a writ of conspiracy would not lie against women, but there is no clear authority for such an inexplicable rule[1]. In Y.B. Mich. 17 Ed. II, f. 509 a writ of conspiracy was brought against two women and four men and it was said in argument, "This writ is not maintainable against women, for the writ has been abated here before now." CANT.[2] said, "What do you reply for the man?" Other arguments followed on this and other points, but nothing more was said as to the women, and no decision is reported. On the other hand, Y.B. 19 Ed. III, 346[3] is against any such view. The writ was against a man, his wife and others, and exception was taken to it on the ground (among others) that it cannot be understood in law that a woman could be supposed to conspire, and particularly a *feme covert*. But the writ was adjudged to be good, and there is evidence that suitors had experimented with a writ in the 14th century[4]. It is difficult to think of any intelligible reason for the alleged immunity, but perhaps a confused analogy with the rule that the writ did not lie against husband and wife—a rule itself of doubtful foundation[5]—may have been the root of it.

### EFFECT OF DEATH OF ACCUSED

§ 38. We are told that Richard III[6] in the inner Star Chamber called before him all his Justices and put to them the question whether, if anyone should have brought a false writ and action against another, whereby he is taken and imprisoned and dies in prison, there would be any remedy for the party, or for the King. The facts raising the question were that Thomas Stanton

---

[1] Reeves, *H.E.L.* II. 328-9 citing Y.B. Mich. 17 Ed. II, f. 509.

[2] The context implies that he is a judge but according to Foss neither of the Cantebrigs, and none of the Cantilupes was at that time a judge, though John de Cantebrig was continually employed in the judicial commissions for Cambs. from 4 Ed. II onwards.

[3] Ed. Pike.

[4] Bodleian MS. Reg. Brev. (Rawlinson, C. 310) writ No. 4 of conspiracy states one of defendants to be the wife of a certain person. Cf. Vidian's *Entries* (1684) where there is a precedent of conspiracy against several, including a widow.

[5] *Ante* § 26.                                    [6] Y.B. 2 Ric. III, f. 9.

had a judgment in Chancery against Thomas Gate for certain lands, and had execution thereof; and that Gate in contravention of this had re-entered the lands, and taken and imprisoned Stanton by colour of a false and fictitious action. The Justices replied that there was no punishment for prosecution of the false action, since it was not ended. This opinion does not in terms apply to the writ of conspiracy, but the question was a general one, and the Justices mention no remedy except attachment by the Chancellor for contempt against the judgment. Their reply is consistent with the general principle that the writ is inapplicable where the plaintiff has not been acquitted.

## COMPROMISE BY THE PLAINTIFF

§ 39. It is probable that compromise by the plaintiff barred the action.

In Y.B. Hil. 18 Ed. IV, f. 24, ten men were sued for conspiracy. One defendant pleaded that an accord had been taken between him and the plaintiff by the mediation of their friends, who agreed that the defendant should pay to the plaintiff 10s. for this procurement and all other offences, and the defendant paid that sum. Each of the other defendants pleaded the same. The plaintiff imparled, and there the report ends. But in Rastall's *Entries* there is a precedent of a bar to the writ by arbitration[1], and Stanford states that concord is a good bar[2].

## MISCELLANEOUS POINTS OF PROCEDURE

§ 40. A count in conspiracy need not specify details of the offence with which the plaintiff had been charged in a false appeal, for the defendants must have been well aware of what it was that they had conspired and procured, and the plaintiff could scarcely be blamed for not repeating *verbatim* the lie which had injured him to the very persons who had invented it[3]. The writ while it had to state the place where the conspiracy was made[4] was good though it did not state the Justices before

---

[1] Consp. f. 125 b.          [2] P.C. 175 A citing the above case.
[3] Y.B. Pasch. 17 Ed. II, f. 544. SCROPE [HENRY LE SCROPE C.J.K.B.] "and if you conspired and imagined an appeal to be sued against him of a thing which was never done, so much the greater is the malice."
[4] *Obiter* in Mich. 24 Ed. III at f. 76. So too the writs in Reg. Brev. f. 134.

whom the plaintiff was arraigned and acquitted on a false indictment[1] nor the manner of acquittal[2], nor that the place where
he was acquitted was in the county over which the Justices
who acquitted him had jurisdiction, for this was presumed in
his favour till the contrary was shewn[3]; and though it alleged
that the conspiracy took place in two towns, for that did not
negative the possibility of its commission at one time[4]. It was
enough that it rehearsed the substance of the false indictment[5].
But if the plaintiff made no mention of the indictment he would
be met successfully by the plea "nul tiel record"[6]. But the
writ should be brought in the county where the conspiracy was
made, and not where the indictment was, or where the deed
was done[7], for if the rule were otherwise it might expose the
defendants to another action on the same set of facts after
judgment in their favour in the first[8]. Purchase of one writ of
conspiracy pending another for the same conspiracy against the
same defendants did not vitiate the former, for a plaintiff could
have "twenty writs of conspiracy or trespass against a man for
one and the same trespass and each pending at the same time"[9];

---

[1] Y.B. Trin. 3 Hen. VI, f. 52. It was queried whether the declaration were
ill for alleging the acquittal to have been before Justices of the Peace instead
of Justices of gaol delivery. Cf. Stanf. P.C. 174 C.

[2] Trin. 47 Ed. III, f. 15. Stanf. P.C. 174 C. This must be qualified by
what has been said as to the difference between "acquietatus fuisset"; and
"quietus recessisset."

[3] Hil. 35 Hen. VI, f. 46. Stanf. P.C. 174 B.

[4] Pasch. 22 Hen. VI, f. 49. F.N.B. 116 M.

[5] Stanf. P.C. 174 C. Mich. 19 Hen. VI, f. 34. By a slip, the plaintiff in
abstracting the indictment in his writ said "felonice cepit" instead of
"cepisset," and it was urged that he thereby admitted that he had taken
what he was charged with stealing, in spite of his acquittal. But the reply
was that the writ need recite only a rehearsal of the indictment.

[6] Conceded *obiter* by the Court in Trin. 9 Hen. VI, f. 26. Br. *Abr.*
*Consp.* 36.

[7] F.N.B. 116 M. Stanf. P.C. 176 E. 22 Ric. II (Bellewe) is shewn by the
fuller report in Fitz. *Abr. Challenge*, 177, not to be in point. Pasch. 42 Ed. III,
f. 14 (conspiracy at Lincoln to bring an assize of novel disseisin in York.
Writ brought in county of Lincoln, and adjudged good, for the conspiracy
had commenced by speaking in Lincoln, though the assize had been sued
in York). In Hil. 15 Ed. IV, f. 20 (a case of maintenance) LYTTLETON J.
said *obiter* that the writ of conspiracy can be brought in the county where
the conspiracy was made, and in Hil. 13 Hen. VII, f. 17, FROWYK (not then
a judge) said that conspiracy in Bucks. cannot be sued upon in any other
county.

[8] FROWYK (*loc. cit.*).          [9] Y.B. Mich. 19 Hen. VI, f. 34.

and the same applied to a statutory writ of procurement[1], nor was any injustice done to the defendants, for "though a man procure another to be indicted a hundred times, he shall receive but once his damages"[2]. It is not certain whether two could join as plaintiffs in a writ of conspiracy; in Y.B. Mich. 47 Ed. III, f. 17, though the argument was that the damages of the one could not be the damages of the other, nor the recovery of the one the recovery of the other, it was held by Robert Knivet, the Chancellor, that they could join, because they were damaged by the conspiracy, but in 19 Ric. II a writ brought in common by two was abated because their grievance was several. MARKHAM[3] contended that as the indictment was common to both plaintiffs, so was the grievance, but RICKHILL J. held that the grievance was several since the imprisonment of the one could not be the imprisonment of the other, and that they could take nothing by the writ[4]. On a verdict for the plaintiff the defendants were taken without further process, though the case was otherwise where they were indicted at the suit of the King[5].

[1] Y.B. Trin. 9 Ed. IV, f. 23. The statute is probably 8 Hen. VI c. 10.
[2] GENNY J. (loc. cit.).
[3] JOHN MARKHAM was made judge of C.P. July 7th, 1396.
[4] Bellewe (ed. 1869), Briefe, pp. 80–81. Fitz. Abr. Briefe, 926.
[5] Trin. 43 Ed. III, f. 33. Fitz. Abr. Consp. 11. Stanf. P.C. 175 B.

# CHAPTER III

## EARLY HISTORY OF CONSPIRACY TO ABUSE PROCEDURE AS A CRIME[1]

### DISTINCTION BETWEEN CIVIL AND CRIMINAL PROCEDURE

§ 1. In treating of conspiracy as a crime, we are met by the well-known difficulty of distinguishing the civil from the criminal proceeding. That there was at the time when the writ of conspiracy originated a perception of the distinction in both theory and practice is clear[2]. That there was no sharply cut division between them is equally clear. The two might be described as a viscuous intermixture, for "every cause for a civil action is an offence" and "every cause for a civil action in the king's court is an offence against the king, punishable by amercement, if not by fine and imprisonment"[3]. The distinction between Pleas of the Crown and Common Pleas was not perfectly certain[4]; nor can it be said that writs connoted civil proceedings—least of all the writs of trespass with which the writ of conspiracy is closely allied both as a matter of historical origin and mechanical arrangement in the Register; and the writ of trespass took the place of writs relating to criminal appeals—probably was born of them—and trespass itself was persistently treated as a crime in the Middle Ages[5]. Again, any fraudulent abuse of procedure in the course of a civil action would be punished by imprisonment, and of this there are examples more than half a century before the writ of conspiracy was invented[6].

When allowance has been made for the blurred line between

---

[1] For the whole topic, see Wright, *Consp.*
[2] Glanv. Bk. I. ch. 1. Bracton, III. f. 115. *Fleta*, lib. 1. cap. 16.
[3] P. and M. II. 572.　　　　　　　[4] *Ibid*. 573.
[5] Holds. II. 434; Mait. *C.P.* II. 157, 164, 165, 168. P. and M. II. 526.
[6] P. and M. II. 519. Bract. *N.B.* pl. 1946 (A.D. 1221) closely resembles conspiracy (Assize of novel disseisin brought by Copsy against husband and wife. This was found to be brought by collusion between Copsy and the husband with a view to defeating wife's marriage portion. Copsy and the husband were committed to prison).

civil and criminal redress, we can still take advantage of the difference between procedure which begins by the writ of conspiracy, and that which is based on the presentment of a local court or before the King's justices[1], and this will be adopted as a test.

## EARLY HISTORY OF THE CRIME AS ABUSE OF PROCEDURE

§ 2. The early history of conspiracy in its criminal, as in its civil, aspect, is closely (but not entirely) implicated with combination to abuse procedure, and the exposition under this section will as far as possible be confined to that. But at the outset it must be noticed that the idea of punishing combinations of a certain—or rather uncertain—kind appears in our law even before the Statute of Conspirators, 21 Ed. I[2] and the Ordinance of Conspirators, 33 Ed. I[3]. Nothing of the sort is traceable in Glanville, but a case of 1225, and another of 1230 from Bracton's *Note Book* bearing upon the point have been already quoted[4]. Bracton himself in speaking of "facta," "scripta," and "consilia" that are punishable exemplifies the last named by "conjurationes"[5], but the passage is a transcript from Roman Law[6]. Elsewhere in discussing the liability of an accessory, he remarks on the rule that there cannot be an accessory without a principal, "quia ubi principale non consistit, nec ea quae sequuntur locum habere debent, sicut dici poterit de praecepto, conspiratione et consimilibus," and adds that these are sometimes punishable if followed by an act, otherwise not[7]. This does not illuminate "conspiratio," nor does Bracton include anything akin to it in the Articles of the Eyre which he gives[8]; and the same applies to other Articles of the Eyre prior to Ed. I which have been examined[9]. According to Britton, inquiry is to be made of "alliaunces" between jurors and the King's officers, or between one neighbour

---

[1] Cf. P. and M. II. 518 et seq.    [2] *Ante* 22.
[3] *Ante* 1.    [4] *Ante* 3.    [5] II. 154–6.
[6] Dig. 48. 19. 16 pr. Mait. *Bracton and Azo* (S. S. vol. VIII), 190.
[7] II. 334–7.    [8] II. 240–253.
[9] E.g. Hoveden, III. 263 (A.D. 1194); IV. 61 (1198); *Rot. Cl.* II. 213 (1227). The *Mirrour* apparently refers to conspiracy as a crime (*ante* 30–31).

and another to the hindrance of justice, and such persons are to be ransomed at the King's pleasure, and their oath is never after to be admissible[1]. Here we are not far from conspiracy in its strict sense. We have combination, and it is combination to abuse procedure; and the germ of the "villainous judgment" which later appears with more detailed severity as the punishment of a convicted conspirator. Yet the mere fact that this is not styled conspiracy shews that lawyers had not then a definite conception of the term. A marginal note to this passage in an early 14th century MS. copy of Britton by a contemporary commentator also shews this fluidity of thought. The note calls the offence to which Britton has referred "conspiracie des assisours & des jurours," and immediately after exemplifies it by an "alliance" in 30 Ed. I between a Sheriff, Sir Robert de Veer and several other persons in the county of Northampton, that some of them should indict persons, and the others save them, for bribes, according as the Sheriff should arrange the panels[2]. Cases have been quoted from the Parliament Rolls mentioning conspiracy in 1290, and in one of these (the complaint of the citizens of London) there is some reason for thinking that the object was abuse of procedure[3]; but no reference to it as a crime *eo nomine* can be found before De Conspiratoribus Ordinatio, 21 Ed. I[4]. This provided that those convicted of conspiracy should be severely punished according to the discretion of the justices by imprisonment and ransom. Coke's belief in the existence of a crime of conspiracy (meaning abuse of procedure) at Common Law has apparently nothing better to recommend it than the *Mirrour* which gave him the equally wrong impression that there was a Common Law writ of conspiracy[5]. The Statutum de Conspiratoribus,

---

[1] Liv. I. ch. xxii. sect. 19.

[2] C. U. Lib. Dd. vii. 6. And see Nichols' ed. of Britton. Introd. xlix, lxi and p. 95, note d.

[3] *Ante* 27.

[4] *Ante* 26. Wright (p. 15) makes the source "the first Ordinance of Conspirators, A.D. 1292, 20 Ed. I." The context shews that this means Statutum de Conspiratoribus (for which we have conjectured the date 21 Ed. I), wherein De Conspiratoribus Ordinatio is recited.

[5] 2 Inst. 382 et sqq. In *O'Connell* v. *R.* (1844), 11 Cl. and F. 155, TINDAL C.J. (at p. 233) says that it was manifestly known to the Common Law. This cannot be extended to conspiracies to abuse legal procedure.

21 Ed. I[1] which followed De Conspiratoribus Ordinatio, levelled its three years' imprisonment and fine rather at champertors than conspirators. Either because the punishment in the Ordinatio was too vague, or more probably because it needed emphasis to check a crying abuse, 28 Ed. I c. 10 (Art. sup. Cart.) passed. It ran thus:

In right of conspirators, false informers, and evil procurers of dozens[2], assizes, inquests, and juries, the King hath provided remedy for the plaintiffs by a writ out of the chancery[3]. And notwithstanding he willeth that his justices of the one bench and of the other, and justices assigned to take assizes, when they come into the country to do their office, shall upon every plaint made unto them, award inquests thereupon without writ, and shall do right unto the plaintiff without delay[4].

Shortly after this, Ordinacio de Conspiratoribus[5] makes its definition of conspirators include those who commit maintenance. These offences are not easy to disentangle historically, and maintenance must be left for future discussion. After the definition, Articles of the Eyre direct inquiry as to conspirators either by description[6] or name, and, in the middle of Edward III's reign, in the string of criminals to be inquired of by inquest of office in the King's Bench are conspirators and confederators who ally themselves by oath, covenant, or other alliance that each shall aid and sustain the other's undertaking,

Mr Bryan points out that on his side of the Atlantic hasty judicial influences have been drawn as to the ancient conception of conspiracy; pp. 11 and 20, notes on *State* v. *Buchanan*, 5 H. and J. 317.

[1] *Ante* 22.

[2] *Termes de la Ley*, tit. "Deciners."

[3] Either the writ under De Conspiratoribus Ordinatio (*ante* 26), or that under Statutum de Conspiratoribus (*ante* 22). Cf. JONES J. in *Smith* v. *Cranshaw*, W. Jones at p. 94. Coke, 2 Inst. 562, takes it to be the writ under the Statutum.

[4] *St. of the Realm*, I. 139. The writ founded upon the Stat. is given in F.N.B. 116 N. There is a commentary on the Stat. in Coke, 2 Inst. 561. Cf. Stephen, *H.C.L.* II. 227–9; Bryan, 17–18.        [5] *Ante* 1.

[6] "Of those who by oaths bind themselves to support or defend the parties, quarrels and businesses of their friends and well-wishers, whereby truth and justice are stifled." *St. of the Realm*, I. 233 (*temp. incert.* Ed. III). Cf. *Rot. Parl.* I. 330 *b* where on a petition from the City of Lincoln and the county, Justices were assigned to inquire into robberies, homicides, murders, disseisins, false judgments, forstallments and conspiracies made by ministers of the King, and others in Lincolnshire (A.D. 1314–1315).

be it false or true; and those who falsely make people to be indicted and acquitted, or falsely move or maintain pleas in manner of alliance[1]. The Statute 4 Ed. III c. 11 had already passed owing to the inadequacy of 28 Ed. I c. 10 to extirpate conspiracies, confederacies and maintenance. We know from its preamble that some lost their lands by these means, while others preferred to abandon their rights rather than risk maim and battery at the hands of their enemies, and jurors were intimidated from returning verdicts. The statute provided that Justices of both Benches and of Assize in their sessions should inquire and determine, both at the suit of the King as well as that of the aggrieved party of such maintainers, undertakers, and conspirators, and also of champertors; if they could not determine the case at *nisi prius* owing to the shortness of their visit, they were to adjourn it to their own courts and settle it there.

## CONFEDERACY

§ 3. Here we may conveniently say something of "confederacy" and "confederators," terms which are constantly encountered in connection with conspiracy on its criminal side. They begin and end in the history of our law with no very technical meaning. An early instance of their use is to signify privity to a felony, as where Nicholas de Appelby was killed by John Fraunceys and others, and an appeal of this by Adam de Prynge was quashed. B. de S. then made inquest on behalf of the King, but took it 60 leagues from the place where the felony was committed, and by the parents and confederates of the felons, to the prejudice of the King and his peace[2]. Again, there is some trace of an idea that confederacy signified the combination in conspiracy to abuse procedure, apart from the abuse itself[3]; on the other hand, at a later period, WYNDHAM J. in *R. v. Starling* took an almost exactly opposite view and spoke as if conspiracy were the mere combination to commit crime, and confederacy or "coadunation" were the consummation of it[4].

---

[1] 27 Lib. Ass. 44.  Cf. pl. 34.
[2] *Rot. Parl.* I. 49 *a* (A.D. 1290). Cf. I. 127 *a* (1290. Complicity in some unnamed wrong-doing against the King).
[3] 19 Rich. II (Bellewe "Conspiracy"), *ante* 65, n. 10.
[4] 1 Keb. 675 (15 and 16 Car. II, B.R.).

Frequently "conspiracy and confederation" appear as a phrase —sometimes without any meaning specified for either word[1], but more usually as synonyms for some wrong the nature of which can be gathered from the context. This wrong certainly involves combination on the part of its perpetrators, and it may be abuse of procedure[2]. Confederacy is sometimes equivalent to maintenance[3], but it is by no means limited to that, and continually appears in the sense of combination to commit a crime or wrong of any sort[4], such as confederation to murder the King[5], or to oppose him[6], confederacies in restraint or to the prejudice of trade[7], or to kill another, as where John of Lancaster complains that five of the Thornburgh family with the assent of their father imagined the death of John by false confederacy, by sleeping armed in the same room where he was spending the night with intent to kill him in his bed[8]; or

[1] *Rot. Parl.* I. 216 *b* (A.D. 1306); IV. 104 *b* (1416). Cf. 28 Lib. Ass. pl. 12 (where they are mentioned distinctly).

[2] *Rot. Parl.* II. 141 *a* (1343), 165 *a* (1347), 259 *b* (1354), 265 *b* (1355); III. 248 *a* (1387–8). So too 18 Ed. III st. 1; 4 Ed. III c. 11; 27 Lib. Ass. pl. 44; *The Poulterers' Case* (Mich. 8 Jac. I) 9 Rep. 55 *b*; *Abb. Plac.* 295 (*ante* 3). Other words to which confederacy is joined are "colligaciones" (*Rot. Parl.* I. 371 *a*, A.D. 1320), "champerty," "maintenance," "alliance." *Rot. Parl.* II. 374 *b* (1376–7); III. 42 *a* (1378); and several of the preceding references.

[3] 27 Lib. Ass. pl. 34. Eyre of Kent, 6 and 7 Ed. II, S. S. vol. XXIV. p. 62. According to Wright (*Crim. Consp.* 15) from very early times "conspiracy" and "confederacy" were distinguished as different crimes under 33 Ed. I, conspiracy becoming appropriated to false and malicious indictments, while confederacy was especially used to designate combinations for maintenance. No doubt this holds of conspiracy, for though it applied to appeals, these rapidly became obsolete; but, with deference to the learned author, it is difficult to admit his specialization of confederacy to maintenance. See many of the passages cited in preceding note, where confederacy often seems to be a variant word for conspiracy as well as for maintenance; also *Rot. Parl.* I. 198 *a* (1306) where conspiracy is used to cover a case of maintenance. The authorities cited in Wright are 27 Lib. Ass. pl. 44 and 29 Lib. Ass. pl. 45. The note to Art. 5 in 27 Lib. Ass. pl. 44 supports his suggestion, but Art. 6 makes confederacy equivalent to conspiracy. 29 Lib. Ass. pl. 45 is a mere opinion or argument that an indictment which alleges only that the accused is a champertor or conspirator is insufficient, "sed non sic de confederatione. Quaere." Cf. Bryan, 54 n.

[4] *Rot. Parl.* I. 201, 202 *a* (1306).

[5] 3 Hen. VII c. 14; certain officials are to inquire by "xii sadde and discrete persones of the Chekk rolle" of confederacies, compassings and conspiracies with any person to murder the King.

[6] *Rot. Parl.* I. 127 *a* (1294).       [7] *Post* 98.

[8] Reply to John's petition is that the Thornburghs are to be bound over not to injure him. *Rot. Parl.* IV. 163 *a* (1421).

to get a man out of gaol[1]; or to disturb the staples[2]; or to rob[3], or to extort money by the detention of goods[4]; or to commit a riot, as where a petitioner in Chancery complains that the two defendants by confederacy and conspiracy made between them and certain persons of a guild to the number of two or three hundred to whom the defendant had promised the petitioner's lands, entered by forcible assemblies upon the petitioner[5]. Sometimes it is difficult to say that the combination is to commit any specific wrong; thus in 1411, the Commons complain on behalf of dwellers on the Severn that certain persons have confederated together to compel the inhabitants to cross the Severn, whose passage till then had been free, in great boats called "trowes" to be hired of the owners[6].     -

Coke, in stating the essentials of confederacy, employs the word as if it were conspiracy in the old strict sense, and also distinguishes it not very intelligibly from "coadunatio" and "falsa alligantia"[7]. In R. v. Best, where the accused were indicted for conspiring to charge another falsely with being the father of a bastard child, the counsel for the accused "took a diversity between a conspiracy and a confederacy; the one must be in judicial proceedings, the other may be in pais"; but HOLT C.J. in his judgment did not pin himself down to such a distinction[8], and a precedent of a similar indictment in West's Symboleographie which was cited in this case is against it, for the description of the crime "unitionis, conspirationis, confederationis, manutentionis," is a mere jumble of words indicating the same idea[9], and in Hawkins' treatise, conspiracy and

---

[1] Rot. Parl. VI. 102 a (1474).          [2] 27 Ed. III st. II. c. 25.

[3] Four men forcibly took from an alien 40 pence "per extorsionem et confederacionem." Leet Jurisdiction in Norwich. S. S. vol. v. p. 64 (1374–5). Cf. p. 68.

[4] R. v. Grimes and Thompson (3 Jac. II) 3 Mod. 200. Detention of goods alleged to be "per confederationem et astutiam."

[5] Select Cases in Chancery, S. S. vol. x. Case 79 (1396–1403 A.D.). Cf. 2 Rich. II st. I. c. 6.          [6] Rot. Parl. III. 665.

[7] Note to The Poulterers' Case (8 Jac. I) 9 Rep. 55 b. "Coadunatio" is a uniting of the wrong-doers together, "confederatio" is a combination amongst them, and "falsa alligantia" is a false binding each to the other, by bond or promise, to execute some unlawful act.

[8] 6 Mod. 186 (3 Ann. B.R.).

[9] Pt. II. sect. 97. POWELL J. and HOLT C.J. differed in their opinions of West's value.

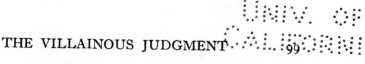
confederacy are used interchangeably[1]. The conclusion is that though no exact meaning can be attached to confederacy apart from its context, it is roughly equivalent to criminal conspiracy in its broad modern meaning, and is not limited to the old sense of that word.

## THE VILLAINOUS JUDGMENT

§ 4. There was at first no definite punishment for conspiracy, for the Statutum de Conspiratoribus, while it imposed three years' imprisonment on champertors, and required them to make fine at the King's pleasure, did not refer to conspirators generally[2]. Very likely the punishment of the *assisa* who swore falsely led to the selection of something similar for the kindred offence of conspiracy[3]; and then by accretions—some perceptible, some imperceptible—this developed into the villainous judgment. Even before the 13th century if the assize perjured themselves in court, and confessed, or were convicted of, the perjury, they forfeited all their chattels to the King, were imprisoned for a year at least, were deprived for ever after of their law, and subject to perpetual infamy[4]. A century later, neighbours who ally themselves to the hindrance of justice are bracketed with jurors who ally themselves with the royal officers for the same purpose, and both are to be ransomed at the King's pleasure, and their oath is never again to be admitted[5]. In Fortescue's time, we hear of additional penalties—their houses and buildings are to be razed, their woods felled and their meadows ploughed[6]. It has been inferred that the penalties against perjured jurors were so inadequate towards the end of Ed. I's reign that it was intended to include them in the definition of Conspirators of 33 Ed. I, though judicial construction of it gave them immunity[7].

[1] 1 P.C. ch. 72, sect. 3 et sqq. especially sect. 9.
[2] *Ante* 22.      [3] Reeves, III. 126.
[4] Glanv. II. xix; and see P. and M. II. 542, n. 1.
[5] Britton, I. xxii. 19.
[6] De Laud. *Leg. Angl.* ch. xxvi. *Termes de la Ley*, "Attaint." Coke (3 Inst. 222) says that the villainous judgment is given in conspiracy and in attaint of a jury, and in those cases only.
[7] Sir F. Palgrave. "Essay upon the Original Authority of the King's Council," sect. xxii. See too the interesting ballad of that period in sect. xxiii.

Conspiracy had scarcely been christened when a scandalous case of it led to a petition recorded on the Parliament Rolls. Several men were indicted of conspiracies and other trespasses and made fine for these; yet they were afterwards placed on the inquest and jury, to the confusion of those who had faithfully indicted them. To the petitioners' request for a remedy, it is replied that if the conspirators have made false confederacies, or procured themselves to be put on inquests for gain, or have taken gifts from either side and have been convicted thereof, they may not in future be put on any jury, inquest or assize[1]. Another short step and we get a fresh instalment of the villainous judgment. In 1314, the Commons complain to the King and Council of conspirators who infested every city, borough, hundred, and wapentake, and were allied by oath to maintain and procure false parties against law and right. It was ordained by the Council that no one convicted of conspiracy should be placed on any jury, assize, or recognition, or get himself admitted to any County, Hundred or other Court, or any "congregationes" or "tractatus," except for pursuing or defending his own affairs, on pain of heavy forfeiture; and every sheriff in England must publicly proclaim this[2]. In Ed. III's reign, the law repeats in substance these penalties, and adds to them further terrors—some of them purely vindictive. Two were convicted of conspiracy at the King's suit. The judgment was that they should lose their "franke ley," to the intent that they should not thereafter be put on juries or assizes, nor otherwise on testimony of truth; that they should transact their business in the King's Court by attorney only; that their lands, goods and chattels should be seized by the King, and stripped if they could not get this mitigated; that their trees should be uprooted, and their bodies

[1] *Rot. Parl.* 1. 201 *a* (A.D. 1306).

[2] *Ibid.* 1. 289 *a*. Those who complain of such convicted conspirators can get a writ of trespass from the Chancery formed upon this ordinance and proclamation. The year before this, two found to be guilty in the Eyre of Kent of conspiracy and maintenance were committed to prison, and afterwards made fine. This leaves it open whether the disabilities mentioned in *Rot. Parl.* 1. 201 *a* were implied on a conviction, and need not be expressed in the sentence. S. S. vol. XXIV. p. 62. And see Henry le Swan's case, A.D. 1325, *post* 103.

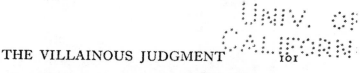

imprisoned[1]. Later still in the same reign, one who was convicted was sentenced in the same way with the refinements that he was not to come within 12[2] leagues of the King's court, and that his wife and children were to be ousted[3]. Here we have the villainous judgment in full flower, a composite product of ordinance and judicial decision[4]. It was said at a later date when the judgment was no more than a legal fossil, that it could not be given except where the conspiracy was to take away a man's life, but the reports of the case are not trustworthy on this point[5]. The name was due to the "villanie et huntie" which it brought upon the criminal[6], and Coke gives as a further reason the loss of freedom and franchise of the law which entailed a kind of bondage and villainy, and he is at some pains to support the moral justice of its severity[7]. This remedy was limited to conviction at the King's suit and did not apply to the defendant in a civil suit[8]. The last recorded instance of it is 46 Lib. Ass. pl. 11, and for it were substituted fine, pillory, imprisonment, and sureties for good behaviour[9]. The Star

[1] 27 Lib. Ass. pl. 59; slightly fuller in Br. *Abr. Consp.* 28. Already in 1343, in response to a prayer of the Commons, the King had declared that no one attainted of confederacy or conspiracy should hold office of the King, Queen, or great men, or be a sheriff, or escheator. *Rot. Parl.* II. 141 *a*. Cited 3 Inst. 222.

[2] Fifteen acc. to Br. *Abr. Consp.* 31. Hudson (p. 133) surmises that he could not prosecute a suit in the Star Chamber.

[3] 46 Lib. Ass. pl. 11. Cf. Br. *Abr. Consp.* 31.

[4] Cf. Stanf. P.C. 175 B. Coke contradicts himself, for in 3 Inst. 143, 222, and 2 Inst. 562, he states that the judgment is given by the Common Law, while in 2 Inst. 384, he bases it on an imaginary Act of Hen. I. Hawkins (1 P.C. 72, sect. 9) attributes it to the Common Law; so does Blackstone (IV. 136). Cf. Wright, p. 15. In *Sydenham* v. *Keilaway* (16 Eliz.) Cro. Jac. 7, it is said that conspiracy is a misdemeanour punishable at Common Law.

[5] *Obiter dictum* in *Savill* v. *Roberts* (10 Will. III, B.R.) 12 Mod. at p. 209. The report in 1 Ld. Raym. at p. 379 makes the Court say, "But in an action for a conspiracy no villainous judgment shall be given, unless the life was endangered by that conspiracy," and Carthew 416 is to the same effect. But the villainous judgment, according to earlier authority, could not in any event be awarded except on conviction at the suit of the King. Mich. 24 Ed. III, f. 34 (note by Shard[elowe?]).

[6] Stanf. P.C. 174 B.

[7] 3 Inst. 143.     [8] Note 5 *supra*.

[9] Leach's note to 1 Hawk. P.C. (ed. 1787) 72, sect. 9; so too Bl. IV. 136-7. It is mechanically repeated in Vin. *Abr. Consp.* (I) 2. In *R.* v. *Best* (3 Ann. B.R.), 6 Mod. 186, it is mentioned.

Chamber punished conspiracy by branding in the face and slitting of the nose[1]. Thus in Henry VIII's reign, a priest was branded with F and A in his forehead for false accusation[2]. So too in James I's reign, Basset and an attorney named Reignolds, were convicted in that Court, and the sentence was that Reignolds be degraded and cast over the Common Pleas Bar, and that both defendants should lose their ears, be marked with a C in the face for conspirators, should stand upon the pillory with papers of their offences, should be whipped, and each of them fined £500. These sentences were executed[3]. It may be added that Edward III consulted his justices and serjeants whether persons indicted of conspiracy for indicting another of felony were mainpernable, and received the express opinion that they were not[4], no doubt on account of the odious nature of the offence[5].

## DEVELOPMENT OF THE CRIME IN ITS ORIGINAL SENSE

§ 5. There is not much wonder that the punishment of conspiracy culminated in the savagery of the villainous judgment. The crime was rife in high places, and the watch-dog too often a disguised wolf. In 1314–15, the men of Romney complain that felons and murderers are received in Romney, that the bailiff lets felons escape, and with his fellows conspires against the petitioners to prevent justice being done to felons and murderers, so that the inhabitants dare not remain there unless a speedy remedy be applied. The Council answers the petition by assigning Henry Spigurnel, Henry of Cobham, Custodian of the Cinque Ports, and Roger le Sauvage to inquire into the petition and hear and determine for the King[6]. Edward II sought the help of the Church in suppressing conspirators and maintainers of false pleas. He issued a writ to the Bishop of

---

[1] Hudson, 224.

[2] Hil. 37 Hen. VIII, acc. to Coke's note to *The Poulterers' Case*, 9 Rep. 57 a. So also one of the conspirators in *Sir Anthony Ashley's Case* (Mich. 9 Jac. I) Moore, 816, was branded.

[3] *Miller* v. *Reignolds and Basset* (11 Jac. I) Godbolt, 205. Hawkins (1 P.C. 72, sect. 2) speaks of branding as one of the punishments for a false and malicious accusation.

[4] 27 Lib. Ass. pl. 12.    [5] 3 Inst. 143.

[6] *Rot. Parl.* 1. 324 b.

Cicester directing him to fulminate the greater excommunication against these and many other offenders, and Parliament a century later recited this in a petition requesting the same remedy against the prevalence of crime in half-a-dozen counties[1]. Henry le Swan, according to another petition at the end of this disorderly reign, whilst " gardein del Murage de Loundres," was attainted in the Eyre of London for false and malicious conspirations, whereby the King's Council ordered that he should hold no office in the realm. Yet he was never so bold, malicious, and oppressive to the people as now. The reply is that if the facts alleged be found on scrutiny of the record in the Chancery, the sheriff is not to put him on assizes, juries, inquests, etc.[2] But the sheriffs themselves had not clean hands. It was but two years after the Definition of Conspirators that the auditors of plaints hear John de Tany's complaint against the sheriff of Essex because he has conspired with another to disseise de Tany of some manors and will not allow him to view the panel or the writ, and for this the sheriff makes fine of £10[3]. This is only an isolated instance, but in 1330 a sweeping provision of the King and Council requires all the sheriffs of England to be removed and not to be received back, and good people and sages of the law to be assigned throughout all England to inquire, hear, and determine, at the suit of both King and party, conspiracies, oppressions, grievances, and trespasses made between 1 Ed. II and 4 Ed. III by sheriffs, coroners, constables, bailiffs, hundredors, and such other ministers, and others[4]. Among the long list of things into which justices assigned for keeping the peace are, in 1343, directed to inquire we find conspiracies, confederacies, champerties, ambidextres, meyntenours, meffesours, false quarrels, and all other falsities made in deceit of the law; and in the same year the writ of *exigent*, which outlawed a defendant who did not appear with moderate promptitude, was made applicable

[1] *Rot. Parl.* IV. 121 a (1433). The petition is met by a promise to consult the Lords.
[2] *Ibid.* 435 a (1325), where the Bishop of Durham is charged with conspiracy and collusion in inducing the petitioner's relations to bring a law suit.
[3] *Abb. Plac.* 305 (35 Ed. I).          [4] *Rot. Parl.* II. 60. Cf. 416 a.

on the prayer of the Commons to conspirators, confederators, and maintainers of false quarrels[1]. But again in 1347, the King is importuned to forbid under a certain penalty great men from maintaining maintainers, conspirators, confederators, embracers, champertors, and others, and he fends them off with the promise of a homoeopathic cure—he will consult with the great men and ordain such remedy as shall please God and man[2].

This cancer of administrative corruption spread to the judicial bench, for in the Parliament of 28 Ed. III, the King assents to the request of the Commons that inquest upon conspiracy, confederacy, and maintenance shall be returned only by the sheriff of the most lawful men, and nearest to the place of the supposed fact, and that all evidence therein shall be openly given at the bar, and no justice or other shall commune with the inquest to move or procure them after their departure[3]. In the next year, the grievance is not corruption of the judges, but their hastiness. Justices assigned to inquire of confederacies, conspiracies, and maintainers, judge "molt reddement"[4], and the Commons ask the King and his Council that the points of confederacies, etc., be declared. The answer is that no one is to be judged or punished for confederacy except in the case where the statute has made express mention on the points contained in the same statute[5].

Sometimes the petitioner is bluntly referred to his Common Law remedy, even where it has conspicuously broken down, as when Sir Hugh le Despenser makes a stranger buy a false writ for certain lands against another, who loses his verdict because the inquest are terrified, and gets imprisoned by Sir Hugh when he sues writ of trespass and conspiracy[6]. In Richard II's reign, Parliament begs the King—not for further

---

[1] *Rot. Parl.* II. 137 a, 141 a.

[2] *Ibid.* II. 165 a. Cf. Palgrave, *King's Council*, 71–75, where two of the commissioners directed to inquire into a conspiracy, and the bailiffs who returned an inquest for that purpose, behaved no better than the conspirators themselves.

[3] *Ibid.* II. 259 b; also 266 a.

[4] "Rapidement" (Godefroy).

[5] *Rot. Parl.* II. 265 b.

[6] *Ibid.* II. 385 b (ann. incert. Ed. III). Cf. ante 56, n. 4.

redress against criminals but—for a general white-washing of them, including those who have committed conspiracies, confederacies, champerties, ambidextries, falsities and deceits[1]; and from a later petition it appears that attempts were made to hoist the law with its own petard, and that the writ of conspiracy, originally designed to stop false accusations was being employed to stifle honest ones. Evil-doers who had been properly indicted procured their acquittal by a favourable inquest, and then sued writs of conspiracy against their indictors[2] and others, alleging the conspiracy to be made in a county where they had powerful friends; and thus good and lawful men dared not speak the truth. The King met this abuse by giving the Chancellor power to make a remedy till the next Parliament[3]. A case something like this had occurred only the year before. Thomas Hardyng was committed to the Fleet by the King and Lords for falsely impeaching Sir John and Sir Richard de Sutton, on the ground that they had wrongly imprisoned Thomas for one year in the Fleet by conspiring to accuse him before the King's Council[4].

A petition by the Commons in 1402 curiously exemplifies the political history of the times. It alleges that conspirators maliciously indict in Middlesex persons resident in other counties, who are outlawed for treason or felony on these indictments before they know of them. The prayer is that the accused when acquitted may get the conspirators convicted by the same inquest which acquits the accused, and that their accusers may be punished. The reply is that the statutes and Common Law are to be observed, and such conspirators, on conviction, must pay damages to the injured parties, and make fine and ransom to the King[5]. It was not long before this that the Despensers had been impeached for procuring false indictments, and, probably as an act of political revenge, packed juries were impanelled without being returned by the sheriff,

[1] *Rot. Parl.* III. 248 a (1387–8); IV. 104 b (1416).
[2] Contrary to the well settled rule that the writ did not lie against indictors. *Ante* 67 et sqq.
[3] *Rot. Parl.* III. 306 a (1392–3). Cf. III. 318 a (1393–4).
[4] *Ibid.* III. 288 b (1391).
[5] *Ibid.* 505 a (1402).

and these juries falsely accused at Westminster persons, some
of whom were outlawed. Such indictments were made void
by 11 Hen. VI c. 9[1], and the sheriffs were made essential
parties to the impanelling of juries. But the device was then
hit upon to which the petition just mentioned refers, and it
was applied with further success in Lancashire where geo-
graphical peculiarities favoured it. Morecambe Bay so splits
that county that juries drawn from either division of it might
well be ignorant of the existence of places in the other, and
indictments and appeals of treason and felony were falsely
procured against persons who were accused of having committed them in a fictitious place. These persons went in such
fear of being beaten and maimed by the procurers that they
dared not appear to answer the accusation. 7 Hen. V c. 1
recites this, and requires every justice having jurisdiction over
such treasons and felonies in Lancashire to inquire before
award of the *exigent* which entailed outlawry whether the place
mentioned existed in the county and, if it did not, such appeals
and indictments were to be void, and the indictors punished
by imprisonment, fine, and ransom at the discretion of the
justices. This ordinance was limited in place to Lancashire
and in time till the next Parliament. 9 Hen. V st. 1, cc. 1 and 2
extended it to England generally, and a later statute provided
that defendants' outlawries, though good in Lancashire, should
not be operative in other counties so as to forfeit their lands
and goods elsewhere. 18 Hen. VI c. 12 made the ordinance
perpetual[2]. Two varieties of the fraud just discussed had also
to be met by legislation. One was to issue a *capias ad respondendum* to the sheriff of Middlesex returnable within so short
a time that a person so indicted who lived at a distance had no
opportunity to appear, and thus forfeited his goods and chattels
on an award of *exigent*[3]. This was remedied by 6 Hen. VI c. 1.
The other was to procure indictments and appeals of treason,
felony, and trespass in counties or franchises unknown to the
parties accused, with the similar result of *exigent* and outlawry.

[1] Cf. *Rot. Parl.* III. 627 b.
[2] See I. S. Leadam, Introd. to S. S. vol. XVI. pp. ciii et seq. The peculiar
exception of Cheshire from 9 Hen. V st. 1, c. 2 is there explained.
[3] I. S. Leadam, *ubi supra*.

8 Hen. VI c. 10[1] gave the acquitted party action upon the case against the procurer with treble damages. Of this more will be said in developing the history of the writ of conspiracy; here it is enough to note that where an appellor appealed one who was not merely out of a particular county, but abroad, there are traces in earlier times of a much more summary procedure, for in a case in which the appellor admitted to the Court that the appellee was in Flanders, it was awarded that he be hanged, for the appellee could not be convicted[2].

The iniquities of jurors and sheriffs break out again under the feeble rule of Henry VI, and statutes of Edward IV, and Richard III were aimed against them[3]. There can be little doubt that it was the Star Chamber that withered conspiracy at its root. As it reaches the zenith of its power for good in the reign of Elizabeth, so does the shadow of conspiracy *stricto sensu* dwindle. In the country, the suitor might have to face magistrates unprincipled and ill-educated, and juries intimidated or corrupted by a powerful opponent; and if he tried to upset the unjust verdict against him, he might, if it were a civil case, resort to an obsolescent remedy[4] and perhaps tread the vicious circle of attempting to attaint one jury by another just as corrupt; or, whether the case were civil or criminal, he would probably have to plunge into further tedious litigation in order to right himself[5]. In the Star Chamber, on the other hand, he was sure of a strong Court and was free from a jury[6] Its jurisdiction over conspiracy was not established without question. In *Rochester* v. *Solm*, Coke maintained that the remedy of the acquitted party was to prefer an indictment at Common Law, but Lord Egerton "did gravely confute that opinion," and shewed that the Common Law remedy did not

---

[1] Stanf. P.C. 176 B; F.N.B. 115 H ("c. 80" is a misprint for "c. 10").
[2] Trin. 1 Ed. III, f. 16.
[3] I. S. Leadam, *loc. cit.* 1 Ed. IV c. 2; 1 Rich. III c. 4. The popular suspicion of juries did not vary much from one century to another. Cf. the verses cited by Palgrave, pp. 58–9, 103.
[4] Sir Thomas Smith said in 1565 that attaints were very seldom put in use. See Thayer, 153.
[5] Palgrave, sect. xxxiv–v; Hudson, 14; Thayer, 149.
[6] The Council had long before been given by legislation a short-lived authority to deal with false suggestions made to it. 37 Ed. III c. 18, 38 Ed. III st. 1, c. 9, 42 Ed. III c. 3.

exclude the Court of Star Chamber from proceeding for the King also[1]. Moreover, the Court was willing to overlook formal defects in pleading in order to save its jurisdiction in such cases[2].

In early times the fool occasionally appears to have received punishment more appropriate to the knave. One Knige, in Edward II's reign, indicted the coroner, Mekelfield and Berneham, whereon the jurors said that they confederated themselves on account of enmity borne by Mekelfield to Knige, and that they falsely and maliciously published that Knige had killed Isabella de Shapstone. Notice of this death reached the incompetent coroner, who, in ignorance of the law, and not by any conspiracy, took an inquisition without inspecting the body. Six other persons honestly but blunderingly consented to the indictment of Knige, who was convicted. Isabella in fact was alive. The six were imprisoned in spite of the lack of malicious intention; so apparently were the coroner, Mekelfield and Berneham. Berneham assigned as errors that he was compelled to be a juror by the coroner, and that he need not reply to the indictment for conspiracy, because conspiracy is always voluntary. The ultimate result does not appear[3].

As conspiracy gradually widens into the crime known at the present day, the cases in which its object is to abuse procedure dwindle in proportion to those where the aim is wrong-doing of other kinds, and modern examples are not easy to find[4].

---

[1] Hudson, 104–5.

[2] *Tailor and Towlin's Case* (4 Car. I). Godbolt, 444. Cases of conspiracy were not always so styled in the S.C., if *Amerideth's Case* (41 and 42 Eliz.) Moore, 562, be correctly reported. There a "combination" of tenants (apparently copyholders) to maintain each other in suits relating to the freehold was punished.

[3] *Abb. Plac.* 322 (9 Ed. II).

[4] *R. v. Teal* (1809) 11 East, 307, seems to be the last case of combination to accuse before a Court as distinct from accusation to the public.

# CHAPTER IV

## DEVELOPMENT OF CRIMINAL CONSPIRACY GENERALLY TO THE END OF THE 18TH CENTURY

### PRELIMINARY

§ 1. It has been shewn that if conspiracy had any strict meaning in early law, it was that of combination to promote false accusations and suits before a Court. This is in extraordinary contrast with the modern law which has expanded the crime so much as to make it almost incapable of definition. The change has come by astute adaptation of a term which never lost its early plasticity[1], and had an equally plastic doublet in "confederacy." Cases occur from the beginning which would later have been called conspiracies, but which have no special name[2]. On the other hand, "conspiracy" and "confederacy" —the latter especially—are traceable at an early date with the broad signification that they were to bear in the developed law. But they are not to be found in the Year Books. The solitary example of any attempt to extend criminal conspiracy beyond its original boundary occurs in Mich. 24 Ed. III, f. 75, where a judgment against two on a presentment for conspiracy was reversed partly because the presentment omitted the day, year and place of the conspiracy, and partly because the chief cause of the offence was not so much conspiracy as wrongful damage and oppression of the people, for the presentment alleged imprisonment of a person till he had made fine.

### THE PARLIAMENT ROLLS

§ 2. It is rather in the Parliament Rolls that evidence of the growth of conspiracy is to be sought. We read there of confederation by oath to oppose the King in 1294[3], and confederation in the sense of combination to commit crime in 1331-2[4].

---

[1] See *Termes de la Ley* for the colourless French and Latin meanings of the word.
[2] *Ante* 3-4.
[3] *Rot. Parl.* I. 127 a.
[4] *Ibid.* II. 65 a.

A curious case illustrating both terms forms the subject of a petition to Parliament in 1306. Four citizens of York were indicted before justices appointed to inquire of a certain confederation made between the four, for having removed a gild [*gildam*] anciently set up for making certain alms, and for this trespass they afterwards made fine to the Treasurer. Four other persons then spread it abroad that the original four were convicted before the Council of conspiracy and collusion, and would not allow them to come among them so that they could not know the plans or secrets of the city. The Mayor, Sheriffs and community of the city are ordered in the reply to the petition to refrain from this civic ostracism[1]. Another petition throws a side-light on the feeble rule of Edward II. It sets out that he had commanded Elizabeth de Burgh to stay with him on Christmas Day, and that by the abetment and ill counsel of Hugh de Spencer, Robert de Baldock, and Sir W. de Cliffe, he had caused her to be arrested and to make a bond obligatory for forfeiture of her property, if she married against the King's wishes. The writ issued by Ed. III in response to the petition recites these facts and that "our said father, by the conspiracy and crafty plotting" of the men mentioned, acted as he did. The script of the obligation is to come before Parliament without delay. Parliament advised that it was against law and reason and caused it "to bee damned"[2]. Next, conspiracy appears as a combination to hinder the realization of the Royal revenue, when, in 1340, punishment is decreed for those who by conspiracy or false covin prevent the sale for the King's benefit of the ninth sheaf, fleece, and lamb granted by the preceding Parliament to the King[3]; and not long afterwards as a combination to contravene the Ordinance of the Staples (27 Ed. III st. 2) c. 25 of which forbids any merchant to make confederacy or conspiracy to the disturbance of the Staples[4]. Conspiracies to commit treason are mentioned several times[5], and the

---

[1] *Rot. Parl.* I. 202 *a*.      [2] *Ibid.* II. 440 *a*.
[3] *Ibid.* II. 117 *b*, and see sect. 3 of the Statute.
[4] So too *Rot. Parl.* II. 251 *a*.
[5] *Rot. Parl.* III. 316 *b* (1393–4); *St. of the Realm*, II. 46–47 *Ibid.* 509 (3 Hen. VII c. 14). So too in later law, *Blunt's Case*, St. Tr. I. 1410 (1600). *R. v. Hardy*, 24 St. Tr. 438 (1794).

Lollards are spoken of as conspirators to subvert the Catholic faith[1]. In 1413, the Commons pray for a remedy against those who by false conspiracy and covin forge false deeds[2]. Keeping greyhounds among the lower classes seems to have lead not merely to Sabbath breaking and poaching, but to conspiracies to disobey their allegiance[3].

## TRADE COMBINATIONS

§ 3. But by far the commonest use of conspiracy and confederacy is in connection with combinations to restrain or to interfere with trade. In 1320, fishmongers complain to Parliament of a confederation among other fishmongers that fish should no longer be sold by retail on a particular wharf[4]; in 21 Ed. III the grievance is against a confederacy of merchants who had farmed the King's wool[5]. Among the Articles of inquiry by inquest of office in the King's Bench, 27 Lib. Ass. pl. 44, is one relating to merchants who by covin and alliance form a "ring" to fix the price of wool annually to the great impoverishment of the people. In a Norwich leet court, there is a verdict in 1390 against some who have cornered wheat[6], and in 1415, Parliament is asked to supervise the dyers of Coventry who have confedered to raise the cost of dyeing[7]. In fact, the prevailing idea was that trade combinations when they interfered with prices were an economic evil to be stamped out by the state, and a Parliament which was parental enough to fix the price of a young capon at threepence, and an old one at fourpence[8] was not likely to shirk this duty. That its attempts to regulate trade were not always satisfactory in result was only to be expected. A statute of 13 Rich. II[9] in effect forbade any tanner to be a shoemaker, or shoemaker a tanner, and shoe-

---

[1] *Rot. Parl.* IV. 106 a, 108 a.
[2] *Ibid.* IV. 10 a. For riot, see *ante* 98.
[3] 13 Rich. II st. 1, c. 13.
[4] *Rot. Parl.* I. 370 a.
[5] *Ibid.* II. 170 b. Cf. 350 b (conspiracy to defraud by the merchants of Florence and Lombardy).
[6] S. S. vol. v. p. 74.
[7] *Rot. Parl.* IV. 75 a.
[8] 37 Ed. III c. 3.
[9] St. 1, c. 12. Partially repealed 4 Hen. IV c. 35 and wholly 5 Eliz. c. 8 and 1 Jac. I c. 22.

makers who disobeyed were to forfeit all leather so tanned. The tanners took advantage of this to form a conspiracy and confederacy to beat down the price of leather and oxen at market, so that they could sell leather at an extortionate price, and thus raise the price of boots. On this the Commons petitioned that shoemakers should be allowed to tan, but the request was not granted[1]. Confederacies of masons in their chapters and assemblies subverted the Statutes of Labourers so seriously that causing the holding of such chapters was made a felony[2]. But 2 and 3 Ed. VI c. 15 surpasses any previous enactment in scope and graduated severity, for it punishes in effect all purveyors of food who conspire to sell their goods only at fixed prices, and all artificers or labourers who conspire not to work except at a fixed wage or for a fixed time[3].

### CRIMINAL CONSPIRACY IN THE LATTER HALF OF THE. 17TH CENTURY

§ 4. The latter half of the 17th century witnesses a swift approach of criminal conspiracy to the meaning it now bears. It was a favourable time for its extension, for on the civil side the writ of conspiracy was obsolete because its work was more efficiently done by the action of case founded upon it, and on the criminal side the Star Chamber had crushed combinations to accuse before a Court. The original meaning was disappearing, save for the idea of combination, and it was not difficult to tack on to that idea almost any conceivable evil object that two or more persons might have. The transitional era is well illustrated in the reports. Even in the earlier half of the century there are signs of the coming change. The Star Chamber in 4 Jac. I had held to be illegal a "combination" of tenants who joined in a petition to the King relating to the

---

[1] *Rot. Parl.* III. 330 b (1394–5).

[2] 3 Hen. VI c. 1. *Rot. Parl.* IV. 292 a.

[3] It is instructive to notice that West's *Symboleographie* (ed. 1647), II. sect. 98, has a precedent of an indictment for a conspiracy of bakers Oct. 2nd, 39 Eliz. that the penny loaf should not weigh more than 2 lb. 6 oz. while sect. 97 is an indictment for conspiracy in the old sense. Again in *Midwinter* v. *Scrogg*, 1 Keb. at p. 756 (1636), the Star Chamber fined the butchers of London £3000 for glutting the markets to the impoverishment of several country farmers.

customs of the manor, and had bound themselves by writing to bear the expenses rateably. The ground of the illegality was not the joining in the suit nor the contribution as such, but giving a blank power to one Perkins to write what he liked in the petition and formulating a claim as to tenure and not merely as to the customs[1]. And Coke, though he confines his definition of conspiracy to its old sense, clearly recognizes elsewhere that it had a wider interpretation[2]. In *R. v. Starling*[3], a case much cited in later authorities, an information was laid against London brewers because they were of confederacy, and had conspired "deprender" the "gallon trade" (by which the poor were supplied), and so caused the poor to mutiny against the farmers of the excise. A jury found the defendants guilty of nothing except the conspiracy to impoverish. One of the grounds of a motion in arrest of judgment was that the defendants had not been found guilty of any offence, since it was no legal offence to impoverish another with intent to enrich oneself as by selling commodities at cheaper rates. But after several debates, it was adjudged by the Court that this was a good verdict upon which judgment should be given for the King. For the verdict related to the information, and the information recited how the excise was part of the revenue and to impoverish the farmers of the excise would make them incapable of rendering to the King his revenue. And HYDE, TWYSDEN, and KELYNGE held that the bare conspiracy in this case to diminish the King's revenue, without any act done, was finable. WYNDHAM J. said that if it was no more than a conspiracy without an act done, it was not punishable, but that here there was more—a confederacy and a coadunation, by assembling themselves for this purpose. Here then, the Court has taken the step of applying to the law of criminal

---

[1] *Lord Greye's Case*, Moore, 788. Cf. Wright, 22. The learned author classifies this under combination to commit maintenance, and perhaps it falls within Coke's definition of this. Co. *Litt.* 368 *b*.

[2] 3 Inst. 143. *Ibid.* 196, where he says that every practice or device by act, conspiracy, words, or news, to enhance the price of victuals or other merchandize, was punishable by law, and also refers to 2 and 3 Ed. VI c. 15 (*ante* 112).

[3] 1 Sid. 174 (15 and 16 Car. II, B.R.); 1 Keble, 650, 655, 675, 682; 1 Lev. 125.

conspiracy in general the principle which had already been
settled in criminal conspiracy to accuse another of crime before
a court—that combination is the gist of the offence; and
WYNDHAM J.'s *dictum* merely relates to the evidence needed to
prove the combination, not to the execution of its purpose.
But it will be noted that there is nothing in the decision which
implies that the purpose of the conspiracy need not be unlawful[1]. In *R. v. Opie* the conspiracy was in the nature of
embracery[2], and soon after cases occur on conspiracy to cheat[3].
A case which was argued on adjournment, but of which no
decision is reported, was *R. v. Thorp*[4], where the information
laid was that Thorp and others had conspired to take an infant
under 18 from the custody of his father and to persuade him
to marry a person of ill name, and the purpose was effected.
All were found guilty except Thorp. It was moved in arrest
of judgment that the information did not contain any matter
of misdemeanour, and that one alone could not conspire as one
only had been found guilty. The discussion seems to have
been centred on the first objection. There had, however, been
a unanimous decision not long before that this was an offence
punishable by fine and imprisonment at Common Law, but
though the offence was committed by several acting together,
there was no allegation of conspiracy[5]. In 10 Will. III, leave
was granted to file an information against several button makers,
for combining not to sell under a set rate, and HOLT C.J. said
that it was fit that all confederacies by those of trade to raise
their rates should be suppressed[6]. Early in Anne's reign counsel
argued that the defendants in *R. v. Starling* were liable because
the conspiracy would affect the public revenue, but that if the
conspiracy had been that none should buy coffee from *B*, it
would not bear an indictment, so too if there were a confederacy

---

[1] Cf. Wright, pp. 11–12, 38, and App. II.
[2] 1 Wms. Saund. 300 e (1671).
[3] *Thody's Case*, 1 Vent. 234 (24 and 25 Car. II). *R. v. Orbell*, 6 Mod. 42
(2 Anne, B.R.). *R. v. Maccarty*, 2 Ld. Raym. 1179 (3 Ann. B.R.) is not a
case of conspiracy; Wright, 106.
[4] 5 Mod. 221 (8 Will. III, B.R.) Comb. 456.
[5] *R. v. Twistleton*, 1 Sid. 387 (20 Car. II, B.R.); 1 Lev. 257. Cf. *Lord
Grey's Case* (1682), 9 St. Tr. 128, and the criticism in Wright, 106.
[6] *Anon.* 12 Mod. 248.

to waylay a man and kill or rob him. But HOLT C.J. denied
the last two instances, and in any event the case was not on
conspiracy; he also said that in *R. v. Starling* the gist of the
offence was its influence on the public, not the conspiracy, for
that must be put in execution before it is a conspiracy[1]. This
must be qualified by his decision next year in *R. v. Best*[2],
where the conspiracy was falsely to charge (but not before a
Court) a man with being the father of a bastard child. It was
urged (*inter alia*) upon demurrer that it ought to appear that
the accusation was before a lawful magistrate. But HOLT said,

> This indeed is not an indictment for a formed conspiracy, strictly
> speaking, which requires an infamous judgment....But this seems
> to be a conspiracy *late loquendo*, or a confederacy to charge one
> falsely, which sure, without more, is a crime.

And the whole Court thought that the mere agreement to charge
a man with a crime falsely was a consummate offence, and
indictable; and that the crime charged need be no more than
an ecclesiastical offence (here fornication), and that the confederacy was the gist of the indictment.

## CRIMINAL CONSPIRACY IN THE BEGINNING OF THE 18TH CENTURY

§ 5. It may be said then that about the beginning of the
18th century, we have decisions or indications in decisions that
criminal conspiracy had been extended to include combinations (1) to accuse, but not necessarily before a Court, of some
offence; (2) to commit embracery; (3) to cheat; (4) to sell goods
at a fixed price (but this is the merest indication)[3]; (5) to extort
money; and that combination was the gist of the offence. In
considering further developments in the 18th century, there is
no need to examine each case in detail, for that has already
been done in the learned monograph of WRIGHT J. The salient
points may, however, be noticed. And first, it was said by the

[1] *R. v. Daniell* (2 Anne, B.R.) 6 Mod. 99.
[2] 6 Mod. 185 (3 Anne, B.R.), 1 Salk. 174. 2 Ld. Raym. 1167.
[3] *Anon.* 12 Mod. 248 (*ante* 114). *R. v. Rispal* (1762) 3 Burr. 1320. Wright
(p. 61) refers to 37 Ed. III c. 5 as the statute which covers this (*Ibid.* 44);
but that chapter was repealed 38 Ed. III c. 2.

8—2

Court in *R. v. Journeymen Taylors of Cambridge* (1721)[1], and
in other cases, that conspiracy is an offence at Common Law.
This must be limited to conspiracy in its extended sense, and
not in its original meaning of abuse of process, for there it is
traceable to "De Conspiratoribus Ordinatio"[2]. The Court held
as a consequence that the indictment need not include *contra
formam statuti*, for the case was that the defendants had conspired to raise their wages, and this was alleged to be a breach
of 7 Geo. I c. 13 which prohibited journeymen from entering
into any agreement for advancing their wages. But the answer
was that the case was outside the statute "because it is not the
denial to work except for more wages than is allowed by
Statute, but it is for a *conspiracy* to raise their wages, for which
these defendants are indicted." These last words raise a
question very difficult of solution. Need the object of any
combination be criminal, or at least unlawful, in order to make
it a conspiracy?

## RESULT

§ 6. The result seems to be:

(1) Where the combination is against the government, or
public safety, it is possible that it may be criminal
although the acts proposed may not be criminal[3]; but
even here, they were perhaps at least unlawful[4].

(2) Where the combination is to pervert justice, otherwise
than by false accusation, though the perversion of
justice may not be criminal apart from the combination, yet this may be criminal conspiracy, though the
actual decisions seem to shew that the perversion must
be at least a contempt of Court[5]. The earliest of these
cases is *R. v. Mawbey* (1796)[6].

(3) Combinations against public morals and decency have
been held to be conspiracies; but there is nothing to
shew that the immoral acts which were the purposes

---

[1] 8 Mod. 11.  [2] *Ante* 94.
[3] Wright, sect. 11. § 7 and cases there cited.
[4] *R. v. Starling* (*ante* 113) is the case which makes this doubtful. All the
other cases shew an unlawful object.
[5] Wright, sect. 11. § 8 and cases there.  [6] 6 T.R. 619.

of such combinations were not in themselves criminal[1].
*R. v. Delaval* (1763) is the earliest case[2].

(4) In combinations to injure individuals otherwise than
by fraud, it is doubtful whether the purpose need be,
apart from combination, criminal[3], such as bribing a
cardmaker's apprentice to spoil his master's cards by
greasing them[4].

(5) There are some indications, but no clear authority
that combinations to raise wages were punishable,
though such demands if made by individuals would
not be[5].

## TEXT-BOOKS

§ 7. The text-books lag behind the reports in taking account
of the expansion of criminal conspiracy. There is no mention
of it in the 1778 edition of Hale's *History of Pleas of the Crown*.
Blackstone contemplates no variety of the original crime[6], and
Hawkins, though he lays it down that all confederacies wrongfully to prejudice a third person are highly criminal, inserts
this statement of questionable accuracy without further discussion in his exposition of conspiracy in its old meaning[7].
So stands the general history of criminal conspiracy to the end
of the 18th century, and, as we are concerned with abuse of
legal procedure only, the statement of the modern law of conspiracy relating to other objects is outside the scope of this
book.

[1] Wright, sect. II. § 9 and cases.
[2] 3 Burr. 1434. See Lord Mansfield at pp. 1438–9. In *R. v. Young* cited
in *R. v. Lynn* (1788) 2 T.R. 733, the conspiracy was to prevent the burial
of a corpse apparently for purposes of indecent exhibition, and there is a
strong probability that this was illegal, as in *R. v. Lynn*, the Court held that
if one carried away a body for mere dissection it was a crime.
[3] Wright, sect. II. § 11.
[4] *R. v. Cope.* Str. 144 (5 Geo. I), which appears to be the first genuine
case. It is not easy to see, on the authorities cited by the learned author, that
such an act was then punishable apart from combination.
[5] Wright, sect. II. §§ 12–14 especially pp. 52–53.
[6] IV. 136.
[7] I P.C. 72, sect. 2. Cf. Wright, 38.

# CHAPTER V

## THE ACTION ON THE CASE IN THE NATURE
OF CONSPIRACY

§ 1. In this chapter we must trace the decay of the writ of conspiracy and the supersession of it to the action upon the case in the nature of conspiracy, which ultimately developed into the modern action for malicious prosecution.

### DECAY OF THE WRIT OF CONSPIRACY

§ 2. Examples may be taken from the Parliament Rolls to shew that the writ of conspiracy was not an entirely adequate remedy in the ordinary Courts. Such cases possibly represent the abnormal, but judging from petitions for amendment of the criminal law *in pari materia*, there is reason to think that the corruption of officers or the fear of great men often made the law in its usual course ineffectual. Thus, in Edward II's reign, a London goldsmith suffered much at the hands of John of Lincoln and his sons. He was insulted, thrashed, maimed and imprisoned till he made a fine of four marks assessed apparently by an inquisition of John's tenants procured by his conspiracy. On another occasion, he was imprisoned by the King's Marshals on a false allegation of speaking disaffection of the King. For this the Council gives him a writ of conspiracy before the King[1]. Oppressors were not invariably great men[2], and occasionally a man in high position was himself oppressed, for the Archbishop of York complains in 1330 that two had by conspiracy and false alliance between them procured the indictment[3]. The petitioner sometimes gets a writ of conspiracy either as a sufficient remedy or as additional to some other remedy[4], sometimes the *subpoena*[5], sometimes a special remedy[6], and occasionally is

[1] *Rot. Parl.* I. 316 *a* (1314–15).
[2] *Ibid.* 320 *b* (same date), where the persons petitioned against were a vicar, a bailiff, and another.
[3] *Ibid.* II. 31 *b*. (He is given a writ of conspiracy.)
[4] *Ibid.* I. 328 *b*.      [5] Palgrave, *King's Council*, 71–75.
[6] *Rot. Parl.* I. 307 *b* (8 Ed. II); 320 *a* (same date).

referred to the Common Law[1]. The writ of conspiracy becomes less and less common as we approach the end of the printed Year Book period, partly because the writ of maintenance was more popular. From that time onwards its place is taken by the action of case in the nature of conspiracy and the history of this must now be traced.

ACTION UPON THE CASE IN THE NATURE OF CONSPIRACY

§ 3. There was always room for the growth of a fresh action from the original writ of conspiracy for it was closely akin to the malleable writs of deceit and trespass, as examples drawn from MS. Registra have already shewn[2], and the narrowness of the old writ in its limitation to two defendants at least, and its requirement of acquittal on the false charge, made the creation of a more elastic remedy a necessity. It is only by processes not very palpable that it comes into being. Thus Fitzherbert, in discussing the writ of conspiracy in his *Natura Brevium*, the first French edition of which was published in 1534, says that there are divers other writs of conspiracy grounded upon deceit and trespass done unto the party. His examples are the writ against two men for conspiring to indict another because he did not arrest a felon, and the application of the writ against one person only, as where the accusation was of trespass or other falsity[3]. But it is worth noticing that the writ in the first of these cases is unseparated in both MS. Registra and the printed Register from the other writs of conspiracy, and that there is no clear decision of conspiracy, or case in the nature of it against one only, before Fitzherbert[4]. Not but what there are signs of action upon the case long before Fitzherbert. In Brooke's Abridgement of 27 Lib. Ass. pl. 73, there is a reference to it[5], and in 30 Lib. Ass. pl. 41, an assize was brought against two, one of whom took the tenancy of a parcel to himself, and

---

[1] *Rot. Parl.* i. 418 a (*ann. incert.* Ed. III). Cf. *Mem. de Parl.* 1305 (ed. Maitland) pet. 197 where John de la Cressovere was indicted and imprisoned on the procuration of three persons. "Let him have a writ according to the ordained form."
[2] *Ante* 57–58.          [3] 116 A.K.L.
[4] *Ante* 57 sqq. See Trin. 11 Hen. VII, f. 25, *post* 120.
[5] Act. sur le Case 81.

successfully challenged a juror. The other did not challenge
the juror and prayed that he should be sworn. The Court
would not do this, for thus they would take different assizes.
STOUFORD J. said that if the tenant who challenged, and the
plaintiff were of one mind for ousting the other tenant of his
advantages, this might be in case adjudged conspiracy. "Query
how?"[1] Mich. 5 Ed. IV, f. 126, seems to shew that the action
was not then particularly well known or at least not clearly
distinguished from conspiracy proper. This was an action on
the case for forging an obligation, and it was said (by whom
does not appear) that if this action were allowed, then the inconvenience would ensue that on every obligation sued, and
every action real or personal, the defendant would have action
upon his case against the plaintiff alleging that he had sued a
false suit against him, and that our law would not maintain this,
for the defendant shall not recover damages against the plaintiff
except in special cases, as in appeal of felony where the defendant is acquitted, or where on indictment he is acquitted,
his remedy is by the writ of conspiracy on St. West. II,
13 Ed. I c. 12[2]. A statutory action on the case in peculiar circumstances has already been mentioned[3]. In Trin. 11 Hen. VII,
f. 25, it was held upon the construction of this statute that the
action under it could be brought against one only, "and so it is
of a conspiracy on an indictment of trespass"[4]. It is not till
Elizabethan times that the reports shew the action on the case
as becoming better known[5]. Coke thought that *Jerom* v. *Knight*[6]
(Trin. 29 Eliz. B.R.) was the first instance of it[7], but *Fuller* v.

[1] In *Smith* v. *Cranshaw*, W. Jones 93 (1 Car. I, B.R.), the Court stated
that it was held in 19 Rich. II that action on the case lay for conspiring to
indict a man though he was not indicted. Neither in Bellewe nor in Fitz.
*Abr. Br.* 926 is the action said to be on the case. In both it appears as a
writ of conspiracy.      [2] *Ante* p. 6.
[3] 8 Hen. VI c. 10 (*ante* 107). It has been said that this statute first
brought the action upon the case into the field heretofore occupied solely
by the action of conspiracy (Bryan, 28–29). This assertion is too bold;
so is the author's criticism of Lord Holt's *dictum* in *Savile* v. *Roberts*, 12 Mod.
209.      [4] FAIRFAX J.
[5] In Rastall's *Entries* (1596) the only precedent for action upon the case
in conspiracy is on 8 Hen. VI c. 10.
[6] 1 Leon. 105, Cro. Eliz. 70, 134 where its *aliases* are *Knight* v. *German*
or *Jermin*.
[7] In *Lovet* v. *Faukner*, 2 Bulst. 270 (11 Jac. I, B.R.).

*Cook* (Pasch. 26 Eliz.) is still earlier[1]; and the decision proceeds upon the assumption that there was no intrinsic objection to the action[2], but in *Jerom* v. *Knight* this was raised as a vital question. The defendant, intending to detract from the name and fame of the plaintiff, and to put his life in jeopardy, maliciously caused a bill of indictment of felony to be exhibited against him, on which he was indicted and acquitted. The plaintiff then sued action upon the case against the defendant and got judgment. Upon this error was assigned in that no action lay upon the matter shewn. The Court were in doubt, but WRAY C.J. thought that it should lie, as the indictment had been written and preferred maliciously, "and if two conspire maliciously to exhibit an indictment, and the party be acquitted, he shall have a conspiracy; so when one doth it, this action upon case lieth." SCHUTE and GAWDY JJ. thought otherwise because every felon who should be acquitted would then sue the action. The case was twice argued later, and the Court seems to have weighed then not so much the question of the action lying at all, as the matter which should be pleaded in defence to it. According to one report, the judgment was affirmed[3]. In *Cutler* v. *Dixon*[4], where articles of the peace had been exhibited to justices, which contained divers abuses and great misdemeanours, concerning other people besides the petitioners, to the intent that the accused should be bound over, it was held that the accused had no action upon the case, for the ordinary course of justice had been pursued, and if actions should be permitted in such cases, those who had just cause of complaint would not dare to complain for fear of infinite vexation. In *Bradley* v. *Jones*[5], however, it was resolved that the action would lie if the articles after being exhibited in the proper Court were pursued in a Court which had no jurisdiction, and in *Allen* v. *Gomersall*[6] the whole Court adjudged the action to

---

[1] 3 Leon. 100.
[2] So too *Bulwer* v. *Smith* (Mich. 26 Eliz.) 4 Leon. 52.
[3] 1 Leon. 105.
[4] 4 Rep. 14 *b* (27 and 28 Eliz. K.B.). Cf. *Buckley* v. *Wood* (33 and 34 Eliz. K.B.). *Ibid.*
[5] Godbolt, 240 (11 Jac. I, C.P.).
Roll. Abr. Act. sur Case (*c*). En Courts de Justice, 1 (17 Jac. I).

lie apparently without even this qualification. The ground there
stated is "deceit and vexation," and on principle there is no
reason why this form of malicious proceeding should not be as
illegal as any other. It has been clearly recognized as actionable
in modern times, and the plaintiff is released from the duty of
shewing that the proceedings before the magistrate ended in
his favour, since they are of an *ex parte* nature and incontro-
vertible[1]. A decade later much the same opposite analogies as
in *Jerom* v. *Knight* were raised in *Throgmorton's Case*[2], where
the action was for procuring the plaintiff to be indicted as a
common barrator. ANDERSON C.J.C.P. held that if one indicted
another, it was to be assumed that he did this lawfully in zeal
of justice, but that if two or more conspired to procure another
to be indicted it should be intended by the law to be maliciously
done. WALMESLEY could see no reason for distinguishing between causeless procurement of an indictment by one person
and by two. The case was adjourned, and no decision is
reported. For some time the law oscillated between appre-
hension of frightening the just accuser, and encouraging the
false one. In *Arundell* v. *Tregono*[3], where there was a verdict
against the defendant for maliciously preferring a bill of indictment against the plaintiff for stealing wheat on which a true
bill was found, it was moved in arrest of judgment that there
was no sufficient cause of action because the defendant had done
nothing but prefer an indictment in the course of justice, and
that was lawful, and the rather so because *non constat* whether
the plaintiff were acquitted or not. This was conceded by the
whole Court, and the plaintiff took nothing by his bill[4]. And
in *Paulin* v. *Shaw*[5], judgment for the plaintiff was stayed by
the Court on the ground that it would greatly discourage the
execution of justice if an action would lie on every *ignoramus*.
So too in *Vanderbergh* v. *Blake*[6], where the defendant seized

---

[1] *Steward* v. *Gromett* (1859) 7 *C.B.N.S.* 191. *Cutler* v. *Dixon* was not cited.
[2] Cro. Eliz. 563 (39 Eliz. C.B.).     [3] Yelv. 116 (5 Jac. I, B.R.).
[4] *Sherrington* v. *Ward* (41 and 42 Eliz. B.R.) Cro. Eliz. 724, is to the same effect.
[5] T. Jones, 20 (*temp*. Car. II).
[6] Hardres, 194 (13 Car. II, Exch.).

the plaintiffs' goods, and falsely and maliciously laid an information in the Exchequer that they had been customed as denizens' goods, though they belonged to aliens, and without notice to the plaintiffs, the Court condemned the goods; HALE C.B. objected to an action upon the case by the plaintiffs that they could have prevented the condemnation of the goods by claiming them before the judgment of forfeiture, "and if such an action should be allowed, the judgment would be blowed off by a side-wind." The view which favoured freedom of prosecution reached its high water-mark in *Hercot* v. *Underhill and Rockley*[1], where CROKE J., though he admitted that action upon the case lies where no felony has been committed and it is falsely alleged that the plaintiff did the act, and the plaintiff is acquitted, said that if a felony were committed and the plaintiff acquitted of it, he should not have the action, because this is in advancement of justice.

§ 4. But the need for stopping malicious prosecution soon shews itself in the reports as a competing principle. In *Henley* v. *Burstall*[2], a defendant to an action upon the case moved unsuccessfully in arrest of judgment that such action does not lie, because it deters a man from prosecuting for the King; and LORD HOLT C.J. in *Savile* v. *Roberts*[3], perhaps the most important case in the development of this action, disposed of the argument that allowing such an action would discourage prosecutions, and that there. was no more reason for allowing it against a prosecutor who had failed to get a conviction than against a plaintiff who had lost a civil action, by pointing out that there is a great difference between suing an action maliciously and indicting maliciously, for in the former the plaintiff claims a right to himself or complains of an injury. Frivolous and vexatious litigation, he said, was hindered at first by amercement of the pledges for the prosecution of the claim, and, when this fell into disuse, by allowing costs to defendants; but there was no amercement upon indictments, and the party had no remedy to reimburse himself except by action. Again,

---

[1] 2 Bulst. 331 (12 Jac. I).
[2] Raym. 180; 1 Ventr. 23, 25; 2 Keble 494 (21 Car. II, B.R.).
[3] 1 Lord Raym. 374 (Mich. 10 Will. III, B.R.).

PARKER C.J. in delivering the resolution of the whole Court in
*Jones* v. *Gwynn*, said, "The only *remora* to those actions is the
fear of discouraging just prosecutions; but to this malice is a
full and sufficient answer"[1].

§ 5. As the action was the offspring of the Common Law
it shewed in its growth both the defects and virtues of that
pliable system, and it requires some groping among a number
of ill-reported cases to follow the changing views of the judges
as to what was the *rationale* of the remedy. At first its analogy
to conspiracy proper influenced both pleaders and the bench.
The declaration in the action closely followed the wording of
the old writ of conspiracy, and according to CLENCH J. in
*Shotbolt's Case*[2], the only difference between conspiracy and
case was that the former must be against two at least, while
the latter might lay against one; and in both actions acquittal
of the plaintiff must be shewn. The Court in *Smith* v. *Cranshaw*[3]
seems to have applied 28 Ed. I c. 10 and 33 Ed. I (the definition
of conspirators) to a decision upon action on the case[4]. But
nearly a century later PARKER C.J. insisted that there was no
arguing from one sort of action to another.

Actions of conspiracy are the worst sort of actions in the world to
be argued from; for there is more contrariety and repugnancy of
opinions in them than in any other species of actions whatever....
There is certainly no arguing from an action which is a formed one,
for which there is a formal writ in the Register, to an action upon
the case, that is tied down to no form at all[5].

In fact, between Elizabethan and Georgian times another
motive for the action besides abuse of procedure was carefully
fostered—that of scandal to the reputation. This was suggested
early in James I's reign. The resemblance between false accusation and defamation had already been noted in *Barnes* v.

[1] 10 Mod. at p. 218 (12 Anne, B.R.).
[2] Godbolt, 76 (28 and 29 Eliz. B.R.).
[3] W. Jones 93 (20 Jac. I, B.R.). Cf. the opinion of COKE C.J.K.B. in
*Lovett* v. *Faukner* (12 Jac. B.R.) 1 Rolle, 109, that where conspiracy will
not lie against two, case will not lie against one.
[4] Cf. Coke *arguendo* in *Knight* v. *Jermin*, Cro. Eliz. 134 (31 Eliz. B.R.).
"The words here, and in a conspiracy, are all one": and reporter's note to
*Skinner* v. *Gunter* (21 Car. II, B.R.), 1 Wms. Saund. 269.
[5] In *Jones* v. *Gwynn* (12 Anne, B.R.) 10 Mod. at p. 219.

*Constantine*[1]. There, one who had been indicted as a common barrator and acquitted sued action on the case in the nature of conspiracy against the prosecutor; and it was said that the action was only for damages for a slander, and well lay, although the indictment were erroneous[2]. In 4 Jac. I, it was laid down that the action lies for the infamy of the false indictment, and was thus independent of the plaintiff's acquittal upon it[3]. It was strongly argued in *Taylor's Case*, where the objection was that the plaintiff did not allege acquittal, that case differed much from conspiracy, and that the indictment was not the cause of the action, but the scandalous words which might have caused loss of reputation, and the damage sustained by the plaintiff was cause sufficient, though the jury had found *ignoramus*. "And this was the opinion of the Court at this time"[4]. A year previously there had been an equally emphatic decision of all the judges of the Common Pleas and the Barons of Exchequer that false, malicious, and causeless exhibition of a bill of indictment for robbery to a grand jury who ignored the bill, was a great cause of slander and grievance and a just ground of action[5]. HOBART C.J. in *Wright* v. *Black*, thought that the giving of false evidence to the grand jury was as great a scandal as the publication of it upon an alebench, and that while the cause of justice ought not to be stopped, so neither ought the good name of a man in things which concern his life to be taken away without good cause[6]. In *Manning* v. *Fitzherbert*, the defendant had caused the plaintiff's wife to be brought before a Justice of the Peace, and had there falsely and maliciously charged her with a felonious theft. The defendant moved in arrest of

[1] Yelv. 46 (2 Jac. I, B.R.).

[2] *Norman* v. *Symons* (10 Car. I) Roll. Abr. Act. sur Case en Nat. dun Consp., shews the close likeness of the action to that of defamation, and the consequent difficulty of classification. The defendant exhibited a scandalous libel stating that plaintiff had committed immorality with her, and thus prevented his marriage. The action was held not maintainable because (*inter alia*) there was no allegation of malice in the libel, but it was only a legal proceeding in a spiritual court.

[3] *Pescod* v. *Marsam* (4 Jac. I, B.R.) Noy, 116.

[4] Vin. Abr. Act. Case. Consp. p. 33. Reference to Palm. 44 is untraceable (17 Jac. I, B.R.).

[5] *Payn* v. *Porter* (16 Jac. I, B.R.), Cro. Jac. 490.

[6] Winch, 54 (20 Jac. I, C.P.).

judgment that the plaintiffs had joined together actions for
words and in the nature of conspiracy, but the Court held that
the action was not in the nature of conspiracy, but an aggrava-
tion of the false and malicious accusation[1]. Here then there
was a tendency to sever the action from conspiracy altogether,
and to base it solely upon the false accusation; and in *Palke* v.
*Dunnyng* there was a further tendency to use this broad general
principle for disposing of technical difficulties which might
arise through modelling the action too closely on the old writ
of conspiracy[2]; and ROLL C.J. in getting rid of a similar flaw
in an anonymous case of 1653 said,

in truth it is not material before what authority he was indicted;
and in this case the trouble the party is put unto by reason of this
indictment, is the cause of his bringing this action, and not his trial
upon it, and therefore the authority is not material; nor is it material
whether the indictment be good or no[3].

Some hesitation was shewn in allowing the action to lie for
malicious indictment of a trespass, and at one time injury to
the reputation seems to have been put forward as the chief
reason for permitting it[4]. It was admitted in *Messenger* v. *Read*
that the action was permissible to one acquitted on an accusation
of common barratry[5]. The plaintiff in *Low* v. *Beardmore*[6] got

---

[1] Cro. Car. 271 (8 Car. I).

[2] Roll. Abr. f. 111 (11 Car. I, B.R.). So too *Atwood* v. *Monger* (1653,
Banc. sup.) Style, 378, where false proceedings were *coram non judice*. In
*Wine* v. *Ware* (12 Car. II) 1 Siderf. 15, one objection was that the Court
which was alleged to have had jurisdiction over the indictment had none.
This was decided against the defendant, and the reporter appends a note
of the justices that even if the Court had had no jurisdiction yet the plaintiff
could have his action because its grounds were the malice and the indicting.
"Mes nihil positive de ceo." Here the idea of scandal to the plaintiff's
reputation seems to have been unnoticed.

[3] Style 372. In *Anon. ibid.* 10 (23 Car. I, B.R.), the Court said that the
action lay against defendant although he procured some one else to indict, and
that it might be grounded on the scandal and trouble to the plaintiff.

[4] *Gardner* v. *Jollye* (1649, Banc. sup.) Vin. Abr. Act. Case Consp. Qc.
sect. 8, is too jejune to make it clear whether defendant objected to the
judgment for plaintiff on the ground that the false indictment was for
trespass, not felony, or on the ground that plaintiff's acquittal was due to
*ignoramus* of a defective indictment. In any event it was held that the
action lay.

[5] Roll. Abr. Act. sur Case. Consp. (10 Jac. I, B.R.).

[6] Raym. 135 (17 Car. II). Siderf. 261. In *Chamberlain* v. *Prescott*, Raym.
135 (*circ.* 1660), judgment for the plaintiff was reversed not because he had

his verdict against the defendant who had indicted him for a rescous. It was moved in arrest of judgment that the action did not lie where the indictment was only for a bare trespass. WYNDHAM and TWYSDEN JJ. held that the action would not lie, and stayed the judgment, though TWYSDEN said that if it had been laid more specially that the defendant, knowing it to be false, did it purposely to vex and draw the plaintiff into trouble, and to cause him expense, perhaps the action would have been maintainable[1]. In *Smithson* v. *Symson*, where the false indictment was for perjury, judgment was for the plaintiff, and there is no hint that the action was inherently inapplicable[2]; and two years after, in *Norris* v. *Palmer*[3], where the plaintiff had been acquitted on an indictment of common trespass, and it was argued on demurrer for the defendant that the action lay only for false indictment of a trespass which involved great scandal, such as battery with intent to ravish[4], the Court agreed that the action would lie after acquittal upon an indictment for a trespass, irrespective of its magnitude. But the distinction suggested by counsel in this case had already been drawn in *Henley* v. *Burstall*[5]. The plaintiff, a Justice of the Peace, had been maliciously indicted for delivering a vagrant out of custody, without examination. Verdict was given for him in an action upon the case, and on a motion in arrest of judgment, his counsel argued that where a malicious indictment contained matter of imputation and slander as well as crime, there the action lay (as in this case), but that it did not lie where the indictment contained crime without slander. All the Court were of this opinion, and judgment was given for the plaintiff. The distinction is also traceable in *Brigham* v. *Brocas*[6], where the indictment was for deceitful sale of hair, and the court refused to stay judgment

been falsely indicted for misdemeanour, but because he had been indicted for something which was not an offence at all (*per* LORD HOLT in *Savile* v. *Roberts* (10 Will. III, B.R.)). 1 Lord Raym. 374.

[1] 1 Lev. 169 *sub nom. Loe* v. *Bordmore*.
[2] 3 Keble 141 (25 Car. II, B.R.). Nor was there in *Atwood* v. *Monger* (1653, Banc. sup.). Style. 378.
[3] 2 Mod. 51 (27 Car. II, C.B.).
[4] *Langley* v. *Clerk* (1658, K.B. No further reference given by the report).
[5] Raym. 180; 1 Ventr. 23, 25; 2 Keble, 494 (21 Car. II, B.R.).
[6] 3 Keble 837 (29 Car. II, B.R.).

for the plaintiff in action upon the case, upon defendant's
motion that the accusation was of mere trespass or trover, and
not of an indictable matter. They held that the matter was
criminal, slanderous, and fraudulent. In an anonymous case of
the next year, the ground upon which the action is based is
slightly shifted, and is said to be the expense to which the
plaintiff was put in defending the charge[1]. In *Moore* v. *Shutter*,
it was ruled by the whole Court that the action lay for a false
information for ill words and a battery, there being no distinction between a false indictment and information[2].

§ 6. *Savile* v. *Roberts*[3] is a land-mark in the history of the
action. The pleadings[4] shew that the action there was trespass
upon the case, and the declaration alleged that Savile

contriving and wickedly and maliciously intending unjustly to
aggrieve him [Roberts] and to weary, oppress, and damnify him
very much with various labours and expenses, by pretence and
colour of justice, and process of law, without a reasonable cause, and
of his malice aforethought [at the Quarter Sessions] the said Roberts
[and others]...did falsely and maliciously cause and procure to be
indicted

of riot till Roberts was acquitted thereof. Roberts then sued
this action against Savile and got £30 damages. Savile moved
in arrest of judgment on the point whether an action lies for
procuring another falsely and maliciously to be indicted of riot,
upon which that other is acquitted. The point was argued two
or three times at Common Pleas Bar, and two judges to one
gave judgment for the plaintiff. The defendant brought error
in the King's Bench. The Court were unanimous that judgment
should be affirmed. HOLT C.J. who delivered their resolution,
carefully examined the grounds of the action, and said that the
point was not *primae impressionis*, but that it had been much
unsettled in Westminster Hall, and that it was very necessary
to set it at rest. He classified damages as of three kinds, any

[1] 2 Mod. 306 (30 Car. II, C.B.). If the report be correct, it seems to have
been held that where a party has a civil remedy, he cannot prosecute an
indictment for it without being liable, if it be a trespass whereof the accused
is acquitted, to an action upon the case.
[2] 2 Show. 295 (35 Car. II, B.R.).
[3] 1 Lord Raym. 374 (10 Will. III, B.R.).
[4] 3 Lord Raym. 264.

one of which might ground this action: (1) Damage to a man's fame, as if the matter whereof he is accused be scandalous; here there was no scandal in the accusation of riot. (2) Damage to the person, as where there is peril of losing life, limb, or liberty, and HOLT appeared to think that conspiracy in its old sense was an example of this. Here, however, there was not this kind of damages. (3) Damage to a man's property as where he is forced to expend his money in necessary charges to acquit himself of the accusation, which was the charge here, and reasonably grounded the action. HOLT then answered the objection that former cases of this kind were based upon conspiracy which of itself was sufficient to support the action, by stating that conspiracy was not the ground of such actions, but the damages done to the party. He added that if the bill of indictment were ignored, where the indictment contains neither matter of scandal, nor cause for imprisonment, loss of life, or limb, no action would lie, but that if there were any of these, it would. The action in *Savile* v. *Roberts* would not have lain, in his opinion, if the grand jury had ignored the bill, because the plaintiff then would not have been imprisoned, scandalized or put to expense[1]. Thus in *Savile* v. *Roberts* three alternative reasons are given for the action, and they are the plinths upon which English Law has been reared—reputation, personal security, and property[2]. *Jones* v. *Gwynn*[3], a well-considered case, carried the law still further. The Court resolved that even if the indictment were insufficient, the action would lie. PARKER C.J. confessed that he had changed his mind before coming to this decision, but justified his final view on the ground that the imprisonment, vexation, and expense are the same upon an insufficient indictment as upon a good one, since a man may not have the power to quash an indictment, and

[1] LORD HOLT disapproved of *Henley* v. *Burstall* on the ground that it decided that no action would lie for falsely and maliciously procuring a man to be indicted of trespass. The case did not decide this. *Ante* 54, n. 3.

[2] "Annoyance, expense, and possible loss of reputation" are suggested as the reason for the action by LORD DAVEY in *Allen* v. *Flood* [1898] A.C. at pp. 172–3. The C.A. adopted Holt's classification in *Quartz Hill Gold Mining Co.* v. *Eyre* (1883) 11 Q.B.D. 674, and *Wiffen* v. *Bailey Council* [1915], 1 K.B. at pp. 606, 610.

[3] 10 Mod. 148, 214. 1 Salk. 15 (12 Anne, B.R.).

demurrer is hazardous, and possibly expensive. According to another part of the Court's resolution, "if scandal be mentioned, it is only mentioned in the nature of damage"[1], and it was held to be immaterial whether the accusation were scandalous or not[2]. A recent decision of the Court of Appeal makes it clear that if the accusation be not scandalous, it must at least involve damage either to a man's person or to his property; in other words, that no action will lie for the malicious prosecution of such an accusation unless it fall under at least one of the heads of damage specified by LORD HOLT C.J. in *Savile* v. *Roberts*. *Savile* v. *Roberts* and *Jones* v. *Gwynn* (where the false indictment was for exercising the trade of a badger without licence) may be taken to settle the rule that the action would lie for malicious prosecution of a misdemeanour, just as much as of a felony. It had already been decided in *Smith* v. *Cranshaw* that it would lie for a malicious charge of treason[3].

§ 7. The action does not seem to have been popular; ROLL C.J. in 1653 regretted its infrequency in view of the prevalence of malicious suits[4]. Perhaps the burden of proof frightened off possible plaintiffs, as it appears to do at the present day; or it may have been because the action was not favoured by other judges[5]. Soon after the Restoration, BRIDGMAN C.J. expressed himself as against all such actions[6], and HOLT C.J. though he allowed the action in *Savile* v. *Roberts*, thought that it ought not to be favoured, but must be managed with great caution[7]. Fifty years later, LEE C.J. was of the same opinion[8].

[1] *Jones* v. *Gwynn* was followed on the point of law in *Chambers* v. *Robinson* (12 Geo. I) 1 Stra. 691, where the action was for malicious prosecution for perjury. A bad indictment, in the Court's opinion, served all the purposes of malice, but none of justice.

[2] *Wiffen* v. *Bailey Council* [1915], 1 K.B. 600. Cf. *Byne* v. *Moore* (1813) 5 Taunt. 187.

[3] W. Jones, 93 (20 Jac. I, B.R.); *ante* 59.

[4] *Atwood* v. *Monger*, Style, 378.

[5] It became too common in Charles II's reign in the opinion of the Judges, who thought that it deterred people from prosecuting on just occasions. Kelyng 3 (16 Car. II).

[6] *Chamberlain* v. *Prescott*, Raym. 135.

[7] 1 Lord Raym. 374 (10 Will. III, B.R.).

[8] *Reynolds* v. *Kennedy* (1748). 1 Wils. 232.

# CHAPTER VI

## MAINTENANCE AND CHAMPERTY
## HISTORICAL OUTLINE

### COKE'S DEFINITION

§ 1. Other forms of abuse of procedure closely connected with conspiracy are champerty and maintenance. According to Coke,

Maintenance, *manutenentia*...signifieth in law a taking in hand, bearing up or upholding of quarrels or sides, to the disturbance or hindrance of common right;...and it is two-fold, one in the country and another in the court.

The former species Coke called *ruralis*, the latter *curialis*[1]. *Manutenentia ruralis* he explains elsewhere as stirring up and maintaining quarrels, that is, complaints, suits and parts in the country other than the maintainer's own, though the same depend not in plea[2], and he exemplifies it from Littleton who puts the case of *F* enfeoffing barrators and extortioners, in the country, of *A*'s house, to have maintenance from them of the house by a deed of feoffment with warranty, so that *A* through fear quits the house[3].

The other kind of maintenance

is called *curialis*, because it is done *pendente placito* in the courts of justice; and this was an offence at the Common Law, and is three-fold. First, to maintain to have part of the land, or anything out of the land, or part of the debt, or other thing in plea or suit; and this is called *cambipartia*, champertie. The second is, when one maintaineth the one side, without having any part of the thing in plea, or suit; and this maintenance is two-fold, general maintenance and special maintenance....The third is when one laboureth the jury, if it be but to appear, or if he instruct them, or put them in feare, or the like, he is a maintainer, and is in law called an embraceor, and an action of maintenance lyeth against him; and if he take money, a *decies tantum* may be brought against him[4].

[1] Co. *Litt.* 368 *b*.     [2] 2 Inst. 213.
[3] Co. *Litt.* 368 *b*.     [4] Co. *Litt.* 368 *b*.

*MANUTENENTIA RURALIS*

§ 2. The distinction therefore between *manutenentia ruralis* and *curialis* is that *curialis* is confined to pending litigation, and it will be shewn that a pretty wide construction was put upon "pending." It appears to have been resolved in the Star Chamber that *manutenentia ruralis* was punishable only at the suit of the King[1]. The offence is akin to common barratry, the chief difference being that the latter is the *frequent* stirring up suits between His Majesty's subjects[2]. Hawkins varies Coke's definition of *manutenentia ruralis* by adding an alternative meaning—assisting another in his pretensions to lands by taking, or holding, possession of them by force or subtlety[3]. This seems to be based either on a loose reference of Coke's to the example given in Littleton[4], or on 4 Hen. IV c. 8 and 8 Hen. VI c. 9 which are considered hereafter.

Perhaps the source of *manutenentia ruralis* is 1 Ed. III st. 2, c. 14 which forbids in particular the King's Councillors, ministers, household officers, and the great men of the realm, and in general all other persons, to maintain quarrels or parties in the country to the disturbance of the Common Law[5]. This was in reply to one of the constant petitions of the Commons on maintenance[6]. The lack of any sanction in the statute was the ground of their petition for one in 1347. The reply is that certain penalties are ordained—presumably under 28 Ed. I (Art. sup. Cart.) c. 11, which however is apparently limited to what Coke called *manutenentia curialis*[7]—and in cases where the law does not certainly fix one, fine and ransom to the King are intended according to the quantity of the trespass[8]. 4 Ed. III c. 11 probably also refers to the same thing. It recites the

---

[1] Mich. 7 Jac. I (Doc. Plac. 240), cited in Co. *Litt.* 368 *b*. Cf. 4 Ed. III c. 11 which might be thought to give a civil remedy. 1 Hawk. P.C. ch. 83, sect. 2 states that it is said not to be actionable. The marginal references are too slovenly to verify, but the only relevant traceable source is Co. *Litt.* 368 *b*.

[2] Bl. *Comm.* IV. 134.     [3] 1 Hawk. P.C. ch. 83, sect. 2.

[4] Co. *Litt.* 368 *b*.     [5] *St. of the Realm*, I. 256.

[6] *Rot. Parl.* II. 10 *b* (1327–8).

[7] And see 3 Ed. I c. 25 and 13 Ed. I c. 49, where punishment is mentioned, but in indefinite terms.

[8] *Rot. Parl.* I. 166 *b* (21 Ed. III).

offences of those who combine "to maintain *parties*, pleas, and quarrels," and empowers the justices of either Bench and Assize to "hear and determine, as well at the King's suit, as at the suit of the party, of such maintainers, bearers, and conspirators"[1]. 1 Rich. II c. 4 also forbids the persons mentioned therein to "undertake or sustain any suit by maintenance in the country, nor elsewhere." Whatever the framers of these statutes may have meant, the wording of them does not express, though it may imply, the meaning which Coke attributed to *manutenentia ruralis*. It is possible that maintenance detached from any idea of litigation is to be found in 4 Hen. IV c. 8 which gave a special assize against one who forcibly entered another's land "by way of maintenance"[2], and in the later confirmatory statute, 8 Hen. VI c. 9, which avoided feoffments by such forcible disseisors[3].

The example which Coke cites from Littleton of this kind of maintenance might well be classified under *manutenentia curialis* of the kind obnoxious to 1 Rich. II c. 9 which would have avoided such a feoffment, except possibly as between feoffor and feoffee[4]. Other instances of *manutenentia ruralis* are not abundant, and there is evidence that the judges of Henry VI's reign—when maintenance reached its zenith—were not familiar with it. MARTIN J. is reported to have said, "there cannot be a maintenance unless he [the plaintiff] has some plea pending at this time"[5]. But Coke's distinction between it and *manutenentia curialis* was referred to by the Lord Chancellor in *Wallis* v. *Duke of Portland* (1797)[6], where an undertaking was alleged between plaintiff and defendant that defendant should contribute to the expense of an election petition against the return of a member of Parliament. His Lordship said that this was maintenance, for maintenance is not confined to supporting suits at Common Law, and he quoted the passage in Hawkins, which as we have seen in based upon Coke[7]. Proceedings upon an election petition were then under the Grenville Act, 1770

---

[1] *St. of the Realm*, i. 264.   [2] Cf. *Rot. Parl.* III. 497 *b*.
[3] *Ibid.* IV. 353 *b*.   [4] *Co. Litt.* 368 *b*, 369 *a*.
[5] Trin. 3 Hen. VI, f. 53. So too Br. *Abr. Maint.* 1.
[6] 3 Ves. 494. Decision affirmed by House of Lords. Brown, *Parl. Cases*, App. 1. 161.   [7] 1 Hawk. P.C. ch. 83, sect. 2 (*ante* 132).

(10 Geo. III c. 16), and the petition was tried by a small committee of the House of Commons. The trial was a legal proceeding, though conducted by persons possibly unacquainted with the exercise of judicial functions. It would not have been difficult, then, for the Lord Chancellor to have classified this maintenance as *curialis*, and there seems to be no doubt that since the present mode of trying petitions was established it could be so treated[1].

But long after statutes had passed dealing with maintenance in its technical sense of interfering with the disputes, litigious or otherwise, of other people, it retained the looser meaning of aiding malefactors. We read in the Parliament Rolls of "maintainers of felons and felonies"[2], of lords who are forbidden to retain or maintain any malefactor[3], of those who have maintained robbers[4], of those whose punishment is demanded for maintaining such as procure extents against the King at under value[5], of those who maintain tenants in villeinage in misbehaviour against their lords[6], or heretics[7], or "the new sect coming from beyond the sea, clad in white garments[8]." Sometimes it means support of rebels by their parents and cousins[9], or of one who breaks a truce or safe conduct[10]. A notable illustration of the use of the word in its strict and its lax significations in the same context occurs in an ordinance which forbids any Lord of the Council from maintaining robbers or felons, or from taking any man's cause or quarrel in favour or maintenance[11]. The more general meaning also appears in the Statute-book. Thus, 10 Ed. III st. 2, c. 3 provides for the imprisonment of notorious malefactors, or maintainers of malefactors[12]. It is shewn too in mediaeval Chancery petitions[13], and in the Star Chamber records[14].

[1] 31 and 32 Vict. c. 125 and 42 and 43 Vict. c. 75.
[2] IV. 421 *a* (1433). II. 446 *a*.      [3] II. 62 *a* (1331). Cf. 446 *a*.
[4] II. 207 *b*.       [5] II. 355 *b*.       [6] III. 21 *b*.       [7] III. 125 *b*.
[8] III. 428 *a* (1399).       [9] *Rot. Parl.* III. 666 *a*.       [10] *Ibid.* IV. 22 *b*.
[11] *Ibid.* IV. 344 *a*. Cf. v. 408 *b*, 435 *a*.       [12] *St. of the Realm*, I. 277.
[13] *Select Cases in Chancery* (A.D. 1364–1471) S. S. vol. x. case 28 (petitioners cannot get their tenant to pay his rent because of "the maintenance of John Skipwyth"); case 81 (defendants described as maintainers of evil doers, robbers, and homicides); and cases 41, 54, 102 and 107.
[14] *Select Cases in the Star Chamber* (A.D. 1477–1509) S. S. vol. xvi. p. 147 (alleged that Sir Robert Harecourt "contrary to the laudable statutes of this

Another meaning in which maintenance approaches a term
of art is that of having a presumptively good ground for supporting legal proceedings, or some particular step in them.
This constantly occurs in the Year Books, and especially in
the 17th century "Tables of Matters" appended to them,
where it is usually distinguishable from the references to
maintenance *stricto sensu* by some such phrase as "Maintenance
del brief"[1], and there are similar titles in the *Abridgements* of
Fitzherbert and Brooke. Thus in Mich. 1 Ed. IV, f. 2,

it was held by the Court that if there are two or three disseisors,
and they make a feoffment according to the statute, and one of them
take the profits of the whole, yet the action is not maintainable
against him[2].

Curiously enough, the case is on maintenance in its strict
meaning, so that it exhibits the word in a double sense. Maintenance is also used in the sense now under discussion in Coke's
*Reports*[3], and in Theloall's *Digest* (1579) which has a title
"Maintenance de briefe"[4]. It survives in legal parlance at the
present day when we speak of an action being maintainable
against a defendant.

There are, of course, plenty of examples in legal literature
of the purely popular meaning of supporting or protecting a
thing[5].

## MANUTENENTIA CURIALIS

§ 3. *Manutenentia curialis* is divided into champerty, maintenance (*stricto sensu*) and embracery. Embracery will be the

lande maynteneth" certain evil-disposed persons. See the learned editor's
note 28 to p. 146 and note 1 to p. 241); and pp. 201, 260.

[1] In Bellewe (ed. 1585), "Maintenance of writ" is a separate title immediately after "Maintenance." The Year Book indexers were not, as a
rule, so particular.

[2] See also Pasch. 4 Ed. IV, ff. 17 and 38; Trin. 15 Hen. VII, f. 8; and
index to 40–50 Ed. III, which refers to nine cases under "Maintenance."
Eight are upon support of an action. The other is untraceable.

[3] *Lord Buckhurst's Case* (1598) 1 Rep. 1 b.

[4] "In this chapter will be included matter to maintain a writ against a
plea pleaded in abatement thereof" (f. 398).

[5] E.g. *Rot. Selecti ex Archivis in Domo Cap. West.* (ed. Jos. Hunter, 1834),
p. 2 (Justice of Ireland is to maintain, protect, and defend the Archbishop
of Dublin); so too pp. 8, 29. Y.B. Hil. 10 Hen. VII, f. 18 ("the King can
maintain his jurisdiction by prescription"). *Borough Customs*, S. S. vol. xviii.
pp. 22, 25.

subject of later treatment, for it is doubtful whether even in early times it may not better be described as an independent offence[1]. Here we are concerned only with the origin and development of champerty and maintenance in its narrower meaning.

§ 4. According to another passage in the Institutes, "maintenance is an unlawfull upholding of the demandant or plaintiff, tenant or defendant in a cause depending in suit, by word, action, writing, countenance, or deed"[2], and this on the whole represents what is to be found in the Year Books. It is true that we read of maintenance being brought against one who was alleged to have improperly interfered in an appeal of mayhem[3], and it might be inferred from this that it applied to officious meddling with criminal prosecutions, as well as civil proceedings. But the appeal must be classified (so far as any such classification is proper in our early law) as a civil proceeding. It is not maintenance to interfere in criminal proceedings at the present day.

## GENERAL AND SPECIAL MAINTENANCE

§ 5. Here we may dispose of Coke's distinction between general and special maintenance[4]. It is not clear what he meant by it. He mentions it not only in his commentary upon Littleton[5], but in the passage just cited from the Institutes, where there is a reference to his exposition of 28 Ed. I (Art. sup. Cart.) c. 11. But in none of these places does he elaborate the distinction, which is reproduced mechanically in some of the later text-books and digests of the law. So far as anything can be extracted from the scraps of arguments and *dicta* in the Year Books, the difference was a procedural one. Maintenance was general, when the plaintiff in his writ and declaration merely alleged that the defendant in a specified trial between the plaintiff and another before specified justices[6] at a particular

---

[1] HANKFORD J. in Hil. 13 Hen. IV, f. 16. MARTIN J. in Mich. 11 Hen. VI, f. 10. 1 Hawk. P.C. ch. 83, sect. 3 follows Coke's division, but deals with the offences in separate chapters.  [2] 2 Inst. 212.

[3] Trin. 3 Hen. VI, f. 53. Mich. 21 Hen. VII, f. 15.

[4] *Ante* 131.  [5] '368 *b*.

[6] Trin. 9 Hen. VI, f. 20 (justices must be mentioned in the writ).

place had maintained that other. It was special when he condescended on further details. Thus in 36 Hen. VI, f. 27, a writ of maintenance was brought against three. Two pleaded not guilty. The other said that he was retained as attorney by the party maintained, and by his command went to a man learned in the law, prayed him to be of his counsel, and gave him forty pence of his master's money. The plaintiff replied that the defendant had given 6s. 8d. of his own money to one of the jurors. Verdict was given for the plaintiff against all three defendants. It was objected that judgment could not be given because damages should have been severed against the three. MOYLE J. acceded to this argument, "for it appears that the one is found guilty of special maintenance, and the others are found guilty generally." PRISOT C.J.C.P. seemed to be of the same opinion, and NEEDHAM J. (in a further report in 36 Hen. VI, f. 29) speaks of the plaintiff alleging special maintenance in the sense of setting out all the circumstances which constituted the wrong. Here the distinction was of practical importance and, if neglected, became a procedural trap.

The same meaning appears in Mich. 19 Ed. IV, f. 5, and in 14 Hen. VI, f. 6, the abridgement of which in Fitzherbert is,

Note, if a man in a writ of maintenance is compelled to shew maintenance specially, such as to shew that he gave certain money to one of the jurors to give his verdict, the defendant ought to traverse that which is specially surmised, as by saying that he did not give any money, and he shall not be driven to the general issue that he did not maintain etc. By the whole Court[1].

[1] Fitz. Abr. Maint. 5. The Y.B. is practically the same, except that it says, "the Court." Plea of the general issue seems to have been permissible where the plaintiff did not allege the particulars of the supposed maintenance. This is not certain but apparently results from the following authorities: 14 Hen. VI, f. 6 (supra); 36 Hen. VI, ff. 27, 29 (supra); 14 Hen. VI, f. 7; one of the prenotaries of the Common Pleas was of opinion that "not guilty" could not be pleaded in maintenance, because this writ was founded upon the Common Law, whereas that of conspiracy was founded on statute. Some apprentices, however, said that the reason was because special matter was alleged in the writ of maintenance. This is not inconsistent with the view that where the writ merely stated the circumstances of the maintenance generally, plea of the general issue was possible. All that the opinion of the prenotary and apprentices shews is that at that time it was usual in the writ and declaration of maintenance to specify details of the alleged wrong; and this possibly explains Pasch. 8 Hen. VI, f. 36, where in a writ of maintenance against two, one pleaded guilty, and the Court held that the plea was

In other passages of the Year Books, special maintenance seems to mean nothing more than unlawful maintenance[1], though it is impossible to pin judges or counsel down to any expression of opinion that "general" maintenance referred to lawful support in litigation.

## WERE MAINTENANCE AND CHAMPERTY FORBIDDEN BY THE COMMON LAW?

§ 6. Coke had no doubt that maintenance was an offence at Common Law, and adduced as notable proof of it 3 Ed. I (St. West. I) c. 28 which stigmatizes maintenance as delaying "commun droiture"[2]. He also says generally that an action of maintenance lay at Common Law, and in particular that one in the nature of trespass "doth lie in ancient demesne, and other base courts at the Common Law"[3]. In his opinion, the statutes

untenable, because the point of the writ should be answered. In Rastall's *Entries* (A.D. 1596), f. 428, a precedent of the general issue being pleaded to a writ of maintenance is given. When the defendant pleaded specially, he had to be careful to put forward some defence which was not merely a statement of what any one might lawfully do; for that was not answering the allegation of the plaintiff at all, and was bad pleading. Thus, in 14 Hen. VI, f. 6, the defendant pleaded that he was the cousin of the person maintained, and became his mainpernor when he was arrested in the original action of debt at the plaintiff's suit. This the Court held to be a good plea, but very much to the astonishment of the apprentices, who did not think that the plea was a good answer to the alleged maintenance. So too, in Mich. 21 Hen. VI, f. 15, the report states that Edward Pomeroy sued a writ of maintenance against the Abbot of Bukfast and that the Abbot was alleged to have maintained Martin Prideaux in an appeal of mayhem which he had brought against Pomeroy and others. *Portington* pleaded that before and at the time of the alleged maintenance, Prideaux was retained by the Abbot as carver for one year, that the Abbot had requested and desired John Wolston and J. Wode, men learned in the law, to aid Prideaux and to be of his counsel against Pomeroy in the appeal, and that they had aided him in consequence, and that this was the alleged maintenance. Markham (then a serjeant) in criticizing this plea said, "This is no plea; for we have declared a maintenance made to us in deed, and what he has alleged for maintenance is not any maintenance, for it is lawful to pray and desire a man learned in the law to be of counsel with another person....But if he had said that he had given money to the said J. and John, this would be a special maintenance, which was not lawful for other strange persons to do."

[1] BABINGTON C.J.C.P. in Mich. 11 Hen. VI, f. 10 ("this is a special maintenance and he did otherwise than appertains to him to do"). Markham in Mich. 21 Hen. VI, f. 15 *supra*. PIGOT in Pasch. 18 Ed. IV, ff. 2, 4. VAVASOUR in Mich. 19 Ed. IV, f. 3.     [2] 2 Inst. 212.

[3] *Ibid.* (commentary on 3 Ed. I c. 25). No example appears in Leet jurisdiction in the City of Norwich, S. S. vol. v.

merely increased the punishment against maintainers. Hawkins
follows Coke in holding that maintenance was restrained at
Common Law, and refers to three remedies—the action of
maintenance for damages, an indictment involving fine and
imprisonment, and committal by a court of record for an act
of maintenance done in the face of it[1]. BABINGTON C.J.C.P.
in Mich. 11 Hen. VI, f. 11, said that the writ of maintenance
was at Common Law, and Rolle's *Abridgement* quotes this and
other authorities of a more doubtful kind[2]. The Star Chamber
spoke of maintenance at Common Law in *Leigh* v. *Helyar*
(1 Jac. I)[3]. The Lord Chancellor in *Wallis* v. *Duke of Portland*
(1797)[4] took the same view, his authority apparently being the
passage in Hawkins just mentioned. LORD ABINGER C.B. in
*Findon* v. *Parker* (1843)[5] implied that there was maintenance at
Common Law, and the Judicial Committee of the Privy Council,
in 1876, and some members of the House of Lords, in 1918,
spoke of maintenance as a Common Law offence[6]. It was
held in *Pechell* v. *Watson* (1841)[7] that a declaration in maintenance need not charge it to have been made *contra formam
statuti*, as it was a wrongful act at Common Law.

The impression that maintenance is a Common Law offence
reinforced in remedies by statute has therefore prevailed for a
considerable time, and other indications support Coke's view.
In 7 Ed. I, the King sent a writ to the justices itinerant of Kent
commanding them to inquire of men who made "detestabiles
confederationes" for maintaining pleas and suits, and a similar
writ was addressed to the other justices in eyre. This has been
regarded as evidence in favour of Coke[8], but it is not clear

[1] 1 Hawk. P.C. ch. 83, sect. 36. In sect. 42 he points out that there was
also a preventive writ founded on 1 Rich. II c. 4. It is given as writ No. 3
on maintenance in Reg. Brev. f. 182 b. *Saulkell's Case* (3 Car. I), Het. 78,
is an instance of committal to the Fleet.
[2] Hil. 22 Ed. III, f. 1 which does not directly support Rolle, and Mich.
8 Hen. V, f. 8 where all that is to the purpose is *Martyn, J.'s dictum* that
"this writ of maintenance is a writ of trespass in its nature."
[3] Moore, 751.
[4] 3 Ves. 494, at p 501.          [5] 11 M. and W. 675, at p. 681.
[6] *Ram Coomar Coondoo* v. *Chunder Canto Mookerjee*, L.R. 2 A.C. 186,
at p. 208. 4 Ind. App. at p. 45. *Neville* v. *London Express Newspaper, Ld.*
[1919], A.C. 368, at pp. 382–383, 389, 392, 405, 406–421.
[7] 8 M. and W. 691.          [8] Vin. *Abr. Maint.* (D), (3).

whether the "confederatio" may not have been looked upon as the gist of the offence aimed at, irrespective of the object of the combination. A document more in point is a petition of the Commons in 1377 complaining of maintenance and livery. The reply is that there are statutes and ordinances for the case, and also the Common Law which the King wishes to be put into execution[1]. Again, Britton tells us that sheriffs who have maintained suits or the parties to actions shall be punished by fine[2]. Yet it is odd that nothing is to be found in Glanvill, Bracton, or Bracton's *Note Book*, on maintenance. These books were written before the statutes passed dealing with that offence, and though Bracton describes what is now called champerty[3] he is silent about maintenance. We have long been told that champerty is a species of maintenance. This is true now, but historically it looks very much like an inversion of genus and species. What really happened seems to have been this. Before Edward I's time, maintenance was used in its purely popular sense of support. Merely to maintain or support the suit of another was probably not a substantive wrong at all. But it was wrongful if the support were for the purpose of sharing the proceeds of the suit. This very soon got the name of champerty, but then it had no specific name and was expressed by some such phrase as maintaining suits for lands to have part thereof, as in 3 Ed. I c. 25. Next, it was seen that officiously aiding another in his suit should be made unlawful irrespectively of the ulterior motive

---

[1] *Rot. Parl.* III. 23 *a*        [2] I. xxii. 7

[3] Etymologically, champerty (properly "champarty") is a derivative of "champart" (Latin *campi pars*) which has two meanings—popular and technical. According to the former, it signifies division of the produce of the land, and is exemplified at the present day in the Channel Islands as a fixed share of produce received by the landlord. So too Britton, II. ii. 4 (Tree owner who takes another person's bees in his tree is bound to restore them or to keep them on terms of divided enjoyment—"garder les a chaumpart"). Its technical meaning is the legal one, and the same as that attached to "champarty," which also occurs in Chaucer with the signification of division of power:

"Thus may ye seen that wisdom ne richesse,
Beautee ne sleighte, strengthe, ne hardinesse,
Ne may with Venus holde champartye."

(*Canterbury Tales*, ed. Skeat, 1894. "Knighte's Tale" l. 1949.) Another variant meaning is that of combination for evil purpose ("A combination and hellish champertie in these powers of darknesse." Bishop Hall, *Contempl. N.T.* III. v. A.D. 1612–15). See Murray, *N.E.D.*

of sharing the gains. This was prohibited, and so we reach the offence of maintenance, and the technical word maintenance[1].

It is also odd that every writ of maintenance in the printed Register has the conclusion "contra formam statuti," or similar words[2]. But possibly the early dates of the statutes forbidding maintenance led to the rapid supersession of the Common Law writ (assuming that one existed) by those based on such statutes.

It is practically impossible to detach the statutory history of champerty from that of maintenance, but before proceeding to consider it, it must be premised that Coke considered champerty to be of Common Law origin, both as a crime and as a civil injury.

It was an offence against the Common Law; for the rule of law is, *culpa est se immiscere rei ad se non pertinenti*. And *pendente lite nihil immovetur*. An action of maintenance did lie at the Common Law, and if maintenance *in genere* was against the Common Law, *à fortiori* champerty, for that of all maintenances is the worst[3].

The scraps of Latin in the first sentence are as unconvincing as the dubious logic in the second. But Coke had better authority for his first proposition. Bracton, in rehearsing the articles inquirable by the justices in eyre speaks

de excessibus vicecomitum, et aliorum balivorum, si quam litem suscitaverint occasione habendi terras vel custodias, vel perquirendi denarios, vel alios profectus, vel per quod justitia et veritas occultetur vel dilationem capiant[4].

This is substantially reproduced in *Fleta*[5], and is the more notable because it is distinct from another article[6] based upon 3 Ed. I c. 25, which had passed after the date of Bracton's work and before that called *Fleta* was written.

It seems then that what we should now call criminal proceedings applied to champerty even apart from statute. But it is by no means clear that there was a writ of champerty at Common Law. There is a solitary writ of champerty in the

---

[1] It is significant that the definition of champerty in Ordinacio de Conspiratoribus, 33 Ed. I, makes no reference to maintenance (*ante* p. 2).

[2] There are three such writs; Reg. Brev. f. 182. A fourth at f. 189 is really a writ of champerty.　　　　　　　　　　　　[3] 2 Inst. 208.

[4] Lib. III. f. 117.　　　　[5] Lib. I. c. 20, sect. 96.　　　　[6] *Ibid.* sect. 81.

printed Register[1] which is based on 28 Ed. I c. 11[2]. It suffered
vicissitudes before it reached its final form, and it may have
been the survivor of a family[3]; but there is no hint that any of
its kin were not of statutory origin[4]. One of the writs of maintenance in the Register[5] recites a portion of 3 Ed. I c. 25, but
it recites 28 Ed. I c. 11 as well. It is really a writ of champerty,
but there is nothing in its patchwork appearance to suggest that
any of its texture is of Common Law origin. In fact, in examining the history of conspiracy, champerty, and maintenance,
one is tempted to conclude that Coke, when he asserted the
existence at Common Law of civil remedies for these wrongs,
was snatching at straws rather than attempting to find a solid
foundation for the breadth of the early Common Law. It is
not here the place to discuss whether this benefited the development of our law; but it is well to bear in mind that the question
of importance in a modern law court is not so much whether
Coke and other writers were historically correct or not, but
whether their version of the law has been adopted as correct.
The maxim *communis error facit legem* may easily be overrated:
it cannot be ignored[6].

We now pass to the surer ground of statutes and ordinances
relating to champerty and maintenance[7]. The first is 3 Ed. I
(St. West. I) c. 25.

No officer of the King by themselves, nor by other, shall maintain
pleas, suits, or matters hanging in the King's courts, for lands,

[1] Britton (I. xxii. 17) refers to the statutory punishment under 3 Ed. I
c. 28, and 13 Ed. I c. 49. Coke also cites the *Mirrour*, Bk. I, c. 1, sect. 5,
but the passage merely states that ministers of the King who maintain false
actions, appeals, or defences, are guilty of perjury.
[2] MS. Add. 3469 E (C. U. Lib.) has the same writ.
[3] F.N.B. 172 A gives the writ of Reg. Brev. and also at 172 N a writ
available against officers of the Court who committed champerty.
[4] In a case of champerty in Mich. 22 Hen. VI, f. 7, the writ was an
original directed to the sheriff, and did not mention the defendant by name,
and the Court were of opinion that, though this was immaterial in the writ
when it was directed to the justices (as is the case in the printed Register),
yet it was a fatal defect here. In the printed Register, however, the defendant's name appears. *Markham* refers to the variations of the Registers—
"Some Registers are like the writ here, and some not."
[5] Reg. Brev. f. 189.　　[6] Broom's *Legal Maxims*, ed. 7, pp. 112–115.
[7] Reviewed in *Neville* v. *London Express Newspaper, Ld* [1919] A.C. 368.
See in particular LORD SHAW's judgment.

tenements, or other things, for to have part or profit thereof by covenant[1] made between them; and he that doth, shall be punished at the King's pleasure[2].

Coke took this to be the foundation of all the acts and decisions that ensued[3]. He infers that "officer of the King" included judges at any rate in Edward I's reign. It will be noticed that neither in this nor in any other chapter of the statute does the word "champerty" occur. The tendency to corruption in high places which we have repeatedly noticed in the history of conspiracy easily explains the mention of the King's officers. The statute referred to them only, not from any wish deliberately to confine its prohibition to them but simply because they were the most conspicuous offenders. Other relevant chapters of the same statute confirm this. Cap. 26 forbids any sheriff or other King's officer to take any reward for doing his office on pain of forfeiting twice the reward, and being punished at the King's pleasure[4]. This is not champerty, but is akin to it. Cap. 28[5] forbids any of the King's Clerks or Justices to receive without royal licence the presentation of any church which is the subject of litigation in the King's Court. The punishment is loss of the church, and of his service. Clerks of any justices or sheriffs are also prohibited from maintaining any suits depending in the King's Courts. In case of disobedience, they are liable to the same punishment, of loss of service, or a more grievous one if necessary. Cap. 33[6] provides that no sheriff shall suffer any barrators or maintainers of quarrels in their shires, nor allow stewards of great lords, or others, except attornies for such lords, to make suit, unless he be requested to do so by all the suitors, and attornies of the suitors at the court; "and if any so do, the King shall punish grievously both the sheriff and him that so doth." The reason for this chapter was that the Statute

---

[1] Construed to mean an agreement by word or writing. F.N.B. 172 L. 2 Inst. 207.

[2] *St. of the Realm*, I. 33. It is still in force. Feoffment after judgment is not within the statute. 2 Inst. 207.    [3] 2 Inst. 209.

[4] Repealed as to sheriffs by the Sheriffs Act, 1887 (50 and 51 Vict. c. 55), to the extent mentioned in sect. 39. Sect. 20 made this necessary, because it allows the sheriff a percentage on sums collected by him under process of any Court.    [5] Unrepealed.

[6] Repealed as to England by St. Law Rev. Act, 1863; as to Ireland by St. Law (Ireland) Rev. Act, 1872.

of Merton, 20 Hen. III c. 10, allowed every free suitor of the county and other courts to employ an attorney to do his suit there. Two mischiefs sprang from this. Barrators and maintainers of suits were encouraged by the sheriff to become such attornies, to give judgment among the other suitors—perhaps even to take the lead in pronouncing judgment on their behalf. Further, stewards of great lords and others who had no letters of attorney as required by the statute would do the like[1].

Advantage was at once taken of 3 Ed. I c. 25, for an article of the eyre founded upon it appears in 3 Ed. I[2]. A petition to Parliament in 1293 shews that the justices in eyre were not always strong enough to enforce it. John de Grey and Andreas de Jarpenuill recite the statute, and complain that Elyas de Hanwyll, a minister of the King, by agreement maintained Hugo de Bray in pleas between Hugo and John de Grey and between Hugo and de Jarpenuill concerning lands, to have champerty thereof. Hugo admitted a general retainer by Elyas for the sum of twopence. Elyas was committed to the Marshalsea to suffer punishment in the terms of the statute[3].

It is doubtful whether any writ were founded on c. 25. A composite writ in the Register shews traces of it[4], and NEWTON J. in Pasch. 20 Hen. VI, f. 30, hinted that such a writ was possible[5].

13 Ed. I (St. West. II) c. 36 forbids lords of courts and their stewards to procure malicious suits against persons with a view to extorting money from them by a forced compromise. The punishment is that they must make fine to the King and restore treble damages to the aggrieved party[6]. In the same statute there is a provision in which champerty is, for the first time, mentioned *eo nomine*. Cap. 49 enacts that,

---

[1] 2 Inst. 225. Reeves, *Hist. Eng. Law*, II. 128.

[2] Bracton (ed. Twiss), vol. II. app. II. It shews the lack of any technical sense attached to maintenance. The statute uses the word "maintene"; this is latinized in the Articles of the eyre by "foverint."

[3] *Rot. Parl.* I. 92 b.

[4] Reg. Brev. f. 189 (*ante* p. 142).

[5] "For we understand that this [writ] shall be warranted by the St. West. I, if it shall be warranted by any statute." The statute did not apply in the circumstances because the writ was not against a minister.

[6] Repealed by 42 and 43 Vict. c. 59.

The Chancellor, Treasurer, Justices, nor any of the King's Council, no Clerk of the Chancery, nor any of the King's House, Clerk ne lay, shall not receive any church, nor advowson of a church, land nor tenement in fee, by gift, nor by purchase, nor to farm, nor by champerty, nor otherwise, so long as the thing is in plea before us, or before any of our officers; nor shall take no reward thereof. And he that doth [contrary to this Act] either himself, or by another, or make any [bargain] shall be punished at the King's pleasure, as well he that purchaseth as he that doth sell[1].

This, says Coke[2], added to, and explained 3 Ed. I c. 25, because it was doubted whether "officer of the King" included the Chancellor, Treasurer, Justices[3], and those of the King's Council, owing to their exalted position. The net is cast widely in 13 Ed. I c. 49, but not widely enough to include any except royal officials[4]. It forbids receiving of the property mentioned (i) by gift, (ii) by purchase, (iii) to farm, (iv) by champerty, (v) by other means. It may seem curious that there was any need to distinguish five things all which to our eyes are only modes of the fourth—champerty. But no doubt the offence was not sharply conceived at this time, and the fact that authoritative definition of it is given in Ordinacio de Conspira-toribus, 33 Ed. I[5], raises the inference that ideas on the topic needed clearing. The chapter marks a further advance on 3 Ed. I c. 25 in punishing not only the taker, but also the giver, of the property. Moreover, it is an extension of 3 Ed. I c. 28, which forbids the Clerks of the King or of the justices to receive the presentation of any church which is the subject of litigation. The mischief aimed at was that litigants were naturally discouraged from proceeding with the suit if the chaplain of the King or of a judge became the defendant in this way[6]. The scandal was all the greater because at that time when the

---

[1] St. of the Realm, I. 95. The brackets are reproduced. This chapter is unrepealed.    [2] 2 Inst. 484.

[3] Coke contradicts his note on 3 Ed. I c. 25 that justices are included (ante p. 143).

[4] 1 Hawk. P.C. ch. 84, sect. 12 cites 2 Inst. 484 to this effect; but Coke does not expressly say that the statute was thus limited in scope.

[5] Ante p. 2.

[6] Ecclesiastical persons at that time were not only clerks in Chancery and in the King's courts, but also acted as stewards of household to noblemen and justices. 2 Inst. 212.

presentation to the living was by a person not having the right to present, and the presentee was admitted, the true patron's only remedy for recovery of the advowson was the writ of right[1], because the peace of the church took precedence over the right of the patron[2]; and if the true presentor were a grantee from the true patron, the former had no remedy whatever[3]. 3 Ed. I c. 28 allowed clerks to receive the presentation with royal licence. This exception is omitted in 13 Ed. I c. 49.

The so-called "Statutum de Conspiratoribus" alleged to have been made at Berwick-on-Tweed in 20 Ed. I has been fully considered in its application to conspiracy[4]. Its recital shews that the previous statutes on champerty were inadequate, and it enacts that all pleaders, apprentices, attornies, stewards of great men, bailiffs, and any other of the realm, who shall be attainted of taking for maintenance or the like bargain any suit or plea against another, shall be imprisoned for three years and make fine at the King's pleasure, and the same penalties apply to such as consent thereto[5]. Then follows a clause which provides that if any one complains of conspirators, inventors and maintainers of false quarrels, and partakers thereof, or brokers of debates, GILBERT DE THORNTON (then probably C.J.K.B.) should cause the offender to be attached by a writ (the form of which is incorporated in the statute) to come before the King to answer the plaintiff[6]. What at once strikes the modern eye is the apparent jumble of conspirators, champertors, and maintainers. The explanation is that none of these terms was at that time clearly defined. Conspirators, we have seen, were roughly speaking those who combined to abuse legal procedure. But what less could be said of champertors and maintainers? A champertor of the late 13th century must always have been a conspirator, for he must always have combined with another person, and it is not intelligible how any man can maintain another's suit without some previous agreement. The "Statutum" differed from its predecessors in fixing a definite punishment for the offences described in it, and perhaps in

---

[1] 2 Inst. 212.  
[2] Bl. *Comm.* III. 242.  
[3] P. and M. II. 139.  
[4] *St. of the Realm*, I. 216 (*ante* 22).  
[5] This part is unrepealed.  
[6] This part was repealed by S.L.R. Act, 1887.

applying to every offender whatever his rank or vocation though the words which warrant this are of doubtful authenticity[1].

Whether writs of champerty and maintenance were commonly issued under the "Statutum" is not known. At a later period, such a writ is spoken of in Pasch. 20 Hen. VI, f. 30. A writ of champerty based upon the statute was issued which omitted reference to the three years' imprisonment and ransom to the King. The Court was of opinion that the writ could not be supported, but the Prenotary unearthed a precedent of Mich. 16 Hen. VI where the defendant got three years imprisonment, though the writ made no mention of it. The Court upon consideration held, no doubt upon this precedent, that the writ was good in spite of the omission, but bad because it was unwarranted by any statute[2]. It is not a fair deduction from this that in Henry VI's reign there was no writ which availed against champertors who were not royal ministers. The report does not reveal whether the plaintiff were trying to apply to civil purposes the criminal remedies of Statutum de Conspiratoribus, and it rather indicates that the Court consulted only the Statutes of West. I and II. It might easily have found the writ to be warranted by 4 Ed. III c. 11.

In 28 Ed. I (Art. sup. Cart.) c. 11 we undoubtedly get a general prohibition of champerty.

And further, because the King hath heretofore ordained by statute, that none of his ministers shall take no plea for maintenance [al. to champertie] by which statute other officers [al. others than officers] were not bounden before this time; the King will, that no officer, nor any other, for to have part of the thing in plea, shall not take upon him the business that is in suit; nor none upon any such covenant shall give up his right to another; and if any do, and he be attainted thereof, the taker shall forfeit unto the King so much of his lands and goods as doth amount to the value of the part that he hath purchased[3].

The statute allows any one to sue on the King's behalf for such attainder, and judgment is to be given by the justices

---

[1] *Ante* p. 22 (words "nor any"). Moreover, the framers of 28 Ed. I c. 11 (*infra*) thought that the statute they were drawing was the first of general application.          [2] *Ante* p. 144, n. 5.
[3] *St. of the Realm*, I. 139. It is unrepealed.

before whom the plea was tried. It expressly reserves the right of any one to have counsel of pleaders, or of learned men, or of his relations and neighbours. The procedure under this statute seems to have been as follows. The King, or the complainant on his behalf sued out an original writ to the justices of the Common Bench. This writ recited the statute[1], and thereupon the justices issued a judicial writ to the alleged champertor who had to appear and answer for his conduct[2]. Several cases shew the law in operation. In *Strode* v. *Prior of Lodres* (Pasch. 4 Ed. II)[3], a writ of champerty was brought to the justices of the Common Bench, and from this original there issued a judicial writ to the sheriff of Dorset to make the Prior come. He appeared and got the judicial writ against him abated, because it was directed to the sheriff of Dorset, whereas the tenements which were in dispute lay in Devonshire. But the original writ held good, and BEREFORD C.J. recommended Strode to sue out another judicial writ to the proper sheriff. In Trin. 12 Ed. III[4], the King sued a writ of champerty against several persons. The writ recited the statute[5], and was directed to the justices of the Common Bench, and out of it issued a writ to the defendants to come and answer the King.

It seems from Trin. 6 Ed. III, f. 33[6], that the writ based upon 28 Ed. I c. 11 was maintainable only by, or on behalf of, the King. "Suit in this case," said HERLE C.J.C.P., "is to

---

[1] See the writ in Reg. Brev. f. 183 which is based on 28 Ed. I c. 11.

[2] F.N.B. 172 A, B. Coke in 2 Inst. 563 notes that the party grieved may upon this statute either have a writ directed to the sheriff, or a writ directed to the justices before whom the principal action depends. The context leaves it open whether "this statute" is 4 Ed. III c. 11 (in which case there is no difficulty) or 28 Ed. I c. 11. The marginal reference to 22 Hen. VI, f. 7, does not clear up the doubt, but another to Reg. Brev. f. 183 goes to shew that he meant 28 Ed. I c. 11. There is the same ambiguity in F.N.B. 172.

[3] S. S. vol. XXVI. pp. 141–3. Four variant reports are given.

[4] *Y.B.* Rolls Series, pp. 538–543, 634–637.

[5] 28 Ed. I c. 11. The learned editor at p. 538 notes it as 3 Ed. I c. 25. This cannot be so, for that statute is not of general application. 28 Ed. I c. 11 is, and the very words that make it so are recited in the writ in this case.

[6] The page heading wrongly gives 5 Ed. III, a mistake repeated in the index. REDE J. in Mich. 13 Hen. VII, f. 8, while admitting that the King could have a writ of maintenance, said that he did not get it by the words of the statute. I do not know to which of the many statutes of maintenance he referred.

the King; for the party cannot have the suit." Piers de Salt-
marche had sued the writ against three others[1], and the argument which called forth HERLE'S *dictum* was that the suit could
not be the King's, because he had not been sufficiently informed
of it[2]. The wording of the statute itself points to the conclusion
that the injured party could recover nothing on his own
account; for the penalty fixed is forfeiture to the King. A note
in Mich. 14 Ed. II, f. 411, "that action of champerty and suit
of it are not given or reserved to anybody by any statute, except
to the King" is to the same effect[3]. A case apparently inconsistent with this occurred three years later. A writ of champerty
had been brought against John Siwist. It was found bad and
was abated. Shardelowe then "said for the King how he had
brought his writ [of *praecipe*] on a certain day etc., and after
purchase of the writ, the said John purchased the land, delaying
his right." To this it was replied that the writ [of champerty]
had been abated, and the Court had no jurisdiction to hear
the plea. But BEREFORD C.J.C.P. said, "The writ is abated
between the parties, but reply now to the plaint of the King"[4],
thus implying that the law recognized a writ of champerty
available to the party injured. It may be that the writ of
champerty in this case was that under Part II of "Statutum de
Conspiratoribus" which is wide enough to include champertors,
but while this suggestion leaves the case consistent with the
remedy under 28 Ed. I c. 11, it does not reconcile it with the
note in 14 Ed. II, f. 411[5].

At the end of the printed copies of Ordinacio de Conspira-

---

[1] "L'estatute de Champertie," which is referred to, is shewn by the
context to be 28 Ed. I c. 11.

[2] POLE raised the same point in Trin. 12 Ed. III. Rolls Series, p. 540.

[3] Per HERLE and STAUNTON JJ., Fitz. *Abr. Champ.* 13 (3 Ed. III, It.
North.) is ambiguous, but probably to the same effect. "Note [that it was]
adjudged by SCROPE that champerty is not given to punish [any one] except at
the suit of the King, and not at the suit of the party, and *Hil.* [Hillary— not then
a judge] said that the action is given only to the tenant for the punishment
of champerty, and here this plaintiff was demandant in the first action etc."

[4] Mich. 17 Ed. II, f. 504. Fitz. *Abr. Champ.* 14 is the same case.

[5] *Supra.* Non-suit of one plaintiff was not non-suit of his co-plaintiff;
Mich. 47 Ed. III, f. 6; Fitz. *Abr. Severauns* 12. *Contra* Coke, at least as to
real actions; 2 Inst. 563 citing Br. *Abr. Sommons and Severance* 7, where the
opinion is expressed that the point is immaterial, because damages are
recoverable in this action.

toribus, 33 Ed. I, there is inserted a definition of champertors: "Campi participes sunt qui per se vel per alios placita movent vel movere faciant; et ea suis sumptibus prosequuntur, ad campi partem, vel pro parte lucri habenda"[1]. This is materially what the offence is at the present day.

At the end of Edward I's reign, we may therefore sum up the law in this way. Under the Statutes of Westminster I (3 Ed. I) and II (13 Ed. I), remedies were given against champertors and maintainers who held official positions. Under 28 Ed. I c. 11, a quasi-criminal remedy was given against champertors of any sort. But under none of these statutes was a purely civil remedy given against champertors and maintainers in general, and such scanty authority as there is in the Year Books confirms this[2]. Theoretically, the Statutum de Conspiratoribus[3], besides fixing criminal remedies in its first part against both, also gave in its second part a writ of a general character that would lie against both. No case in which the writ was used has been traced in this period. There remains the assertion of Coke and others that writs of maintenance and champerty existed at Common Law. The evidence for this is, as has been shewn, questionable.

## REMEDIES DOWN TO THE REIGN OF RICHARD II

§ 7. Edward III's reign opens with a statute prohibiting any one from committing what Coke calls *manutenentia ruralis*[4]. Maintainers and barrators seem to have been such a pest that according to one reading of 1 Ed. III st. 2, c. 16 care was taken to exclude them from the newly created Keepers of the Peace[5]. But the Statute-book and Parliament Rolls from this reign to the middle of the Tudor dynasty are long registers of constant failures to scotch evils of this kind. King after king tried to extirpate them, but never wholly succeeded. 4 Ed. III

---

[1] *Ante* p. 2. Reeves (*H. E. L.* II. 243) states that no original text of the Statutes appears to warrant the inclusion of this definition, and suggests that some reader added it to explain the enactment of uncertain date variously known as Statutum de Conspiratoribus (*ante* 146) or the Statute of Champerty.
[2] Pasch. 17 Ed. II, f. 455 (writ of champerty brought at suit of King).
[3] *Ante* p. 146.
[4] 1 Ed. III st. 2, c. 14. *St. of the Realm*, I. 256. *Ante* p. 132.
[5] *St. of the Realm*, I. 257.

c. 11 enacts that the justices of either Bench and of Assizes, whenever they come to hold their sessions or to take inquests upon *nisi prius*, shall inquire, hear, and determine, as well at the King's suit as that of the party, of (*inter alios*) maintainers and champertors[1]. Here at length an undoubted civil remedy is conferred on the persons injured.

In 20 Ed. III[2] another attempt is made to kill the canker of corruption which spread even to the judicial bench. Cap. 1 forbids the judges to take bribes in the way of their office. Cap. 4 is a comprehensive prohibition of maintenance by any one of another's suits for "gift, promise, amity, favour, doubt, fear, or any other cause in disturbance of law." Cap. 5 requires lords and great men to discharge from their retinue all maintainers. Cap. 6 ordains that the justices of assize shall have commissions to inquire of (*inter alios*) maintainers, and to punish them as law and reason require as well at the King's suit as that of the party; "and thereupon we have charged our Chancellor and Treasurer to hear the complaints of all them which will complain, and to ordain that speedy remedy thereof be made." Once again, then, we have an enactment as to both criminal and civil remedies for maintenance. But the invertebrate administration of the law made it little more than a dead letter. In a petition of 1376, the Commons pray that the statute touching actions of champerty may be more fully declared, and that the Chancellor be commanded to grant writs thereon at the suit of the party, and that the party may recover damages in the said suit[3].

1 Rich. II c. 4 prohibits maintenance (1) by the King's

---

[1] *St. of the Realm*, 1. 264. Repealed 44 and 45 Vict. c. 59, sect. 3.
[2] *Ibid.* 1. 304–5. Repealed 44 and 45 Vict. c. 59, sect. 3.
[3] *Rot. Parl.* 11. 336 *b*. Reply; the King "se vorra adviser" till the next Parliament. 4 Hen. IV c. 8 deals with coarser forms of oppression by the powerful. If any person forcibly enters another's lands by way of maintenance to another's use, the aggrieved party may be given a special assize by the Chancellor without suing to the King. If the disseisor were attainted, he was liable to one year's imprisonment, and must pay double damages to the other party. This was confirmed by 8 Hen. VI c. 9 (*ante* p. 133). Both statutes are now repealed—the first by S.L.R. Act, 1863 (England), and S.L.R. Act, 1872 (Ireland), the second by 42 and 43 Vict. c. 59, sect. 2. The last-named statute also repealed 31 Eliz. c. 5, sect. 4 which restricted in favour of informers, 1 Rich. II c. 4.

great officers, upon a penalty to be ordained by the King
himself with the advice of the Lords; (2) by the King's minor
officers, upon penalty of loss of their offices, imprisonment, and
ransom at the King's will according to their degree and desert;
(3) by any other person, on pain of imprisonment and ransom
as aforesaid[1]. Cap. 9 recites complaints that many people,
great and small, having a good title to lands or goods are delayed
in actions for their recovery because the defendants convey
such property to lords or other great men, and the plaintiffs
are thus frightened from pursuing their claims. It also recites
that many disseise others of their tenements, and then alienate
them to lords and great men to have maintenance, and sometimes to persons whose very names are unknown to the disseisees. It then enacts that in future any such alienation for
fraud or maintenance shall be void, and the disseisees shall
recover from the first disseisors the lands and double damages,
provided they began their suit within a year after the disseisin.
This time limit was found to be mischievous and prejudicial
because of its shortness, and 4 Hen. IV c. 7 extended it to the
life of the disseisor. The statute was also weakened in its
operation by the inference of some lawyers that it applied to
nothing except writs of assize of novel disseisin. 11 Hen. VI
c. 3 settled this doubt by making it cover all manner of writs
grounded upon novel disseisin[2]. It was held upon the construction of these statutes that if there were a number of joint
disseisors, one of whom took the profits, the action lay against
him alone for the whole, but that the case was otherwise with
feoffees of the disseisor who made a feoffment. If one only of
them took the profits, action must nevertheless be brought
against all the tenants[3].

At this stage, therefore, there was abundant statutory warrant
not only for the criminal punishment of champertors and maintainers of any rank or position, but also for their civil liability.
It remains to consider the writs by which this civil liability

[1] *St. of the Realm*, II. 2. Confirmed 7 Rich. II c. 15. Unrepealed.
[2] 1 Rich. II c. 9, 4 Hen. IV c. 7, and 11 Hen. VI c. 3 have all been
repealed as to England by S.L.R. Act, 1863, as to Ireland by S.L. (Ireland)
R. Act, 1872.
[3] Mich. 1 Ed. IV, f. 1.

was enforceable. The printed Register has three writs of maintenance[1]. All are founded upon 1 Rich. II c. 4[2]. This expressed no sanction, as regards laymen generally, except imprisonment and ransom to the King. Whether damages could be awarded on this writ by virtue of 4 Ed. III c. 11 is not known. Even if that were not so, probably there were other writs of maintenance which do not appear in the printed Register, for that was not a complete catalogue of contemporary writs in its first edition of 1531, or in its reprints of 1595 and 1687[3]. Turning to the writs on champerty, the Register gives one which is the original writ issued to the justices based upon 28 Ed. I c. 11[4], and one other (including a variant) which is a skilful interweaving of 3 Ed. I c. 25 and 28 Ed. I c. 11[5]. The first of these statutes applied to champerty by royal officers, the second to champerty generally, and the sutures which mark the recitals of them are plainly discernible in the writ. The defendants mentioned in it are two bailiffs of Winchester and two private persons—hence its composite character[6]. Both these statutes were penal, and one can only speculate why the Register includes no writ of a purely civil kind. We know that there was such a writ from Fitzherbert and Coke, and both appear to base it on 28 Ed. I c. 11[7]. It is certainly mentioned in the Year Books, as in Mich. 22 Hen. VI, f. 7, which has already been cited[8]. This case arose 87 years before the first printed edition of the Register, and it is impossible to say of such an organic document, whether the judges in Mich. 22 Hen. VI, f. 7, were

---

[1] f. 182. Another (together with its variant) at f. 189 is strictly a writ of champerty. The third writ at f. 182 was preventive. Cf. 1 Hawk. P.C. ch. 83, sect. 42.

[2] They refer to a statute "apud Westm̄. nuper aeditam." Of course this does not necessarily imply that the statute is that of West. I or II. The usual phrase in the Register for those statutes is "cum in statuto Westm̄. primi [or secundi] inter caetera contineatur," etc. Cf. Rastall's *Entries*, *sub tit*. Maintenance. The precedents there are all upon this statute or 32 Hen. VIII c. 9.       [3] Maitland, *Coll. Pap.* II. 172–3.

[4] f. 183.       [5] f. 189.

[6] It is addressed to the sheriff, but it cannot be regarded as the complementary judicial writ of the original writ on 28 Ed. I c. 11 (*ante* p. 147). It may be noted here that there was no need (if it were undesirable) to join those who gave up their rights under a champertous agreement as defendants with those to whom they gave them. 30 Lib. Ass. pl. 15.

[7] *Ante* p. 148, n. 2.       [8] *Ibid*. p. 142, n. 4.

rageous multitude of embracers and maintainers, "who are as Kings in the country," and their doubt of Richard's good faith in meeting their wishes is implied in their request to see his intended ordinance against these criminals[1]. Statutes affirming previous ones passed[2], but in his reign the maintainer appears as a liveried servant in many baronial households, and exercised a vocation in return for which he was boarded and clothed. He thus became an infinitely greater plague spot upon society, for he had the definite protection of a man who could shield him from the law by a display of brute force, and he had the further security which companionship and *esprit de corps* could give him. His relation to his lord was a grotesque inversion of that borne by the ancient Roman *patronus* to his *cliens*[3]. The distinctive mark of service of this sort was a hat or some kind of badge, and the sense of corporate strength which a uniform gave these retainers is easily intelligible at the present day. It was much more forcible in an age when heraldry was part of a man's education, and its elements were understood by those who could neither read nor write[4].

The abuse had already been dealt with by statute[5], and had preoccupied Parliaments held at Cambridge and Westminster, and by 13 Rich. II st. 3, lords were required to oust from their retinue these professional litigants, and livery and maintenance were again prohibited. Imprisonment, fine and ransom were added as penalties. One of Henry IV's first acts was to forbid the giving of livery of cloth to any man except menials and councillors[6]. Under the incompetent rule of Henry VI and in the stormy reign of Edward IV, matters were at their worst.

---

[1] *Rot. Parl.* III. 100 *b* (1381); 104 *a*. For similar complaints see II. 136 *b* (1343), III. 339 *a*, III. 184 *b* (1384).

[2] 7 Rich. II c. 15 affirming 1 Ed. III st. 2, c. 14, 4 Ed. III c. 11 and 1 Rich. II c. 4.

[3] Cf. Muirhead, *Hist. of Roman Law*, sect. 3.

[4] See Stubbs, III. sect. 471, and sect. 473 for the household economy of great baronial castles.

[5] 1 Rich. II c. 7.

[6] 1 Hen. IV c. 7. Even the King's son required special legislative permission to confer his badge of a swan on his domestic servants; 2 Hen. IV c. 21. Military uniform in time of war was excepted from another penal statute on livery, 7 Hen. IV c. 14. This statute was repealed 3 Car. I c. 5, sect. 8 (c. 4, sect. 27 in Ruff.).

The Year Books are a notable reflection of this. In Edward III's reign there are not ten cases of maintenance and champerty all told. In Henry VI's shorter reign there are nearly forty, and in Edward IV's over twenty. 8 Hen. VI c. 4 strengthened the statutes of Henry IV and excepted from them the Mayor and Sheriffs of London while in office. It subjected to the penalties of those statutes persons who clothed themselves at their own costs in the liveries of any lord, lady, or esquire for maintenance in any quarrel[1]. "Livery and maintenance, apart or together, were signs of faction and oppression, and were two of the great sources of mischief for the correction of which the jurisdiction of the Star Chamber was erected in the reign of Henry VII"[2]. A Year Book record of Mich. 1 Hen. VII, f. 3, is instructive. It tells us that after dinner all the justices were at Blackfriars, and discussed whether many good statutes profitable to the realm could be executed. These were the statutes compiled in Edward IV's time and sent to the Justices of the Peace in each county to proclaim and execute. They related to robberies, felonies, riots, forcible entry, vagabonds, signs, liveries, maintenance and embracery. The question was how these laws should be executed. The Chief Justice said that this would never be, until all the lords, spiritual and temporal, agree to execute them; and he added that when he was Attorney to Edward IV, he had seen all the lords swear to protect the statutes made by the commandment of the King and with others, and yet within an hour afterwards when they were in the Star Chamber, divers of the lords had made retainments by oath directly contrary to their oaths.

## SUPPRESSION OF THE OFFENCES

§ 9. The Star Chamber did not immediately wipe out these offences, for the cases shew only a slight proportional decrease under that King[3], and not only did statutes pass in 8 Ed. IV confirming previous statutes and forbidding under pecuniary penalties any person giving such livery or retaining any person

---

[1] Repealed 3 Car. I c. 5, sect 8 (c. 4, sect. 27 in Ruff.).
[2] Stubbs, III. sect. 471.
[3] There are 16 in the Y.B.

except a menial servant, officer or man learned in the law[1], and in 19 Hen. VII fixing a £5 penalty on any one giving or taking livery otherwise than as a household servant[2], but as late as 33 Hen. VIII complaint is made of the neglect of statutes against retainers, livery, maintenance, and embracery. A law of that year required Justices of the Peace to hold Sessions in every quarter six weeks before the general Quarter Sessions, for the purpose of inquiring into these offences[3]. It was well meant, but proved such an expensive interference with the routine of local justice that it was repealed four years later by 37 Hen. VIII c. 7. But another earlier statute, 32 Hen. VIII c. 9, had revived all the statutes concerning maintenance, champerty, and embracery. Yet it is very significant that no reference to the oppression of great lords appears in it, and there can be no doubt that the strong Tudor government gave abuse of procedure a crushing blow through the channel of the Star Chamber. It survived, but rather as a pettifogging means of swindling or annoying a neighbour than as an emblem of baronial power and a monument of royal weakness[4]. This last-mentioned statute also fixed a penalty of £10 for unlawful

---

[1] C. 2. *Inter alia* are also excepted liveries given at the coronation, the installation of an archbishop or bishop, the creation or marriage of any lord or lady, the commencement of any clerk in any university, the making of serjeants at law, and liveries given by any corporation or in defence of the Realm. The statute was repealed by 3 Car. I c. 5, sect. 8 (c. 4, sect. 27 in Ruff.).

[2] 19 Hen. VII c. 14.          [3] 33 Hen. VIII c. 10.

[4] Cf. Stephen, *Hist. Crim. Law*, III. 234–240. The learned author points out that India affords a historical parallel. Before the establishment of British rule there, the litigant was often intimidated from pursuing his legal remedies. Since then, what he has to fear is legal chicanery rather than physical violence. The changed attitude of the English Courts towards maintenance is marked in many cases from the judgment of BULLER J. in *Master* v. *Miller* (1791) 4 T.R. at p. 340, to that of FARWELL L.J. in *Defries* v. *Milne* [1913] 1 Ch. at p. 110. See, for example, BEST L.C.J. in *Williams* v. *Protheroe* (1829) 2 M. and P. at p. 786; LORD ABINGER C.B. in *Findon* v. *Parker* (1843) 11 M. and W. at p. 679; LORD COLERIDGE C.J. in *Bradlaugh* v. *Newdegate* (1883) at p. 7; COZENS-HARDY M.R. in *British Cash &c. Ld.* v. *Lamson & Co. Ld.* [1908] 1 K.B. at p. 1012. But it would be a mistake to assume from these *dicta* that officious meddling in litigation is less objectionable than in earlier times. See TINDAL C.J. in *Stanley* v. *Jones* (1831) 7 Bing. at p. 378; LORD ESHER M.R. in *Alabaster* v. *Harness* [1895] 1 Q.B. at p. 339; BRAY J. in *Scott* v. *N.S.P.C.C.* (1909) 25 T.L.R. at p. 790; LORD SUMNER in *Oram* v. *Hutt* [1914] 1 Ch. at p. 106; LORD FINLAY L.C. in *Neville* v. *London Express Newspaper, Ld.* [1919] A.C. at pp. 382–383.

maintenance. And it provided that no one should sell, or buy, or otherwise get any pretenced right in lands, unless the grantor, or his predecessor in title had been in possession for one whole year previously. This part (sect. 2) was repealed by the Land Transfer Act, 1897, sect. 11, for otherwise the powers of alienation given by that Act to a man's personal representatives, who were thereby made his real representatives as well, would have been seriously limited; for "pretenced" right might include even those sales in which the buyer acted in good faith[1]. The statute of 32 Hen. VIII allows a person who is in lawful possession by taking yearly farm rents or profits of lands to get by any reasonable means the pretenced right or title of any other person. The penalty for trafficking in titles under the Act was forfeiture of the lands by the buyer who took knowingly, and of the value of the lands by the seller. The action on it was penal, as half the forfeitures enured to the King, the other half to the party suing. According to Coke, the statute included terms of years, but not a lease for years to try the title in *ejectione firmae*[2], though this was held by the Star Chamber to be maintenance at Common Law in *Leigh* v. *Helyar* (1 Jac. I)[3], and this, though the lease which had been sealed had not yet been delivered, nor anything further done[4]. At a later date there is a juristic opinion that, quite apart from 32 Hen. VIII c. 9, buying and selling of any doubtful title to lands known to be in dispute, to the intent that the buyer may carry on the suit, is a high offence at Common Law; but the authority cited for the opinion is not convincing[5].

[1] Co. *Litt.* 369 a. Cases illustrative of the repealed section are *Cholmondeley* v. *Clinton* (1821) 4 Bligh N.S. 1; *Doe d. Williams* v. *Evans* (1845) 1 C.B. 717; *Cook* v. *Field* (1850) 15 Q.B. 460; *Kennedy* v. *Lyell* (1885) 15 Q.B.D. 491. There are many others, see n. 5 *infra sub fin.*

[2] *Ibid.*          [3] Moore, 751.

[4] Hudson, p. 91, quotes without detail, or further reference, *Sir Oliver Lee* v. *Lidyard* (4 Jac. I) as deciding the same point in the same Court.

[5] 1 Hawk. P.C. ch. 86, sect. 1 (the chapter is on "The offence of buying or selling a pretended title"). The references are to *Shelden* v. *Handbury*, Moore, 751, which is on 27 Eliz. c. 4; *Flower's Case*, Hob. 115, which is on 32 Hen. VIII c. 9 and is a Star Chamber case which concludes with a query if it would have fallen under the statutes in the Common Law Courts; *Partridge* v. *Strange* in Plowden at pp. 80, 88; p. 80 is merely argument; p. 88 contains an *obiter dictum* of MOUNTAGUE C.J. that 32 Hen. VIII c. 9 affirmed, but did not alter, the Common Law. This was made the basis of

The statute is still in force except as to sect. 2 above-mentioned, a part of sect. 3 relating to subornation of a witness to maintain a cause[1], and sect. 5 which required proclamation of the statute at the assizes[2].

his decision by TINDAL C.J. in *Doe d. Williams* v. *Evans* (1845) 1 C.B. 717, 734, that a particular conveyance was void both by the Common Law and by 32 Hen. VIII c. 9. Cf. Dart, *V. and P.* (ed. 1905), I. 265–266. The authorities on this statute down to 1793 are collected in Vin. *Abr. Maint.* (E), 22 note, 24, 30–32, 36, 37 and (T) 22–27. Hawkins deals fully with it in the chapter above-mentioned. The statute was discussed in *Neville* v. *London Express Newspaper, Ld.* [1919] A.C. at pp. 386–387, 397–399, 410–412.

[1] Perjury Act, 1911 (1 and 2 Geo. V c. 6), sect. 17.
[2] S.L.R. Act, 1863.

# CHAPTER VII

## EMBRACERY AND MISCONDUCT OF JURORS

§ 1. This chapter may conveniently be divided into two heads—embracery and misconduct of jurors.

### EMBRACERY

§ 2. Embracery may be defined for the purposes of the law at the present day as the actual or attempted corrupt or forcible influencing of jurors. Any attempt to corrupt or influence or instruct a jury in the cause beforehand, or in any way to incline them to be more favourable to one side than the other, by money, promises, letters, threats, or persuasions, except only by the strength of the evidence and the arguments of counsel in open Court at the trial, is an act of embracery[1]. The law relating to this offence is in as nearly a cataleptic state as the rules with respect to some other forms of abuse of legal procedure with which we have dealt.

There was an indictment for embracery at the Central Criminal Court in 1891[2], but that appears to be the only reported case of it in the 19th century. For various reasons it has fallen into obsolescence, and we may say of it, and of most of the offences which form the subject matter of this book, that the more obsolete the law is with respect to them, the better it is observed. Maintenance, champerty, livery, embracery, barratry, and conspiracy (in its original sense) were commonest at times when the law was constantly set at naught,

---

[1] 1 Hawk. P.C. ch. 85, sect. 1. Cf. Bl. *Comm.* IV. 140; St. Dig. Cr. Law Art. 139; Russ. I. 598; Arch. 1144. The word is derived from O.F. "embracer," meaning "instigator," which is formed on "embraser," the literal meaning of which is "to set on fire." *N.E.D.* "Embracery."

[2] *R.* v. *Baker*, 113 C.C.C. Sess. Pap. 374, 589. In 1801, counsel, in *R.* v. *Higgins*, 2 East at p. 14, referred to *R.* v. *Young* as a case in which an information had been lately exhibited against one for attempting to influence a juror. In *R.* v. *Davis* (1909), 150 C.C.C. Sess. Pap. 736, there was an indictment for perjury and attempting to obstruct and prevent the due course of law and justice, an attempt to influence a juror being alleged. The accused was acquitted.

the government was weak, and the kingdom was very near
anarchy. [That the law now rarely has any need to use its
weapons against these offences is satisfactory, but that it would
be unwise to abandon them altogether no one can doubt.] Even
now, it is easily possible to imagine parts of the United Kingdom
where legal procedure might be warped by corruption or over-
whelmed by violence.

§ 3. The first legislative mention of embracers occurs in
"De Conspiratoribus Ordinatio" of 1293 (21 Ed. I), the
opening words of which speak

de conspiratoribus in patria placita maliciose moveri procurantibus,
ut contumelie braciatoribus placita illa et contumelias ut campipartem vel aliquod aliud commodum inde habeant maliciose manutenentibus et sustinentibus.

From the very first, then, there is a close connection between
embracery, maintenance, and champerty, and the importance
of this connection will appear later[1].

§ 4. If embracery can be regarded as distinct from maintenance, its statutory history begins 20 Ed. III c. 6, which
ordains that justices of assizes shall inquire of (inter alios)
maintainers, embracers, and jurors who take gifts, rewards, and
hire of the parties, and that they shall punish all who are found
guilty of such practices according as law and reason require, as
well at the suit of the King as that of the party[2]. This did not
satisfy the Commons, for in the very next year they petitioned
the King for an ordinance against traitors, felons, robbers,
trespassers against the peace, barrators, maintainers, "em-
braceours des busoignes," conspirators and champertors. The
King replied that he would ordain such remedy as should be
pleasing to God and man; but there is no record of any immediate steps having been taken in that direction[3]. Embracery,
in fact, was only one of the signs of the internal disorder of the
kingdom at this time, for later in this reign we find an attempt
to check it in 38 Ed. III st. 1, c. 12. Four years previously,
34 Ed. III c. 8 had provided that if any party to a plea should

---

[1] For the rest of the Ordinance, v. ante p. 26.
[2] Repealed by 6 Geo. IV c. 50, sect. 62.
[3] Rot. Parl. II. 165 a (A.D. 1347).

complain that any juror in it had been bribed by either party to give his verdict, the party complaining could sue before the justices before whom the jurors swore, and recover damages by assessment of the inquest. Any person other than a party to the suit could also sue on behalf of the King, and was entitled to half the fine.

38 Ed. III st. 1, c. 12 runs thus:

Also, as to the article concerning jurors made in the four-and-thirtieth year; it is assented in addition to the same, that if any jurors in assizes, juries, and other inquests to be taken between the King and party, or party and party, do any thing take by them or by others of the party plaintiff or defendant, for giving their verdict; and thereof be attainted by process contained in the same article, be it at the suit of the party that will sue for himself, or for the King, or of any other person whatever, every one of the said jurors shall pay ten times as much as he shall have taken; and he that will sue shall have the one half, and the King the other half. And that all embraceors to bring or procure such inquests in the country for gain or profit to be taken, shall be punished in the same manner and form as the jurors; and if the juror or embraceor so attainted have not whereof to make satisfaction in manner aforesaid, he shall have imprisonment of one year. And the intent of the King, of the great men, and of the Commons is that no Justice nor other Minister shall inquire of office upon any of the points of this article, but only at the suit of the party, or of other, as afore is said.

This is quoted *in extenso*, because, though only the latter part of it expressly treats of embracers, yet that part fixes their liability by reference to that of the jurors mentioned in the earlier part; and this earlier part again refers to 34 Ed. III c. 8. Hence, though nothing is said about embracers in 34 Ed. III c. 8, it is open to question how much of it was incorporated by reference in 38 Ed. III st. 1, c. 12. The result of that statute was that a juror who takes a bribe for his verdict from plaintiff or defendant was liable to forfeit ten times the bribe, half to the King, half to anybody who instituted the action against him. If the juror could not pay that amount, he was to be imprisoned for a year. An embracer "shall be punished in the same manner and form as the jurors." This certainly made him liable to the ten-fold penalty, or, in default thereof, to the year's imprisonment. But did it also make him liable to the fine *and* the imprisonment for one year mentioned in 34 Ed. III c. 8? Did 38 Ed. III st. 1, c. 12 embody the earlier enactment as far as that? This cannot be determined. In any event, the point is merely of antiquarian interest, for both statutes have been repealed[1].

§ 5. The writ framed as a remedy on 38 Ed. III st. 1, c. 12 was baptized *decies tantum*, the name being derived from the ten-fold penalty claimed under it. Judging from the reported cases, it was of fairly frequent application in mediaeval times, and there is a great deal more to be found about it in the books than about embracers. This is because it was sought far oftener against jurors than embracers, or, at any rate, against both of them rather than against embracers alone[2]. If the embracer or juror took bribes from both parties to the suit, he was an "ambidexter"[3].

§ 6. Litigation occurred on the statute soon after it passed, for in Trin. 40 Ed. III, f. 33, we are told that four of the defendants who were jurors and others, who were barrators and embracers of the original plea, each took 20s. from the defendant in it[4]; and an obscurely reported case of the next year is interesting as shewing that the penalties were ruinous enough to scare away intending offenders, for one of the defendants was adjudged to pay £300 to the King and £300 to the party[5]. But the very severity of the statute is a hint at once of the prevalence of the crime at which it strikes and of the weakness of the executive. Indeed, wherever we find in the mediaeval Statute-book a batch of exceptionally harsh statutes, we can nearly always infer that there were at that period a feeble or

---

[1] 34 Ed. III c. 8 by 6 Geo. IV c. 50, sect. 62 (England) and 3 and 4 Will. IV c. 91, sect. 50 (Ireland); 38 Ed. III st. 1, c. 12 by S.L.R. Act, 1863 (England), and S.L.R. Act, 1872 (Ireland).

[2] The writ in Reg. Brev. f. 188 *b* (a *pone*, with a variant) is against both, and is so drafted as to make it adaptable against either. Cf. F.N.B. 171 G, where the writ is also against both and is founded on 38 Ed. III st. 1, c. 12.

[3] F.N.B. 171 H.

[4] It was contended that receipt of one defendant could not be receipt of the other. *Non allocatur.*

[5] Pasch. 41 Ed. III, f. 9, Br. *Abr. Dec. Tant.* 5. The writ was against jurors and embracers.

absentee King and a lawless baronage. It is the mark of such
times that the punishments for many of the worst crimes
against public order are in theory tremendous, and that the
laws which fix them are little more than a dead letter owing
to the venality or weakness of those charged with their execution. So it was with embracery. The misrule of Richard II
provoked a petition of the Commons in 1381, expressing their
conviction that if the government of the kingdom were not
amended, the kingdom would for ever be utterly lost and
destroyed. They complain of the outrageous multitude of
"braceours des quereles, et maintenours," who are like Kings
in the country. So little are they satisfied with the monarch's
good faith in redressing their grievance that they ask for a view
of the ordinance intended as a remedy against the malice of
jurors, embracers of pleas, and maintainers[1].

§ 7. The other party to the embracery, where it took the
form of a corrupt bargain, also attracted the Commons' attention. The transaction between embracer and juror would
naturally be difficult to trace. This probably led to the fruitless
petition of 1413 that, in every inquisition, jurors should be
questioned on Oath whether any of them had received anything
for his trial of a challenge or verdict[2]. In the next year, this is
followed by a complaint of the powerful embracers, champertors, and maintainers in Middlesex and of the qualification
of jurors in that county being so low that they had nothing to
lose if attainted of a false oath. For once, the petition is successful, and assent is given to an ordinance raising the qualification to 40s. where the amount in dispute is 40 marks or
upwards[3].

Some of the justices of *nisi prius* appear to have had as itching
a palm as jurors, for *decies tantum* is said to have lain against
them[4]. But there were greater men than judges who mocked
the law. The King's Council might fine and imprison the Earl
of Devonshire for threatening justices and jurors with violence,

---

[1] *Rot. Parl.* III. 100 *b*, 104 *a*. See too the complaint as to John Rokell
who was committed to the Tower for embracery and maintenance in 1391.
*Ibid.* 287 *a*.
[2] *Ibid.* IV. 11 *a*.      [3] *Ibid.* IV. 52 *a*.      [4] F.N.B. 171 D.

but as he was of the royal blood, he could look to Richard II
for pardon. Nay, whilst his own trial was pending, he could
attend the meetings of the very body which was to try him and
deliberate on the King's business[1]. And the Council might
annul the acts of maintenance and collusion with jurors by
which Clifford, a Gloucestershire squire got his neighbour,
Atte Wood, committed to prison, and then robbed him of his
land and goods; but before the property is restored, Clifford
murders Atte Wood by a hired assassin. The King's Bench
convicts Clifford of this, and imposes a fine of £1000 which
the King commutes for 200 marks, and this proves to be the
price of Clifford's licence to resume his practices. Yet he "was
an honoured man in the county, serving in the King's commissions and keeping the castle of Caldecote"[2].

§ 8. It was only natural that among the offences singled out
for special attention by the famous act "Pro Camera Stellata"
(3 Hen. VII c. 1) embracery should find a place, and that the
vigorous action of the Court of Star Chamber should be a
strong element in its suppression[3]. "Infinite are the punishments of jurors and those who have embraced juries," says
Hudson in his treatise on the Court, "for as the reverend Lord
Egerton would often remember, *vendere justitiam infamia est,
vendere injustitiam nequitia*." And Hudson recollected that the
Solicitor-General to Queen Elizabeth was standing behind
Robert, Earl of Leicester, among other lords when a cause was
being heard concerning the writing of a letter to a juror to
appear, and the great Earl asked if that were a fault, and swore
that he had committed it a hundred times[4].

§ 9. The statute 32 Hen. VIII c. 9 includes embracery in
its preamble among the evils hindering the administration of
justice, and forbids embracery of freeholders or jurors on a
penalty of £40 for each offence, half to go to the King, half
to him who sues by action of debt, bill, plaint, or information

[1] *Esturmy* v. *Courtenay* (1392). *Select Cases before the King's Council*
(S. S. vol. xxxv), Introd. ci. and p. 77.
[2] *Atte Wood* v. *Clifford* (1402–3), *Ibid.* civ. and p. 86.
[3] 11 Hen. VII c. 3 also notices embracery and maintenance as obstacles
in the way of justice.
[4] Pp. 92–93.

for it (sect. 3). The action must be brought within one year
after the offence (sect. 6). The statute is still in force

§ 10. The writ of *decies tantum* disappeared when the statute
38 Ed. III st. 1, c. 12 creating it was repealed by the Juries
Act, 1825. This Act also repealed 20 Ed. III c. 6 and
34 Ed. III c. 8; but it contains a proviso that embracers and
jurors who wilfully or corruptly consent to embracery are liable
to indictment or information and punishable by fine or imprisonment just as before the Act[1]. There is an almost total
lack of decisions on embracery since the Juries Act, 1825, and
the law can only be illustrated now by such decisions of earlier
times on the writ of *decies tantum* or otherwise as are likely to
be suitable to changed circumstances[2].

§ 11. The law, then, as it now stands depends upon the penal
action under 32 Hen. VIII c. 9[3] and the Common Law.
Whether embracery as distinct from maintenance ever existed
as a Common Law offence is debatable. "De Conspiratoribus
Ordinatio" of 1293 and the statutes 20 Ed. III c. 6 and
38 Ed. III st. 1, c. 12 spoke of embracers as if they were
offenders known to the law apart from enactment[4]. And the
same conclusion has been reached by another line of reasoning.
Coke regarded embracery as nothing more than a species of
maintenance. We have shewn that the balance of the evidence
is in favour of his view that maintenance is a Common Law
offence. If then embracery be only a variety of maintenance, it
could, as a matter of logic, be classified with it as obnoxious
to the Common Law. The first point, therefore, is whether the
following passage from Coke be correct. The third kind of
*manutenentia curialis*

---

[1] 6 Geo. IV c. 50, sects. 61, 62.

[2] Extinct procedural points worth mentioning are that the plaintiff was
obliged to prove how much had been received, otherwise the Court would
not know the amount for which judgment must be given (*per* COKE J. in
*Partrige v. Straunge* (6 and 7 Ed. VI) Plowd. *Comm.* 85); and that the
defendants ought not to plead the general issue, but specially that they did
not take the money (1 Hawk. P.C. ch. 85, sect. 17). The King might sue
for the entire forfeiture in *decies tantum* (*per* REDE J. in Mich. 13 Hen. VII,
f. 8). On the other hand, if the subject instituted the action, he got his
moiety of the penal sum before the King, for the latter's moiety was due
to him as a fine, not as a debt (1 Hawk. P.C. ch. 85, sect. 18). As the action
was popular, the King's release before it was brought barred it; not so the
release of the party grieved (*ibid.*).

[3] *Ante* § 9.          [4] *Ante* pp. 162 sqq.

is when one laboureth the jury, if it be but to appeare, or if he instruct them, or put them in feare, or the like, he is a maintainer, and is in law called an embraceor, and an action of maintenance lyeth against him; and if he take money, a *decies tantum* may be brought against him[1].

This classification of embracery is supported to a certain extent by some of the Year Book cases. It is true that HANKFORD J. took a distinction between maintenance and embracery in Hil. 13 Hen. IV, f. 16, and said that an embracer is properly one who takes upon himself to make the people of an inquest appear, and that such an one is called in English "a leader of inquests." This appears to have made the defendants who had come to distribute fish among the jurors maintainers and not embracers. And it was queried in Pasch. 21 Hen. VI, f. 54, whether maintenance or *decies tantum* were the correct writ against one not sworn as a juror. But later cases do not adhere to Hankford's distinction. Mich. 11 Hen. VI, f. 10, is inconclusive. An attorney had bribed two of the inquest with 10s. apiece. MARTYN J. thought that this was embracery, not maintenance, but added that if the attorney had given of his own goods to maintain the plea, he would have been a maintainer. BABINGTON C.J.C.P. thought that even if the attorney's gift were of his master's goods, it was special maintenance, and PASTON J. took the same view. On the other hand, in a case reported at some length in Mich. 21 Hen. VI, f. 15, and Mich. 22 Hen. VI, f. 5, an Abbot's gift of 40s. to W. E. to labour the jurors was held by all the judges to be maintenance. And in Clement Tailour's case, where Tailour had given 100s. of his own money for distribution among the inhabitants of the county for the purpose of maintenance, it was held that this was maintenance[2]. Finally, in Mich. 17 Ed. IV, f. 5, it was laid down by all the Court that if a juror give money, be it his own or that of another, to his companions, he commits maintenance[3].

It seems then that mediaeval judges made no marked division between maintenance and embracery, and it is unreasonable to expect that they should have done so in an age not addicted

---

[1] Co. *Litt.* 368 *b*.
[2] Trin. 28 Hen. VI, f. 12; Trin. 31 Hen. VI, f. 8. See too Jenk. 101.
[3] Pasch. 18 Ed. IV, f. 4, is to the same effect, though the statement of facts on which the decision is based appears to be defective.

to scientific classification. Perhaps Coke's neat subordination of embracery to maintenance as species to genus is more artificial than history warrants, and perhaps, too, the deduction from this that embracery subjects the offender to all the legal proceedings appropriate to maintenance, is a sweeping inference of a later time when embracery was little known[1].

§ 12. The particular mode of influence which the embracer adopts, or attempts to adopt, is not material. The crudest form is naturally the earliest—a money bribe whether given or promised[2]. But it might well be that threats could do more cheaply and quite as effectually what bribes could. "Speaking great words" to jurors was held not to be maintenance in Hil. 13 Hen. IV, f. 16, but we are not told what the great words were. And in Mich. 22 Hen. VI, f. 5, NEWTON J. put the hypothetical case of a man of great power in the county coming before the jury, and stating openly that he wished to spend £20 for a certain party, or to labour the jury. This he thought would be maintenance, though nothing were given, nor were the jury laboured, for possibly they would not dare to give a verdict unfavourable to the great man. True, this is a general offer of bribery rather than a threat, but there is a veiled threat, and if a promised reward be objectionable, a threatened evil ought to be more so. Moreover, Fitzherbert describes an embracer as one who comes to the bar with the party, and talks in the cause, or stands there to survey the jury, or to put them in fear[3].

The mere writing of a letter urging a juror to appear and to act according to his conscience was held in the Star Chamber to be embracery. But even in the Star Chamber, if the party himself laboured the jurors to appear, this was not unlawful, though the jurors were never summoned to appear[4], and this distinction was recognized by the Court there in *Jepps* v. *Tunbridge*, where the defendant was fined and imprisoned for delivering a "brief" of the cause to jurors[5]. This throws some

---

[1] 1 Hawk. P.C. ch. 85, sect. 7.
[2] Trin. 40 Ed. III, f. 33; Pasch. 41 Ed. III, f. 9; Mich. 11 Hen. VI, f. 10. F.N.B. 171 A. 1 Hawk. P.C. ch. 85, sect. 5.
[3] F.N.B. 171 B. 1 Hawk. P.C. ch. 85, sect. 5.        [4] Dyer, 48.
[5] (9 Jac. I) Moore, 815. Hudson, 91–93. *Hussey* v. *Cook* (18 Jac. I) Hob. 294. Co. *Litt.* 157 *b*, 369 *a*. 1 Hawk. P.C. ch. 85, sect. 2.

light on what "labouring" means. Merely shewing a juror an exemplification in proof of the case, at the same time forbidding him to read it, was not embracery[1]. Coke is credited with the opinion that it is lawful to tell a juror what the issue was, if that be no more than what was contained in the record at *nisi prius*[2]. Soliciting a juror not to appear is punishable, no matter who it is that solicits; for that both delays justice, and is a mode of packing the jury[3].

Whatever be the manner of the alleged influence, it should be detailed in the indictment for embracery. In *R. v. Baker*, one of the objections was that the mode of influence was not stated. All that was alleged was that the accused unlawfully and knowingly attempted to corrupt and influence a jury by persuasions, entertainments, and other unlawful means. The Recorder considered it needless to deal with this objection, as he quashed the indictment on another ground[4]; but the inference to be drawn for future indictments can scarcely be ignored[5].

§ 13. At what moment must the pernicious influence be brought to bear upon the juror? Does a man commit embracery not only if he corruptly approach the juror during the proceedings, but if he do so before the juror be sworn, or after the verdict be returned? Upon the whole, it seems that, if the juror has been summoned, this is enough for the purposes of embracery, even though he has not been sworn. Against this view it may be urged that it was a good plea in bar to the writ of *decies tantum* that there was no record of the previous action shewing that the juror was sworn, for an essential of the offence was its commission in a previous action[6]; and that Fitzherbert's commentary on *decies tantum* states that the jury must have been sworn[7]. Pasch. 21 Hen. VI, f. 54, may be taken either way. It records a statement of counsel that some of the justices

---

[1] *Becket v. Rashley.* Hudson, *ubi sup*.          [2] *Ibid*.

[3] *Hussey v. Cook* (18 Jac. I) Hob. 294.

[4] (1891) 113 C.C.C. Sess. Pap. 374. Upon a fresh indictment, the form of which is not given, the accused was convicted. *Ibid*. 589. From the evidence then given, it appears that he tried to persuade the jurors to favour the prisoner whom they were trying.

[5] The Indictments Act, 1915 (5 and 6 Geo. V c. 90), Sched. I, rule 9, requires the particulars of the offence to indicate with reasonable clearness to the accused the occasion and circumstances of his crime.

[6] 1 Hawk. P.C. ch. 85, sect. 11.

[7] F.N.B. 171 A, B.

were of opinion that though a defendant had not been sworn
as a juror, *decies tantum* would yet lie, while others thought
that the appropriate writ was maintenance. If it be correct
that embracery is only a kind of maintenance, the difficulty is
one of form, not of substance, and would not be likely to trouble
a modern pleader. And there is some show of authority that
it is embracery to tamper with jurors before they are sworn.
Hawkins states that gift or promise of money to, or menaces
or instruction of, the jury beforehand is unlawful[1]. In *Jepps* v.
*Tunbridge*[2], the two Chief Justices and the Lord Chancellor
were of opinion that instruction of jurors verbally or in writing,
or promising them any reward for appearance, whether by the
party himself or by a stranger, is embracery.

If a reward be given to the jurors after their verdict has been
returned and this is done in pursuance of a previous offer or
contract, it is embracery[3]. It is also said that the gift of money
without any preceding contract savours of the nature of embracery, because, if such practices were allowed, it would be
easy to evade the law, by secretly intimating to jurors an intended
reward for their services, which would be as bad as giving
money beforehand[4]. This is no more than saying that if a
preceding agreement or offer can be inferred, the offence is
committed. But on principle it should be immaterial whether
there be any such agreement. It may be conceded that if the
jurors receive no reward till after their verdict, this cannot
affect their verdict in that particular proceeding. Yet it would
be highly inexpedient to raise any expectation of a gratuity for
doing their legal duty in future cases. It is possible that they
may be impanelled in a later case in which the person who
rewarded them is again concerned. Moreover, if such conduct
were of common occurrence, it would have an evil effect on the
integrity of jurors in general.

[1] 1 P.C. ch. 85, sect. 5. Hudson, 91–93. It was also a ground of principal
challenge. Co. *Litt.* 157 b.　　　　　　　[2] (9 Jac. I) Moore, 815.

[3] In Edward III's reign, where there was no previous agreement, the
jurors were fined, and the only matter of surprise to the reporter was that
they were not imprisoned as well, as the proceedings were upon 34 Ed. III
c. 8; 39 Lib. Ass. pl. 19; Br. *Abr. Dec. Tant.* 15. But this decided nothing
as to the liability of him who gave the money.

[4] 1 Hawk. P.C. ch. 85, sect. 3, 14.

§ 14. *Decies tantum* did not lie against an embracer who took
money from another for bribing the jurors, but never distri-
buted it[1]. But at the present day, such an act would probably
be a conspiracy to defeat the ends of justice. If the money were
given to the jurors, it was immaterial that the plaintiff was
non-suited[2], or that the verdict were a true one, for the return
of the verdict was not the cause of the action of *decies tantum*,
but what the jurors took for returning it[3]. It is submitted that
this represents the principle of the law just as much now as it
did in Henry VI's reign.

§ 15. Some acts of interference with a jury are not embracery.
Lawyers, of course, may plead in a cause for their fees, but
they become embracers if they "labour" the jury and take
money for doing it[4]. In the Star Chamber, it was affirmed
that a party to the suit, his son, servant, or near kinsman might
exert himself to procure the jury to appear, if there were no
other ill-qualified circumstance in it[5]; but no man might write
to another to get him to appear in a case in which the persuader
was not interested[6]. But this, and other like opinions are of
little value at the present day. They were uttered in an age
when the jurors were still in a sense witnesses and not merely
judges of the facts. Now that they are solely the latter there
would presumably be no objection to urging them to appear,
but such an act would be rather unintelligible in view of the
punishment with which the law would visit them if they did
not obey its summons.

There are traces of this old theory that the function of jurors
is that of witnesses in an opinion of the 18th century that the
giving to them reasonable expenses for travelling and so forth
which they may fairly expect from the successful party is in no

---

[1] Danvers J. in Trin. 37 Hen. VI, f. 31 ("Ad quod curia concessit"),
F.N.B. 171 c.

[2] *Per* Prisot C.J.C.P. in case last cited.

[3] Paston J. in Mich. 21 Hen. VI, f. 20; F.N.B. 171 c; Co. *Litt.* 369 *a*.
Dyer, 95 *b*. 1 Hawk. P.C. ch. 85, sect. 15.

[4] F.N.B. 171 b. Mich. 6 Ed. IV, f. 5 (Counsel was alleged to have taken
£20, only 6s. 8d. whereof was given to him as his lawful fee).

[5] *Hussey* v. *Cook* (18 Jac. I) Hob. 294. Cf. Dyer, 48. 1 Hawk. P.C.
ch. 85, sect. 6. *Lord Cromwell and Townsend's Case* (28 Eliz.) 2 Leon. 133.

[6] *Bayneham* v. *Lucas* (1603) Baildon, *Cases in Star Chamber*, 165.

way criminal, because if they could look to no such allowance, it would be often difficult to prevail upon persons to serve on juries at their own charge; and that experience had shewn that it was necessary to allow the parties to give some amends for the jurors' charges[1]. Hence, no objection seems to have been taken to a payment of £65 to a jury for coming up in very bad weather from Dorsetshire[2]. But this was more generous than was customary. Usually the party who secured their verdict regaled the jury with a dinner, and that was all that they got, though they might have been obliged to travel 40 miles or more[3]. At the same time, it was well to bear in mind that this, like many other acts which involved no liability for embracery, might raise a question as to whether the verdict ought not to be set aside. And in Charles II's reign, the Court, though it refused to take that course, thought that the practice of giving refreshment to the jury by one of the parties was objectionable[4]. At the present day, a new trial would be procurable in similar circumstances.

The discharge of a juror's duty is now a public duty, for which he is presumptively paid nothing. This holds unqualifiedly where issue is joined between the Crown and a person charged with a criminal offence, except where an indictment is removed by *certiorari* into the King's Bench Division and ordered to be tried by a special jury. Nor has any fee ever been paid to a jury which has asked to be discharged because it could not agree upon a verdict. Apart from these cases, the jurors' fees are as follow. Subject to the discretion of the judge, a special juror's fee is one guinea. It cannot exceed that amount except in causes where a view is directed and shall have been had by the juror[5]. Common jurors are accustomed to receive on each cause tried in the High Court at London 1s., at *nisi*

---

[1] 1 Hawk. P.C. ch. 85, sect. 3.

[2] *R.* v *Inhabitants of Hermitage* (4 W. and M.) Carth. 239, 242.

[3] Forsyth, *Trial by Jury*, c. 18.

[4] *Duke of Richmond* v. *Wise* (23 Car. II) 1 Vent. 124. In *Vickery* v. *L.B. and S.C.R. Co.* (1870) L.R. 5 C.P. 165, the question of jurors' fees was discussed historically.

[5] 6 Geo. IV c. 50, sect. 35. It was said by BOVILL C.J. in 1870 to go back as far as living memory, and to have been recognized by the Courts as well as by the legislature. *Vickery* v. *L.B. and S.C.R. Co. ubi sup.* at p. 171.

*prius* on circuit 8*d*., upon writs of inquiry before the sheriffs
of London 4*d*., at the Mayor's Court, London, 2*d*., in County
Courts 1*s*., and on inquiries to assess compensation under the
Lands Clauses Consolidation Act, 1845, 10*s*. 6*d*. Upon views,
wherever held, there may be paid, in addition to reasonable
travelling expenses and 5*s*. a day for refreshment, to each
special juryman one guinea *per diem*; to each common juryman
5*s*. *per diem*[1].

§ 16. Embracery is a misdemeanour punishable by fine and
imprisonment without hard labour[2]. This appears to be
warranted by the Juries Act, 1825, which contained a saving
clause that embracers are liable to indictment or information
and punishable by fine and imprisonment as before the Act[3].
Whether the draftsman of the Act had clearly in his mind what
the possible punishments were before the Act, and whether
they included all the remedies for maintenance, on Coke's
principle that embracery is a kind of maintenance, is unknown.
This principle is pressed to its logical conclusion if it be
argued that the civil remedies for maintenance would apply to
embracery as well[4].

The penal action under 32 Hen. VIII c. 9, sect. 3, 6, still
survives[5].

§ 17. In *R.* v. *Baker*, the last reported case of embracery,
there was a motion to quash the indictment because (i) The
names of the jurors influenced were not mentioned. The
offence, it was urged, consists in influencing individual jurors,
whereas the indictment alleged an attempt to influence a jury.
(ii) The mode of influence was not sufficiently stated. The
indictment was quashed on the first ground. The accused was
re-indicted, convicted and fined £100[6].

§ 18. Conduct which might possibly be embracery, or which
falls outside it, but is yet improper with respect to jurors, may
be dealt with as contempt of Court. Hence, where the brother
of a convicted prisoner went to the foreman of the jury shortly

---

[1] *Laws of England*, vol. XVIII. §§ 650–651.
[2] Russ. I. 598.                    [3] 6 Geo. IV c. 50, sect. 61.
[4] 1 Hawk. P.C. ch. 85, sect. 7. *Ante* § 11.
[5] *Ante* p. 170.
[6] (1891) 113 C.C.C. Sess. Pap. 374, 589.

after the trial and accused him of having bullied his fellow
jurors into finding the prisoner guilty, and challenged him to
mortal combat, an Irish Court decided that this was a contempt
of the Court itself, and was also of opinion that such conduct was
an indictable misdemeanour punishable by fine and imprisonment[1]. So too, counsel who in the course of his address to the
jury, insulted its foreman, was fined for contempt of Court[2].

§ 19. Another way of attacking many offences which might
be regarded as embracery is through the law of conspiracy.
In modern times this has outgrown its original conception
almost beyond recognition. Where the act of embracery takes
the shape of a corrupt agreement, there seems to be no reason
why it should not also be the offence of conspiracy to defeat
the ends of justice. This, so far from demanding any extension
of the law, would be returning to the meaning with which
conspiracy started. More than a century ago, it was said that
all fraudulent contrivances to secure a verdict are high offences[3];
and a century before that, an information for an offence in the
nature of embracery was laid against four persons who had
conspired that two of them should procure themselves to be
sworn *de circumstantibus*, and should give their verdict for the
defendant. This was carried out, and, on conviction of all four,
HALE C.J. would not even hear a motion in arrest of judgment,
because he thought the offence so serious; and the most he would
do was to leave the parties to bring a writ of error if they
liked[4]. It is submitted that the Courts in our own day are not
likely to regard such offences with any less seriousness.

## MISCONDUCT OF JURORS

§ 20. In addition to the statutes which dealt with embracers
and incidentally with jurors, there was one peculiar to jurors,
which enacted that if they took of the one party and of the
other, they should never again be put on juries or inquests,

---

[1] *R.* v. *Martin* (1848) 5 Cox, 356.
[2] *Ex parte Pater* (1864) 5 B. and S. 299. The question whether embracery
could be treated as contempt of Court was discussed *In re Dunn* (1906)
Victoria, L.R. 493.
[3] 1 Hawk. P.C. ch. 85, sect. 4.
[4] *R.* v. *Opie* (21 Car. II) 1 Saund. 301.

and should be liable to fine and imprisonment[1]. This, like the other statutes, has been repealed[2], and there is nothing to add to what has already been said on their history[3].

§ 21. The misconduct of a juror has a double aspect. It may be a ground for punishing him for contempt. It may also have the effect of annulling the verdict in which he takes part. Most of the forms of misbehaviour which are now to be treated have been regarded as contempts by Hawkins, though several of the decisions do not go quite so far[4].

§ 22. If a juror, after being summoned, made default, the practice seems to have been settled as early as Edward III's reign that those who did appear should ascertain the yearly value of his lands, and that he should be amerced to that amount[5]. But before this step was taken he was given a chance of appearing under a penalty which was forfeited if he still made default[6]. That penalty, it is said, was fixed by reference to the value of his lands found as above (or some less sum), and it is also said that a fine of the like amount might be imposed without any further proceeding[7]. The old rule—not entirely unchallenged—was that, if neither party wished the defaulter to be summoned under the penalty, the Court would not summon him[8].

Modern statutes have made this account of merely historical interest. The Juries Act, 1825, provides that if any one duly summoned to attend on any kind of jury in any of the Courts in England or Wales mentioned in the Act[9] shall not attend being called shall not answer, or if he or any talesman after

[1] 5 Ed. III c. 10.
[2] As to England, by 6 Geo. IV c. 50, sect. 62; as to Ireland by 3 and 4 Will. IV c. 91, sect. 50.
[3] *Ante* pp. 162 sqq.
[4] 2 P.C. ch. 22, sect. 1, 13 sqq.
[5] 20 Lib. Ass. pl. 11.     [6] 30 Lib. Ass. pl. 3.
[7] 2 Hawk. P.C. ch. 22, sect. 14.
[8] Mich. 4 Hen. VI, f. 7. Mich. 4 Ed. IV, f. 37 (CHOKE and LYTTLETON JJ. DANBY C.J.C.P. thought that he should still be summoned on the King's account. No decision is reported). Hawk. *ubi sup*.
[9] Apparently any of the King's Courts of Record at Westminster, the Superior Courts of Counties Palatine, all Courts of Assize, *nisi prius*, Oyer and Terminer and Gaol Delivery, Courts of Sessions of the Peace. 6 Geo. IV c. 50, sect. 1. The fine is from 20s. to 40s. in Courts of Record other than these. *Ibid.* sect. 54.

having been called shall be present but not appear, or after appearance shall wilfully withdraw, the Court shall fine him as it thinks meet, unless he prove by oath or affidavit some reasonable excuse. If he be a viewer, the fine must be £10 at least[1]. Similar power is given to every Court of *nisi prius*, oyer and terminer, gaol delivery and sessions of the peace held for the City of London[2]. Absence of the juror must not be commuted by a reward promised or given to the sheriff or other officer[3]. A juror who makes default at an inquiry under the Lands Clauses Consolidation Act, 1845, forfeits a sum not exceeding £10, in addition to being liable to the same penalty as a juror at any of the Superior Courts[4].

The Mayor's Court of London Procedure Act, 1857, punishes a defaulting juror in that Court by a fine not exceeding £5[5]. This is the limit also in County Courts[6] and Coroners' Courts[7].

No juror is liable to the penalty for non-attendance, unless the attendance summons be served six days before the day on which he is required[8]. Nor will the fine be estreated for 14 days, and not then unless within that period the proper officer of the Court shall have informed by letter the juror of the imposition of the fine, and required him, within six days after receipt of the letter, to forward him an affidavit of the cause of non-attendance with a view to the remission of the fine[9].

§ 23. A juror's refusal to be sworn on appearance is also said to be a contempt of Court. The authority for this might be stronger, but the principle is so palpably sound that it may well fall within a resolution of the whole Court in Elizabeth's time that if any contempt or disturbance to the Court be

---

[1] *Ibid.* sect. 38. The Municipal Corporations Act, 1882 (45 and 46 Vict. c. 50), sect. 186, sub-sect. 7, has a similar provision with respect to borough juries.

[2] *Ibid.* sect. 51.    [3] *Ibid.* sect. 43.    [4] 8 Vict. c. 18, sect. 44.

[5] 20 and 21 Vict. c. clvii. sect. 49.

[6] County Courts Act, 1888 (51 and 52 Vict. c. 43), sect. 102.

[7] Coroners Act, 1887 (50 and 51 Vict. c. 71), sect. 19.

[8] Juries Act, 1870 (33 and 34 Vict. c. 77), sect. 20. It is said that this does not apply to a Coroner's jury. *Laws of England*, IX. sect. 661. At any rate, the law would scarcely be workable if it did.

[9] Juries Act, 1862 (25 and 26 Vict. c. 107), sect. 12. As to the mode of enforcing recovery of the fine, see the Juries Act, 1825 (6 Geo. IV c. 50), sect. 54–55, and the Coroners Act, 1887 (50 and 51 Vict. c. 71), sect. 19, sub-sect. 4.

committed in any Court of record, the judges may set upon the offender a reasonable fine. The actual decision, however, was that the constable-elect in a leet Court who would not take the oath in the Court could be fined[1].

§ 24. If a juror departed after appearance, he was held very early in our law to have committed a contempt; and at the present day if he withdraws himself from the Court without leave after appearance he is liable to a fine at the discretion of the Court, as has been noticed already[2]. The intermediate history begins with a case of Edward III's reign, where one of a jury in an action of trespass went away to drink, after he and his companions had been sworn and brought to a room. He was apparently suspected of having been with the defendant during his absence, but on his return swore that this was not so. He was ultimately fined 40d. and his companions were reprimanded for not watching him better, and were ordered to find mainprize for their appearance on the succeeding day[3]. The case is a curious example of co-operative responsibility not uncommon in other branches of ancient law.

About a century later, both parties wished to have a juror challenged who had departed after being sworn and who did not reappear on being demanded. PRISOT C.J.C.P. thought that this could not be permitted because, if it were, the King would not have the fine for which the juror was answerable for his contempt. But the judges of both Benches were unanimous that he ought to be fined for his contempt, and they inquired of his brethren of the value of his lands with a view to assessing the fine by that[4].

There was a remarkable discussion before all the judges of both Benches in the Exchequer Chamber in Trin. 14 Hen. VII, f. 30, as to the causes which would justify the jurors in departing from the Court. In the course of an action between the Bishop

---

[1] *Griesley's Case* (30 Eliz.) 8 Rep. 38. In Mich. 7 Hen. VI, f. 12, Cotesmore said *arguendo* that if a juror at the bar will not be sworn, the Court would fine or imprison him at its election. See 2 Hawk. P.C. ch. 22, sect. 15.
[2] Juries Act, 1825. *Ante* p. 177.
[3] Mich. 34 Ed. II, cited in Fitz. *Abr. Office del Court.*
[4] 36 Hen. VI, f. 27.

of N. and the Count of Kent, a thunderstorm of such violence arose, that some of the jurors departed from the Court without permission, there being nobody left to give it[1]. One of them came to a house where several persons told him that he should take care what he did, for the Count's cause was better than that of the Bishop; and they prayed him to drink with them, which he did. After the tempest, he and the other jurors returned and, not being challenged, were agreed upon their verdict. The Count of Kent revealed what had occurred to the justices, to whom the jurors confessed. They were asked if they were agreed, and replied that they were, and returned a verdict for the Bishop. The question was whether the verdict were good or not. Five of the eight judges thought it good, three held it to be bad. Of the five, WOOD and DANVERS JJ., while they upheld the verdict, considered that the jury were punishable by fine or imprisonment. FINEUX C.J.K.B. and REDE and TREMAYLE JJ. took the more rational view that circumstances might excuse the departure, the storm being comparable to a sudden affray before the justices. Of the three judges who held the verdict bad, BRYAN C.J.C.P. did so on the ground that the departure was unreasonable; and the other two (HODY C.B. and VAVASOUR J.) do not appear to have contemplated departure of any sort as reasonable[2].

More modern decisions shew that if the jurors go away without leave, this may be ground for ordering a new trial in a civil case if it can be so regarded as to shew that justice was not done between the parties; as where they returned smoking cigars and had been seen talking to the plaintiff's attorney in a public-house, and there was no acquiescence by the defendant in this aberration[3].

As to criminal cases, a distinction must be taken between the departure of a particular juror, and the general separation of the jury at the end of the day or otherwise. In the former event, if his absence be discovered before the summing-up, the

---

[1] Judgment of FINEUX C.J.K.B.
[2] *Et adjournantur.* Further discussion, but no decision, is reported in Hil. 15 Hen. VII, f. 2. Other grounds dealt with were (i) drinking by the juror; (ii) lateness in taking the objection.
[3] *Hughes* v. *Budd* (1840) 8 Dowl. 316.

jury must be discharged and a fresh one impanelled[1]; if after the summing-up, the conviction must be quashed, though it is open to the Crown to recommence the proceedings[2]. The question as to the effect of a general separation of the jurors was raised in *R. v. Kinnear*[3], where the jury on a trial of the defendant for misdemeanour, and without the defendant's consent, separated at night, and their verdict was held to be good and a new trial was not granted. The practice of separation before the summing-up in the case of misdemeanours had then become common, and it was pointed out that while dispersal without the judge's consent would be a misdemeanour, yet it should not disturb the verdict.

The true rule is, that it is left to the discretion of the judge to say whether the jury are to be permitted to separate or not: of course, if in his judgment that separation is likely to be detrimental to the ends of justice, he will not permit it to take place[4].

Such is the practice as to misdemeanours, and now the rigid rule which made jurors on a trial for felony more like prisoners than the accused himself, if he were released on bail, has been modified by the Juries Detention Act, 1897. This allows the Court, if it sees fit at any time before the jury consider their verdict upon the trial of a felony (except murder, treason, or treason felony), to permit them to separate in the same way as the jury upon a trial for misdemeanour are now permitted to separate[5]. And it has been held that even in a trial for murder, a juror may separate from his companions on such an emergency as sudden illness[6].

After the jury have retired to consider their verdict, separation is not permissible[7].

§ 25. It is said that jurors are liable to a fine for refusing to give a verdict at all[8]. This must be taken to refer to obstinate

---

[1] *R. v. Ward* (1867) 10 Cox, 573.

[2] *R. v. Ketteridge* [1915] 1 K.B. 467.

[3] (1819) 2 B. and Ald. 462.          [4] BEST J. at p. 467.

[5] 60 Vict. c. 18. See the result of the Act discussed in *R. v. Twiss* [1918] 2 K.B. 853.          [6] *R. v. Crippen* [1910] 1 K.B. 149.

[7] *R. v. Ketteridge* [1915] 1 K.B. 467. *R. v. Twiss* [1918] 2 K.B. 853. In *R. v. O'Connell* (1843) 1 Cox, 410, the famous Irish case, they were not allowed to separate *during* the summing-up in a trial for misdemeanour.

[8] 2 Hawk. P.C. ch. 22, sect. 16 citing *Bushell's Case* (1670) Vaughan, 135, 152.

evasion of their duty, not to honest and irreconcilable difference of opinion.

§ 26. The older law which forbade the refreshment of jurors during a trial is accurately stated by Coke. If after evidence they ate or drank at their own charge, whether before or after they were agreed on their verdict, they were liable to a fine, but the verdict was unaffected. But if before agreement on the verdict they ate or drank at the charge of one of the parties, that avoided the verdict, unless it were cast against the party treating the jury[1]. It is true that VAVASOUR J. in Mich. 14 Hen. VII, f. 1, granted a fresh *venire facias* where the jury had eaten and drunk, and that he adhered to this view in a later case of the same year where the verdict was against the party on whose account, but without whose authority or privity, the juror had been given some drink. But this view did not commend itself to the majority of Vavasour's legal brethren, though BRYAN C.J.C.P. and HODY C.B. were of his opinion[2]. REDE and DANVERS JJ. held that the drinking produced no partiality, as the jurors found against the party on whose behalf it was given. There is no traceable dissent from the opinion of FINEUX C.J.K.B. (who also thought the verdict good) and REDE J. that the juror was liable to a fine for the drinking[3].

Other cases of the Tudor period also illustrate the rule. In Mich. 20 Hen. VII, f. 3, where all the jurors ate and drank together after departing from the bar, three judges held that their verdict was good, and they referred to the Bishop of Lincoln's Case where one juror departed, and a stranger gave him drink, and prayed him to favour the Bishop; the verdict stood, as he found against the Bishop. FROWYK C.J.C.P. saw less danger in all drinking than in a few only so doing, for "if all drink together, each is in the good plight of resisting the malice of the others....But when two only drink, it can be presumed that they will be more obstinate than the others." This rather doubtful inference did not secure the assent of

[1] Co. *Litt.* 227 b.
[2] Cf. PRISOT C.J.C.P. *obiter* in Hil. 35 Hen. VI, cited in Fitz. *Abr. Examinacion*, 17.
[3] Trin. 14 Hen. VII, f. 30, and Hil. 15 Hen. VII, f. 2. No decision is reported. *Ante* pp. 178–179.

VAVASOUR J. In Henry VIII's reign, the Court regarded the rule as long settled that jurors were fineable for refreshing themselves at their own cost, but that their verdict held good[1].

It was immaterial to their liability for contempt that the jurors had not eaten food concealed about their persons. Thus, jurors who had eaten figs were fined £5 apiece, while others who had pippins, but had not eaten them, escaped with the less penalty of 40s. each. It was only after a weighty debate that the judges held that this surreptitious refreshment did not upset the verdict[2].

The mode in which the victuals are procured may be such a scandalous piece of misbehaviour as to justify the Court in ordering a new trial. In *Cooksey* v. *Haynes*[3], the jury, having retired, covertly procured food and beer by means of a string let down out of a window. It was contended that this should not avoid the verdict, but POLLOCK C.B. while he admitted that it would not be ground for error, held it to be good cause for a motion for new trial; for this was an application to the discretionary jurisdiction of the Court. In delivering the judgment of the Court, he said that it concerned the interests of justice itself that such gross indecencies in its administration should not be allowed.

But there may be circumstances in which jurors are entertained by the party who afterwards secures their verdict which do not affect that verdict. Two jurors before the summing-up dined and slept at the house of the defendant in the case in which they had been impanelled. There was but one inn which afforded very insufficient accommodation. No allegation was made that they had been adversely affected by their visit, nor was there any reason to suspect unfairness. The Court, acting in its discretion, refused to set aside the verdict[4].

[1] *Trewennarde* v. *Skewys* (34 and 35 Hen. VIII) Dyer, 55 *b*.
[2] *Mounson* v. *West* (30 Eliz.) 1 Leon. 132. In *Sely* v. *Flayle* (21 Jac. I) Godbolt, 353, three jurors had sweetmeats in their pockets and were for the plaintiff till they were searched and the food discovered. Then they agreed with the other nine in a verdict for the defendant. Held: whether they ate or not, they were fineable, for it was a very great misdemeanour.
[3] (1858) 27 L.J. Exch. 371.
[4] *Morris* v. *Vivian* (1842) 10 M. and W. 137. LORD ABINGER'S opinion that the cases applied only where the whole jury had been refreshed seems

There seems to have been a judicial opinion of Henry VIII's reign that if the jurors ate and drank at the expense of parties other than the litigants, this induced suspicion and affection which would annul their verdict[1]. This is not inconsistent with a case of the next century, where the jurors had bottles of wine brought to them before they returned their verdict, and the plaintiff's solicitor paid for the wine after the verdict had been returned. It was held that the verdict was good. The judges were unanimous that refreshment of the jury at the cost of the party for whom they found avoided the verdict. Here, however, it did not appear that the plaintiff or his agent had ordered the wine, and the after-payment only raised a presumption that the solicitor had bespoken it. Indeed the gift of a dinner by the successful litigant to the jury was admitted to be the usual practice. Nor was their privy verdict[2] to be set aside because the solicitor had treated them at a tavern before they affirmed it in open Court. Had they changed it, it would have been a different matter[3]. But while the verdict remained undisturbed, the Court thought that the jury had been guilty of a great misdemeanour for which they should be fined, and that the solicitor had carried himself with much blame and indiscretion. Two tipstaffs who had connived at the matter were fined[4].

What if the treating were the unauthorized act of some person who professes to act as agent for the plaintiff or defendant? If the verdict be against the alleged principal, it would hold good by the rule already stated; but if it be for him, it seems harsh to say that he should be put to the expense of a new trial for the corrupt act of a meddlesome stranger which might conceivably have had a trivial effect on the verdict. Yet who is to measure whether the effect were trivial or not? And how can his opponent's grievance be any the less merely because the jurors took their bribe from a supposed agent instead of a real

---

consistent with neither authority nor principle. If this were the rule, as counsel pointed out, a party might safely treat any number of the jury up to eleven.

[1] *Trewennarde* v. *Skewys* (34 and 35 Hen. VIII) Dyer, 55 *b*.

[2] A verdict given to any one of the judges, but not in open Court. None such could be given in a criminal case. Co. *Litt.* 227 *b*.

[3] *Ibid.*      [4] *Duke of Richmond* v. *Wise* (23 Car. II) 1 Vent. 124.

one? "The law intends that, by the receipt of such money for eating, hearing, or other matter, the jurors will be more favourable to that party." Such were the words of Gascoigne C.J.K.B. 500 years ago on facts of this kind. It is true that the case had not got so far as a finding by the jury, for we are told that 12 *tales* were awarded; it is true also that the functions of jurors of the 15th century were far otherwise than those of the 20th century. But the soundness of the general principle has been undermined neither by the lapse of time nor by change of circumstances[1].

Even in ancient times, it is likely that there was some perception of the distinction between physic taken by jurors and food "for their sensual appetites and desire"[2], and at a much later date, where one of a jury that had been locked up in a capital case fell ill, the judge allowed a medical man to see him and give him medicine, but not sustenance[3].

The position of juries has been made more tolerable by the Juries Act, 1870, by which the judge in his discretion may allow them at any time before verdict the use of a fire when out of Court and reasonable refreshment at their own expense[4]. As a matter of custom the cost is usually borne by the County.

§ 27. Coke gives a fair summary of the law down to his own time as to the reception by the jury of information other than that laid before them in Court. If, he says, the plaintiff or one for him, after evidence given and the jury departed from the bar, deliver any letter from the plaintiff to any of the jury concerning the matter in issue, or any evidence or escrow touching the matter in issue, which was not given in evidence, it shall avoid the verdict if it be found for the plaintiff, but not if it be for the defendant, and *sic e converso*. But if the jury carry away any writing unsealed, which was given in evidence in open Court, this shall not avoid their verdict, albeit they should not have carried it with them[5].

Long before Coke, it had been held that the jury after they

---

[1] Hil. 13 Hen. IV, ff. 12–13.
[2] *Arguendo*, Mich. 20 Hen. VII, f. 3.
[3] *R.* v. *Newton* (1849) 3 Car. and Kir. 85.
[4] 33 and 34 Vict. c. 77, sect. 23.
[5] Co. *Litt.* 227 b.

were sworn ought not to see or take with them other evidence than that delivered to them by the Court and by the party put in Court upon the evidence shewn. Judgment for the plaintiff was refused because he had shewn an escrow to a juror after he was impanelled, but before he was sworn. It did not matter that the escrow was to the same effect as the evidence given at the bar[1]. This last part of the judgment was shaken as an authority by an Elizabethan case in which it was decided that a verdict for the plaintiff should stand, although his solicitor had delivered to the jury before they left the bar a church book which had been put in evidence at the trial[2]. But there is other evidence of Coke's time, and later, that the law preferred the more stringent rule which avoided the verdict given for a litigant who had merely reminded the jury out of Court of facts which they had already heard in it. Thus, where depositions taken in Chancery were delivered to the jury after they had departed from the bar by a solicitor to one of the parties, the verdict was quashed, even though they read only what had been read to them in Court[3]. And, in 1653, additional written evidence similarly delivered by the plaintiff's witness to a jury, who found for the plaintiff, was held to avoid the verdict, although the jury did not so much as read the evidence. More, they were held to have committed a misdemeanour in not having informed the Court earlier of the communication[4]. Possibly a modern Court would not go further than a reprimand of the jury in such circumstances, though there are traces of severer treatment in earlier times[5]. That the party himself who tampers with the jury in this fashion is criminally liable there is no doubt[6]; and much more so is a stranger. It is a plain case of embracery either way[7].

---

[1] GASCOIGNE C.J.K.B. and HULS J. in Mich. 11 Hen. IV, f. 17.

[2] *Vicary* v. *Farthing* (37 and 38 Eliz.) Cro. Eliz. 411 (three judges to one). Moore, 451 (Court evenly divided).

[3] *Pratt's Case* (circ. 21 Jac. I) Roll. *Abr.* 716, pl. 19 (no further reference).

[4] *Webb* v. *Taylor*, Roll. *Abr. Trial*, 714, pl. 6 (no other reference).

[5] Fitz. *Abr. Examinacion*, 17, citing Hil. 35 Hen. VI, where, after the jurors had been sworn, it was alleged that they had received a letter from the defendant, and PRISOT C.J.C.P. said that if this influenced their verdict, the verdict was null, and the jurors should be fined.

[6] *Goodson* v. *Duffill* (10 Jac. I) 2 Bulst. at p. 25 (Private instruction of one of the jurors after he was impanelled held punishable in the Star Chamber). [7] *Anon.* (undated) Noy, 102.

At one time, there seems to have been a tendency to distinguish between words said to the jury out of Court which might be regarded as an attempt to put fresh evidence before them and words which fell short of this. Hence, we are told that if one of the parties said to the jury after departure, "You are weak men, it is as clear of my side as the nose in a man's face," this was new evidence and would quash the verdict[1]; but that mere speaking by the plaintiff to jurors did not avoid the verdict unless it were proved that he gave evidence concerning the matter[2]. The law now adopts a different line of cleavage more suited to the altered circumstances in which it operates. Separation of the jury before summing-up has long been permissible where the trial is for misdemeanour, and, since the Juries Detention Act, 1897, in most felonies[3]. It would be absurd to ignore the probability of converse by the jurors during this separation with other persons, even though it be with reference to the trial. It is not enough to upset the verdict that the juror spoke to some one, or that the person to whom he spoke was a witness, although, in the latter case, the matter needs more careful examination by the Court. The true test is whether what was said might have prejudiced the accused. Such is the inference from *R. v. Twiss*[4], where, before the judge's summing-up and during the luncheon interval, a juryman conversed with some of the witnesses for the prosecution. The judge accepted his explanation that the conversation had reference solely to the duration of the case and the length of a previous trial which had been mentioned in the course of the proceedings. Another juryman had talked with the prisoner's landlady, who was also a witness for the prosecution, but the nature of the talk was such that it would tend to remove any bad impression which the juryman might have formed of the prisoner. The Court of Criminal Appeal upheld the prisoner's conviction; but they added an emphatic opinion that, although

[1] Roll. *Abr. Trial*, 716, pl. 20 (no other reference). *Hunt* v. *Locke* (14 Car. II) 1 Keble, 300 is perhaps on the same side. Verdict for defendant set aside because defendant's servant had talked to juror and the jury were inclined to plaintiff before the speaking. But the report ends, "Adjornantur."
[2] Roll. *Abr. Trial*, 715, pl. 17 citing Mich. 7 Jac. I *per Curiam* (no further reference).
[3] *Ante* sect. 24.
[4] [1918] 2 K.B. 853.

jurymen are allowed to go about while the trial is proceeding and cannot be prevented from doing so, nothing said by the Court should be taken as encouraging them to discuss the evidence given at the trial. "They should talk of other topics, discussing the trial with the other jurymen only until it comes to a close." "They had much better keep their own counsel and not speak to anybody else[1]."

The principle of this decision is wide enough to justify the inference that the mere fact that somebody has spoken *to* a juror during a separation of the jurors prior to summing-up does not form a ground for quashing the conviction. It is true that in 1910 the deputy chairman of the London Sessions discharged a jury because a woman had spoken to one of them during an adjournment; but what was alleged to have been said by the woman might have been construed as an attempt to influence the juror[2].

Unauthorized separation of a juror from his fellows after the summing-up, with its possibilities of converse with third persons, is a very different matter. The Court of Criminal Appeal characterized as wholly irregular the conduct of a clerk of assize who had had a discussion with the jury after they had retired. They referred to the plain principle that the trial of a criminal charge must be in public, not in secret, and they held the discussion to have been so serious an interference with the jury as to necessitate a quashing of the conviction[3]. And the same Court quashed a conviction where a juror, after the summing-up, had separated himself from his colleagues for a quarter of an hour, even though it did not appear that he had actually conversed with strangers but had been merely in a

[1] *Ibid.* at pp. 859, 860. In *Armstrong* v. *R.* (1914) 30 T.L.R. 215, the Judicial Committee refused special leave to appeal from a conviction of murder on the ground of alleged misconduct of the jurors in communicating during the trial with persons not their custodians. The conversations did not relate to the trial, and were no such violation of the principles of natural justice as would justify the Judicial Committee's interference.

[2] *R.* v. *Shepherd* (1910) 74 J.P. (Journal), 605. Not cited in *R.* v. *Twiss.* In the light of the latter case, what the learned deputy chairman said in reply to an explanation tendered by the foreman of the jury, after the jury had been discharged, was too wide a statement of the law. In any event, it was unnecessary to his decision.

[3] *R.* v. *Willmont* (1914) 30 T.L.R. 499.

position to do so. It was pointed out, however, that it was open to the Crown to recommence proceedings[1]. This case was distinguished in *R. v. Twiss*[2], as the facts of it shewed an absolute breach of the whole procedure governing the conduct of the Court at the time of, and after, the summing-up; for a bailiff is sworn to keep the jury together and to see that they do not converse with any one except each other.

The decisions just discussed were in connection with criminal trials. As to civil cases, it is equally "a cardinal principle of the jury system that a jury must deliberate in private"; and an order was made for the new trial of a County Court action where the town serjeant in mistaken zeal remained for 20 minutes in a room in which the jury were considering their verdict[3]. Conversations with third parties by the jurors before summing-up and during an adjournment of the Court seem to be just as objectionable as in criminal trials.

§ 28. It is possible that a juror may possess knowledge of a fact not put in evidence at the trial. This was more likely to occur at a time when jurors were in a sense witnesses as to the facts in issue than at the present day, when they appraise the testimony of others. That such individual knowledge might be taken into account by the jury at large does not appear to have been doubted. But the method by which it should be submitted to them has varied.

In an Elizabethan case, it was held not to be assignable as error that a juror had shewn an escrow in his possession to his brethren after their departure from the bar, although it had not been proved in Court. It had been given to him neither by any party to the proceedings nor by any representative of such party[4].

But as the line between witnesses and jurors became less blurred, this was probably regarded as an irregular mode of receiving such evidence. A couple of cases under the Commonwealth shew a hesitancy in the Courts which perhaps resulted from the lingering influence of the ancient idea as to a juror's

[1] *R. v. Ketteridge* [1915] 1 K.B. 467.
[2] [1918] 2 K.B. 853.
[3] *Goby v. Wetherill* [1915] 2 K.B. 674.
[4] *Graves v. Short* (40 and 41 Eliz.) Cro. Eliz. 616.

functions. In 1650, it was said by the Court that if either of the parties to a trial desire a juror to give evidence of something of his own knowledge, he must be examined on oath openly, in Court, and not in private by his companions[1]. Six years later, a barrister serving on a jury, who had heard evidence in a case decided 20 years earlier relevant to the case in hand, was ordered to come into Court and to state what he knew, but he was not sworn again, his oath as juror being regarded as enough[2]. But practice appears to be hardening in the direction of requiring such evidence to be given on the oath of a witness as distinct from that of a juror, in a case of Charles II's reign[3].

The rule now is that, while a juror may use his general knowledge, he must be sworn on special knowledge, e.g. that of a particular trade[4]; and if he suspect that a stamp on a bill of exchange is forged, he must be sworn, or his suspicion must be rejected[5].

§ 29. The next kind of misconduct may be described as endeavouring to impose on the Court[6]. This is exemplified by improper methods in finding the verdict.

There was very little sympathy in our early history with jurors who could not make up their minds. Jurors who returned a verdict which was not unanimous were fined and might be kept in custody till they could agree[7]. Another way of clearing their wits was for the judge to carry them about in carts from town to town on the circuit[8]. Nor could they take refuge in a hedging verdict. Where the Court found that a jury had alternative verdicts ready, it sent back the jury, and fined and

---

[1] *Bennet* v. *Hundred of Hartford*, Style, 233.

[2] *Duke* v. *Ventris* (1656) Duncomb, *Trials per Pais*, c. 12 (no further reference).

[3] *Fitz-James* v. *Moys* (15 Car. II) 1 Siderf. 133. It is worth noting that the reporter adds that the juror "uncore continue del jury," thus implying the distinction between juror and witness.

[4] *R.* v. *Rosser* (1836) 7 C. and P. 648.

[5] *Manley* v. *Shaw* (1840) Car. and M. 361. Cf. *Bushell's Case* (1670) 6 St. Tr. 1012 note.

[6] 2 Hawk. P.C. ch. 22, sect. 17.

[7] 29 Lib. Ass. pl. 27; 40 Lib. Ass. pl. 10 (Br. *Abr. Jurors*, 28 cites this case, but makes the verdict one given in a writ of conspiracy. The other report states that it was given in an indictment for trespass de baterie).

[8] 41 Lib. Ass. pl. 11.

imprisoned all of its members except two who were originally
for a verdict of guilty (which was that ultimately returned) and
on whose confession the matter was discovered. They escaped
with a censure[1].

Honest inability to agree is, of course, no offence now, and,
as the law recognizes its possibility, juries are much less likely
to resort to means of concealing it. But where they make no
real effort to decide on the fact, a new trial would probably be
ordered in a civil case[2].

Casting lots seems to have been a pretty frequent piece of
impropriety committed by jurors who were puzzled by the
facts. In one case, where there was an even division of opinion,
the bailiff picked one of two sixpences out of a hat, and the
verdict was given accordingly. WYNDHAM J. thought that as
the jury were equally divided, this method of reaching their
verdict was as good as any by the strongest body and suitable
to the law of God; and despite the doubt of TWISDEN J. that
it would be a bad example a new trial was denied[3]. But later
authority is decidedly the other way, and not only has a verdict
been set aside which was arrived at "on throwing cross and
pile," or by other chance determination, but the jurors em-
ploying such means have been fined[4]; nor is it material that the
verdict is according to evidence and coincides with the judge's
opinion[5].

§ 30. Personal bias on the part of a juror is a ground for
ordering a new trial. But the Courts have scarcely interpreted
bias in the sense which a moralist would attach to it.

A plain enough instance is that of the foreman of a jury who
declared that the plaintiff should never have a verdict whatever

---

[1] *Watts* v. *Brains* (42 and 43 Eliz.) Cro. Eliz. 778.
[2] *Hall* v. *Poyser* (1845) 13 M. and W. 600 (*Semble*: splitting the difference
between the rival claims of the parties as a compromise of conflicting opinions
among the jurors is a ground for a new trial).
[3] *Prior* v. *Powers* (16 Car. II) 1 Keb. 811. But the reporter adds that a
new trial was granted in Sir Philip Acton's Case where the verdict was "on
fillip of counter."
[4] *R.* v. *Fitz-Water* (27 Car. II) 2 Lev. 139. *Foster* v. *Hawden* (29 Car. II)
*Ibid.* 205. *Foy* v. *Harder* (29 Car. II) 3 Keb. 805, and *sub nom. Fry* v.
*Hordy*, T. Jones, 83.
[5] *Hale* v. *Cove* (1725) 1 Stra. 642.

witnesses he produced[1]. So is that of a juror who said he would give a verdict for the plaintiff right or wrong[2]. In both these cases a new trial was granted. Such too was the decision in *Allum* v. *Boultbee*[3], where, before conclusion of the trial, one juryman was heard to say to another at a public-house that the defendant would get served out[4]. But in *Onions* v. *Naish*[5], the Court refused a rule to set aside the verdict on the affidavit of an unsuccessful plaintiff that one of the jury was a relative of the defendant, was on terms of intimacy and friendship with him, and had frequently expressed himself strongly in the defendant's favour. No reason was given except that it would be very dangerous to set aside a verdict on these grounds. In *Ramadge* v. *Ryan*[6], the Court conceded that if a juror, before being sworn, express a determination to give a verdict one way, this is cause for a new trial; but it held that the rule had no application to the facts before it, which consisted in a juror entertaining a strong opinion on a former verdict; for that was not incompatible with his concurrence in a correct verdict on the case which was to come before him. So too, an anticipatory statement by a juryman of what he thinks is likely to happen in a criminal case may be unwise, but unless he says that whatever the evidence may be he is resolved to come to a certain result, it cannot be a ground for interfering with the conviction[7].

The mere fact that the jury, at the conclusion of the plaintiff's case, express an opinion in his favour to the Court, without having heard the defendant's evidence, is not such misconduct as will justify the defendant's counsel in refusing to go on with the case and afterwards claiming a new trial[8].

Where attempts have been made in a criminal case to canvass persons on the jury panel list, the indictment may be removed

---

[1] *Dent* v. *Hundred of Hartford* (8 W. III) Salk. 645.
[2] *Wynn* v. *Bishop of Bangor* (1728) 2 Comyns, 601.
[3] (1854) 9 Exch. 738.
[4] The decision, which was that of POLLOCK C.B., PARKE and PLATT BB. also rested upon the trial judge's dissatisfaction with the verdict. MARTIN B.'s dissent was partially based on the curious ground that the bias of one juror against the defendant could be set off against the bias of another in his favour.
[5] (1819) 7 Price, 203.          [6] (1832) 9 Bing. 333.
[7] *R.* v. *Syme* (1914) 10 Cr. App. R. at p. 287.
[8] *Campbell* v. *Hackney Furnishing Co.* (1906) 22 T.L.R. 318.

into the Central Criminal Court under the Central Criminal
Court Act, 1856[1].

§ 31.  It has long been a settled rule that where there has been
misconduct of jurors either by exhibiting partiality or by irregular methods in arriving at their verdict, the evidence of such
misconduct must not be that of the jurors themselves. Words
spoken which shew prejudice should be proved by those who
heard them, for such expressions are so improper that the juror
ought not to be asked whether he used them[2].

An affidavit by one of the jurors that the verdict had been
tossed for has been rejected, for conduct of this kind is also
a serious misdemeanour[3]; and an affidavit that two of the jurors
had confessed to deciding their verdict "by hustling halfpence
a hat" met a like fate[4]. Much less is evidence admissible where
it consists of an affidavit by an attorney of an admission made
to him by one of the jury, for that is hearsay, and if it were
allowed hardly any verdict would be safe[5]. In fact, with one
early exception, there appears to be no case in which even
affidavits by persons other than the jurors themselves have
been regarded as sufficient[6]; and affidavits in support of an
application for a new trial have actually been rejected precisely
because parts of them alleged misconduct on the part of the
foreman of the jury[7].

The Court of Criminal Appeal has given some indication of
what kind of evidence will support an appeal on this ground
in a criminal case. It has held that, while evidence of the
jurors as to their having been interfered with after returning
is not admissible, the report of the clerk of assize who had been
guilty of the interference is[8]. They are also reported as having
allowed witnesses to attend to speak to the alleged prejudice of

---

[1] *R. v. Barnett* [1919] 1 K.B. 640.
[2] Treby L.C.J. in *R. v. Cook* (1696) 13 St. Tr. 338. Tindal C.J. in
*Ramadge* v. *Ryan* (1832) 9 Bing. at p. 339.
[3] *Vasie* v. *Delaval* (1785) 1 T.R. 11.
[4] *Parr* v. *Seames* (8 Geo. II) Barnes, 438.
[5] *Straker* v. *Graham* (1839) 4 M. and W. 721.
[6] In *Dent* v. *Hundred of Hartford* (8 Will. III) Salk. 645, a new trial was
granted on an affidavit that the foreman declared that the plaintiff should
never have a verdict, whatever witnesses he produced.
[7] *Hartwright* v. *Badham* (1822) 11 Price, 383.
[8] *R. v. Willmont* (1914) 30 T.L.R. 499.

two jurymen, but they did not wish this permission to be taken as a precedent[1]. But they have laid it down that evidence of jurors' misconduct should only be admitted very cautiously, and that it must be such that, if admitted, it would compel the Court to quash the conviction. An application for this must be based on substantial information, and not on something which is little better than mere gossip[2].

Though a juryman's affidavit of what occurred in the jury-box during the trial cannot be received, yet his affidavit explaining the circumstances in which he came into the jury-box is admissible[3].

§ 32. The personation of a juror will lead to the award of a *venire de novo* in a criminal case, for, in effect, the prisoner has been tried by 11 jurymen instead of 12[4]. And the personator commits a Common Law misdemeanour, though he has no corrupt motive and has nothing to gain by his conduct. His intent to deceive is sufficiently proved by the mere fact of his personation, the necessary consequence of which is to deceive the Court. He also commits the Common Law misdemeanour of taking a false oath as a juror[5].

§ 33. If the jury have returned a satisfactory verdict, subsequent misconduct of one of them, even though it be gross, is no ground for disturbing the verdict where the party to the action has been guilty of no collusion. Writing a letter to a successful defendant asking for a sum of money is scandalous enough, but it would be hard on the defendant to set aside a verdict in his favour, when he takes no notice of the request except to bring it before the Court[6].

§ 34. Up to this point what we have considered has been misconduct of jurors in their ministerial rather than their judicial capacity. It remains to sketch briefly the history of the law relating to false verdicts.

---

[1] *R. v. Hancox* (1913) 29 T.L.R. 331. It is not easy to make out from the report what exactly did happen.

[2] *R. v. Syme* (1914) 10 Cr. App. R. 284.

[3] *Bailey* v. *Macaulay* (1849) 19 L.J.N.S. 72, 83.

[4] *R. v. Wakefield* [1918] 1 K.B. 216. *R. v. Mellor* (1858), Dears. and B. 468, 473, 474.

[5] *R. v. Clark* (1919) 82 J.P. 295. The accused was the personator in *R. v. Wakefield, ubi sup.*

[6] *Sabey* v. *Stephens* (1862) 7 L.T.N.S. 274.

In Bracton's time, a juror committed perjury if he swore a false oath, but he was not liable for a foolish one; for he swore according to his conscience and might believe facts to exist which did not[1]. Where there was a false verdict, it could be punished—and severely punished—by the process of attaint, which is discoverable in judicial records as early as 1202, though not in legislation till 1268[2]. The 12 jurors who were suspected were accused before 24 jurors and, if they were convicted of a false oath, their verdict was replaced by that of the 24.

But a distinction was drawn between the *assisa* and the *jurata*. The former was the outcome of ordinance, while the latter, in theory, depended on the consent of the parties. Therefore, while the *assisa* was liable to an attaint, the *jurata* was not; for it would have been unreasonable to allow those, who had pledged themselves in advance to abide by the verdict, to reprobate it merely because it dissatisfied either or both of them. But it became plain that the consent of the parties to the *jurata* was only nominal[3]. And the attaint is said to have been extended by 3 Ed. I (St. West. I) c. 38 to all juries in real actions. Even then the people cried for a broader application of the remedy. It was cramped because it did not cover the expanding forms of action, and by piecemeal legislation of the 14th century this was amended. That it proved to be very inadequate in the 15th century almost goes without saying. Every known remedy for abuse of legal procedure broke down in that period, and the attaint was no exception to the general rule. And owing to the unwieldy number of the jurors concerned in it, and its clumsy machinery, it was better fitted for delay and fraud than were other writs. Moreover, the attaint jury did not relish their duties. They feared the prospect of being hoist with their own petard, for if they could attaint one jury, they could be attainted by another; and they disliked the brutality of the punishment. The attainted juror forfeited his movables to the King, was imprisoned for a year at least, lost his *lex terrae*, and became

---

[1] Bracton, 288 *b*. *Fleta*, lib. v. ch. 22, sect. 9 repeats this with the qualification that if there be lack of skill or gross ignorance, the jurors should not be heavily punished. Cf. P. and M. II. 541–542, 623, 665.

[2] 52 Hen. III c. 14. Thayer, *Evidence*, Pt. I. 141.

[3] Thayer, 146.

infamous. The severity of these penalties became more disproportionate as a change took place in the functions of the juror. He ceased to be a mere witness of what he had seen and heard. He had to listen to other witnesses and to weigh what they said. And it seemed hard to punish a mistaken inference as if it were a lie. In 1495, the punishment was mitigated. During the next century, attaints fell into disuse, and in 1665 were thought by HYDE C.J. to be so fruitless that he was strongly of opinion that jurors should be fined. Lord Mansfield, in 1757, regarded the writ of attaint as "a mere sound in every case." In 1825, it was abolished[1].

As to the attaint in criminal cases, it was said by Bracton, and four centuries later, by Hale, that the King may have an attaint if the case go against him. But there is a lack of reported cases on the point[2]. Besides, in criminal cases, the dice were already cogged in the King's favour, and he had little need of the attaint. A man accused of treason or felony could have no counsel, and, later, while the King could call witnesses, he could not. On the other hand, the rule that he should not be in jeopardy twice for the same offence would work in his favour against the idea that the jury which acquitted him should be attainted.

§ 35. It is not clear whether, apart from attaint, there existed at Common Law any other method of punishing a jury for an unacceptable verdict. VAUGHAN C.J. in *Bushell's Case* (1670) was positive that they could not be fined.

That the Court could not fine a jury at the Common Law, where attaint did not lie (for where it did, is agreed he (*sic*) could not) I think to be the clearest position that ever I considered, either for authority or reason of law[3].

But this must be taken as ignoring the practice of the Star Chamber[4], and even then there is some show of the contrary

---

[1] 6 Geo. IV c. 50, sect. 6.

[2] The possibility of attaint by the second jury of 24 seems to be recognized by BEREWYK (an itinerant justice) in Y.B. 30 and 31 Ed. I, 522 (Rolls Series). For a different view of this opinion, see Thayer, 162, and, for the history of attaint generally, Thayer, ch. IV. See also St. *H.C.L.* I. 306–307. Hudson (sect. vii) thought that no attaint lay for acquittal of a felon or murderer.          [3] 6 St. Tr. 1010.

[4] VAUGHAN C.J. was of opinion that there had been no punishment there merely for finding against evidence. 6 St. Tr. at p. 1020. But *Throckmorton's Case*, to mention no other, is contrary to this.

practice in the Common Law Courts, and still more as to imprisonment of jurors. The authority is admittedly slender, but some of the efforts to explain it away seem to be strained[1].

In Edward III's reign, a juror who delayed his companions a day and a night without reason was sent to the Fleet[2]; and where 11 jurors agreed that the defendant in trespass was not guilty, and the twelfth juror differed from them, HERLE C.J.C.P. took the verdict of the 11 and adjudged all 12 to prison[3].

On the other hand, a juror in an assize, who was sent to prison by the justices on assize, because he said that he would sooner die than agree with his fellows after two days' difference, had his committal set aside by the Common Bench[4]. And, in Richard II's reign, though TRESILIAN C.J.K.B., on the acquittal of one who had been indicted, told the inquest that the accused was known as a common thief and that they should be bound for his good behaviour from that time onwards, the reporter queries by what law[5]. The fact that a statute passed in Henry VIII's reign requiring jurors in Wales who gave an untrue verdict against the King upon the trial of any traverse, recognizance or forfeiture contrary to good and pregnant evidence to be bound to appear before the Council of the Marches for fine or ransom is evidence of a sort that no power of fining existed at Common Law[6]. And in 3 and 4 Philip and Mary, it was agreed that the justices of assize had no power to fine jurors for a false oath before them, but the justices might appoint a day for their appearance either before themselves or the King's Council. The inference seems to be that if they could not be fined, they were punishable in some way or other[7].

[1] 2 Hawk. P.C. ch. 22, sect. 20 sqq.
[2] 8 Lib. Ass. pl. 35.
[3] Fitz. *Abr. Verdit* 40 citing 3 Ed. III, It. North. The proceeding seems unintelligible, but perhaps the report is too much abridged. In 41 Lib. Ass. pl. 11, the Court strongly reprobated the practice of taking a verdict of 11, and refused to affirm it.
[4] 41 Lib. Ass. pl. 11. It was said that the jury should have been taken from town to town on the circuit till they agreed.
[5] Fitz. *Abr. Corone*, 108 citing Trin. 7 Rich. II (no further reference). 2 Hawk. P.C. ch. 22, sect. 20. Tresilian's evil reputation as a judge makes it more likely that the ruling was a hasty one.
[6] 26 Hen. VIII c. 4, sect. 2. VAUGHAN C.J. in *Bushell's Case* (1670) 6 St. Tr. at p. 1019.    [7] 2 Hawk. P.C. ch. 22, sect. 20.

According to *Wharton's Case* (44 and 45 Eliz.)[1], upon a verdict of not guilty, the judges were very angry, and all the jurors were committed and fined and bound to their good behaviour; but a collateral report shews that some of the jurors were suspected of being friends of the prisoner, and the case is then reducible to one of misconduct[2].

Sir Thomas Smith, Elizabeth's famous Secretary of State, remarks that jurors who returned perverse verdicts might be rebuked by the judges, who might also threaten punishment; but their bark was seemingly worse than their bite, provided the jurors protested their good faith with sufficient humility[3]. Whatever uncertainty appears in the Common Law practice, there was none in that of the Court of Star Chamber. In the reigns of Henry VII, Henry VIII, Mary, and in the beginning of Elizabeth's reign, scarcely a term passed without some grand inquest or jury being fined in the Star Chamber for acquitting felons or murderers[4]. A well-known example occurred in 1554 when Sir Nicholas Throckmorton was acquitted of high treason[5]. The Court was displeased with the verdict, and committed the jurors to prison. Eight who refused to submit were heavily fined by the Council in the Star Chamber[6].

Many of these cases may be regarded as a mere warping of the law for political purposes, and what was done in *Throckmorton's Case* was extreme even for that period of our history[7]. After the Star Chamber fell, there was still some judicial vacillation as to punishing jurors. Grand jurors were occasionally fined for not returning true bills[8]. Petty jurors also were fined in *R. v. Wagstaffe* for returning a verdict against the judge's direction[9], but it was agreed by all the judges of England, except

[1] Yelv. 23.  [2] Noy, 48.
[3] *De Republica Anglorum* (ed. Alston), Bk. III. c. 1.
[4] Hudson, sect. vii. Coke refers to the Star Chamber practice in *Floyd v. Barker* (5 Jac. I) 12 Rep. 23.
[5] 1 St. Tr. 869.  [6] Thayer, 162–163.
[7] One of the charges against Empson was that he had imprisoned a jury and fined each member £8 for refusing to convict a person of larceny on sufficient evidence. Yet he did this with the consent of the King's Council. 2 Hawk. P.C. ch. 22, sect. 20.
[8] *R. v. Brown* (16 Car. II) 1 Siderf. 229. *R. v. Windham* (19 Car. II) 2 Keb. 180.
[9] (17 Car. II) 1 Siderf. 282. T. Raym. 138. 1 Keb. 934, 938.

one, that this fine was illegal[1]. In *R. v. Selby* (1664)[2], the Court ordered an information against petty jurors for a verdict contrary to clear evidence. And we are told that KELYNG C.J.K.B. was obliged to answer a complaint in Parliament that he had fined jurors, and that it was only the mediation of his friends that prevented an angry House of Commons from bringing him to trial[3].

To sum up, no decided conclusions as to the law on this point down to 1670 can be stated. Juries were often punished in the Star Chamber for verdicts distasteful to the trial judges. Apart from this, the practice of the Common Law Courts wavered, but with an inclination against the punishment of jurors. There was no positive recognition that it was legal. Hale's conclusion is that although long use may possibly have given the King's Bench a jurisdiction of fining jurors in criminal cases, yet this did not extend to other Courts of sessions, of gaol delivery, oyer and terminer, or of the peace or other inferior jurisdiction[4].

So stood the matter when *Bushell's Case* came before the Courts in 1670. Bushell was one of a jury which had acquitted prisoners of unlawful assembly against full and manifest evidence and against the direction of the Court in a matter of law. The justices of oyer and terminer fined him 40 marks and committed him to the Old Bailey. He sued out *habeas corpus*. The return, which alleged the above facts, was held to be incomplete on technical grounds, and Bushell was discharged. But the Court went further, and resolved that petty jurors are in no case finable for a verdict against evidence delivered in Court, whether they be liable to attaint or not, because the jury are by law judges of fact and therefore ought to be free, and it is not possible that the judge should know certainly that the verdict is corrupt[5]. With the decay of the attaint and the

---

[1] 2 Hale P.C. 313.                                    [2] 1 Keb. 769.
[3] 1 Siderf. 338 note. Foss *sub tit.* "Kelyng." Kelyng notes in his Reports (p. 50) a case in which he fined a jury £5 apiece for returning a verdict of manslaughter instead of murder (18 Car. II).
[4] 2 P.C. 313. Hale died in 1676. The first publication of P.C. was in 1739.
[5] VAUGHAN C.J. in 6 St. Tr. 999, 1021.

impossibility of punishing jurors for a perverse verdict after *Bushell's Case*, the law had no control over a verdict except by the grant of a new trial. There were also exceptional cases to which *Bushell's Case* did not apply.

(i)  It might perhaps be an offence if an inquest of office refused to find an office for the King against clear proof; for such inquests were not subject to attaint, and determined no man's rights[1].

(ii)  It was said that if a jury find the facts and then refuse, against the judge's direction, to find an inference of law from those facts, they are fineable[2].

[1] VAUGHAN C.J. in 6 St. Tr. at p. 1021. *Lamnois' Case*, Moore, 730. See 2 Hawk. P.C. ch. 22, sect. 23 for a criticism of the principle.

[2] VAUGHAN C.J. (6 St. Tr. at pp. 1008–1009) recognized such an exception, but thought it only possible in theory. Cf. 2 Hawk. P.C. ch. 22, sect. 21.

# CHAPTER VIII

## COMMON BARRATRY AND FRIVOLOUS ARRESTS

§ 1. The legal definition of Common Barratry is no older than the time of Elizabeth, though the terms "barrator" and "barret"—especially the former—were known to our law centuries earlier with a meaning so vague as to be wellnigh unascertainable. Nor does the Elizabethan definition carry us much further. It occurs in the *Case of Barretry* reported by Coke[1], who states that it was held by the Court that a common barrator is a common mover or stirrer up, or maintainer of suits, quarrels, or parties, either in Courts or in the country: in Courts of record, and in the county, hundred, and other inferior Courts: in the country in three manners:

- (i) In disturbance of the peace.
- (ii) In taking or detaining of the possession of houses, lands or goods, etc., which are in question or controversy, not only by force, but also by subtilty and deceit, and for the most part in suppression of truth and right.
- (iii) By false invention, and sowing of calumny, rumours and reports, whereby discord and disquiet arise between neighbours.

The report is of a type not uncommon in Coke. No facts are given, and how much of it is Coke and how much what the Court said, is not easy to determine. Its general diffuseness, scraps of Latin, and citation of the Pentateuch indicate the reporter rather than the bench. The definition in it is repeated in Coke upon Littleton as part of the comment on a passage in which Littleton says that if *F* enfeoff certain barrators and extortioners in the country, to have maintenance from them of the house by a deed of feoffment with warranty, by force whereof *A* (the lawful tenant) dare not abide in the house, the warranty commences by disseisin[2].

So far as the definition given in the *Case of Barretry* refers

---

[1] (30 Eliz.) 8 Rep. 36.   [2] Co. *Litt.* 368.

to stirring up litigation in Courts, so far is it intelligible. But when it goes on to describe barratry "in the country," it seems to poach upon other preserves of the law to an astonishing extent. It would include the common brawler, the land-grabber, the forger, the slanderer, the sedition-monger, the lying journalist. Of course, no judicial decisions have gone to such lengths as these, and common barratry has fallen into such oblivion that no Court is likely to have a chance of trimming the Elizabethan definition. There have been few enough decisions on common barratry at any time, and most of them fell in the period of indifferent law reporting. In none of them except the *Case of Barretry* does an analysis of the term appear to have been attempted.

Whether the Court in that case gave the loose description reported, or whether Coke edited what they did say into something very different, is not of much moment. What is important is that Coke probably reproduced a current legal idea or something like it, and that the history of the term "barrator" fully excused considerable vagueness in expressing its meaning. And to that history we now turn.

§ 2. Before confining ourselves to barratry in the only sense here relevant, we must note that it has several other legal meanings. In Scots law, it has been used to signify the purchase or sale of ecclesiastical preferment or of offices of state; and also acceptance of bribes by a judge. In English maritime law, certain forms of fraud and misconduct by masters and mariners are designated barratry.

The origin of "barrat" from which these meanings, and that of stirring up suits, spring, is doubtful. According to one view, the original sense in Romanic is "traffic, commerce, dealing"; another connects it with πράττειν; a third with the Welsh "brad" (betrayal or treachery); and the Old Norse "barátta" (fight, contest, strife) appears to have influenced the word in the sense of "strife." Be this as it may, in the commonest meaning of the word—which is also its legal one—the idea of cheating seems to be combined with that of fighting, the latter predominating[1].

[1] *N.E.D.* "Barrat," "Barratry." Cf. Coke in 8 Rep. 37 *a*.

§ 3. Early statutes take the meaning for granted. The Statute West. I (3 Ed. I) c. 33 provides that no sheriff shall suffer any barrator [or maintainers of quarrels][1] in their shires[2], nor stewards of great lords nor others, who are not attornies for their lords, to give judgments in the counties, unless they be specially prayed so to do by all the suitors and attornies of the suitors at the Court. For disobedience, both the sheriff and the offender are to be punished grievously by the King.

This statute, which is now repealed[3], is said to have been the result of abuses which sprang up from the Statute of Merton (20 Hen. III) c. 10[4]. This allowed every free suitor of the county and other Courts to appoint an attorney to act for him there. Two mischievous consequences ensued. Barrators and maintainers were encouraged by the sheriff to become attornies, to give judgments among the other suitors and occasionally perhaps to take the lead in giving such judgments. And stewards of great lords and others who had no letters of attorney as required by the statute would do the like. It was to check this perversion of agency in litigation that 3 Ed. I c. 33 passed[5].

Another chapter of the same Statute of Westminster[6] struck at misconduct of the sheriffs in another direction. It appeared that when the justices in eyre had amerced the whole county for false judgments or other trespass, sheriffs and barrators had assessed the amount of the penal sum at a much higher rate than was just, presumably pocketing the difference. This was stopped by requiring that the sum should be assessed in the presence of the justices in eyre, and before their departure, by the oath of the knights and other honest men[7].

The Statute called Rageman, which has been dated 4 Ed. I, instructs the justices of assize as to the object of their inquiries, and enjoins them that no complainant or defendant is to be

[1] "To maintain" is the variant in *St. of the Realm*, I. 35.
[2] As "conte" is the word in the text, Dalton (*Sheriffs*, p. 31) seems right in suggesting this to be a mistranslation for "county courts."
[3] S.L.R. Act, 1863 (England). S.L. (I) R. Act, 1872 (Ireland).
[4] *St of the Realm*, I. 4.
[5] Coke, 2 Inst. 225. Reeves, *H.E.L.* II. 128.
[6] 3 Ed. I c. 18. *St. of the Realm*, I. 31.
[7] Repealed S.L.R. Act, 1863 (England). S.L. (I) R. Act, 1872 (Ireland).

surprised or troubled by "hoketours[1] ou barettours," whereby
the truth may not be found out, and offenders remain un-
punished till the next Parliament.

We have seen that sheriffs and barrators were coupled together in statutes in a way that did not flatter the probity of
the former. From Magna Carta onwards, the duty of the
sheriff in his tourn or circuit through the hundreds of the
county was to take indictments against prisoners, and not to
try them. He abused his power by falsely charging persons
with having been indicted in his tourn. A series of complaints
redressed by remedies more or less effectual culminated, in
1327, in the King's justices being ordered to take cognizance
of false indictments, and in the establishment of the county
magistracy from which maintainers of evil and barrators were
to be excluded[2], and which reduced the sheriff's influence and
gave him a subordinate part in the administration of justice[3].

34 Ed. III c. 1, in defining the powers of those assigned to
keep the peace, enables them to restrain offenders, rioters, and
all other barrators, and to pursue, arrest, take, and chastise them
according to their trespass or offence, and to cause them to be
imprisoned and duly punished according to the laws and customs
of the realm, and to what they think best in their discretion[4].

Soon after Richard II's accession, certain lords and others
were commissioned in every county with power to arrest, among
others, barrators, and to imprison them without bail till the
coming of the justices[5]. But this statute speedily illustrated the
axiom that it matters little whether the law ignores or threatens
a rogue so long as its administration is in his hands. Peaceful
people were more frequently arrested and imprisoned by the
commissioners than were evil-doers, partly because some of
the commissioners themselves were corrupt, partly because
false accusations were made before them. The Commons requested and obtained the repeal of the statute.

---

[1] According to Coke, an ancient French word for a knight of the post
(worthy to be knit to a post), a decayed man, a basket-carrier. 3 Inst. 175.
So too *N.E.D.* "Hockettor."

[2] 1 Ed. III st. 2, c. 16. *St. of the Realm*, I. 258. It was in reply to a
prayer of the Commons. *Rot. Parl.* II. 11 a. It is still in force.

[3] *Select Cases before the King's Council*, S. S. vol. XXXIV. pp. lxxxiv–lxxxv.

[4] Unrepealed.          [5] 2 Rich. II st. 2, c. 2. Cf. *Rot. Parl.* III. 65 a.

§ 4. Such are the early statutes which relate to, or mention, barrators[1]. One thing that is clear is that they attach no technical meaning to "barrator." A barrator perhaps signified to the lawyer, generally but not invariably, a rascal in litigation, though he could not be ear-marked as a maintainer, champertor, conspirator, or embracer. What in modern law the bully is to the man who commits an assault, the scamp to the man who steals, the swindler to the fraudulent company promoter, that in ancient law was the barrator to the man who committed champerty or embracery. And just as modern law does not embark on futile attempts to punish all bullies, scamps and swindlers, so the early law has very little to say about the punishment of barrators. When the justices were empowered by 34 Ed. III c. 1 to arrest and punish "rioters and all other barrators," probably the legislator understood barrators to be brawlers of some sort, perhaps brawlers connected with litigation. The age was not one in which there was any craze for exact legal definition, as we have seen in the case of conspiracy. In popular speech, a barrator might be a hired bully or quarrelsome person[2], and in legal texts we get similar variations. When we are told that barrators and embracers each took 20s. from the defendant in an action, we are left in the dark as to what the barrators did for their pay[3]; but we have no doubt that it was some sort of perversion of legal process. Elsewhere, they appear as persons who disturb the collection of an aid[4], as those who by false suggestion in the King's Courts delay the King's servants in rendering their accounts[5], as those who are agents of great men for the purpose of threatening physically such as wish to recover lands of which the great men have been enfeoffed for maintenance[6]. As late as the 17th and 18th centuries, judicial decisions were needed to settle that "common barrator"

[1] Ordinatio de Conspiratoribus, 33 Ed. I (*St. of the Realm*, I. 145; *Rot. Parl.* I. 183 *b*) includes, in its definition of conspirators, stewards and bailiffs of great men who undertake to maintain or sustain pleas or "baretz" for parties. *Ante* p. 1.

[2] *N.E.D.*                                        [3] Trin. 40 Ed. III, f. 33.
[4] *Rot. Parl.* II. 117 *b* (A.D. 1340).          [5] *Ibid.* 167 *a* (A.D. 1347).
[6] *Ibid.* III. 21 *a* (A.D. 1377). In II. 165 *a* (A.D. 1347), an ordinance is asked for by the Commons against great men maintaining *inter alios* barrators, maintainers of quarrels and "baretz," embracers, conspirators, confederators, and champertors.

was a technical term which had no such equivalent as "common oppressor of his neighbours"[1], "common and turbulent brawler, and sower of discord among her neighbours"[2], "calumniator and turbulent disturber of the peace, and mover and inciter of actions, brawls and fights"[3].

§ 5. The question whether common barratry is a Common Law or statutory offence has been answered in a curious way. No one who drew an indictment for it had the courage to omit *contra formam statuti*[4]. No opponent succeeded with the argument that the offence was one at Common Law, and that therefore the draftsman's conclusion was wrong. No Court would give a positive decision that the offence was a statutory one, and only a statutory one. The result was a number of cases in which a familiar path came to be trodden. What appears to be one of the earliest may be taken as a specimen. A man was indicted as a common barrator *contra formam statuti*. Coke (then counsel) took exception that there was no statute making this an offence, but that it was at Common Law, and that 34 Ed. III c. 1[5] did not make it an offence, but merely appointed the punishment. But the indictment was held good, and it was said that there were many precedents to that effect[6]. While however the Courts had no doubt that it was a statutory offence, they would not pin themselves to any particular statute. They passed an indictment *contra formam diversorum statutorum* because common barratry, they said, was an offence against the statutes of maintenance and the like[7], and they even swallowed a barbarism like *contra formam statuti de Good-behaviour* as being the constant form of such indictments[8]. But the mere fact that the draftsman resorted to such a desperate expedient, and that the Court adopted it without denying that common barratry was a Common Law offence, shews on the

[1] *R. v. Hardwicke* (18 Car. II) 1 Siderf. 282. *R. v. Ledginham* (20 Car. II) 1 Mod. 288. [2] *R. v. Cooper* (19 Geo. II) Stra. 1246.
[3] *R. v. Taylor* (3 Geo. II) Stra. 849.
[4] The last instance is exceptional. Arch. (ed. 22) 1027 (indictment in *R. v. Bellgrave* (1889), Guildford Assizes). [5] *Ante* sect. 3.
[6] *Burton's Case* (31 and 32 Eliz.) Cro. Eliz. 148. *Bowser's Case* (15 Jac. I) 2 Roll. Abr. 79, pl. 3 is to the same effect.
[7] *Chapman's Case* (9 Car. I) Cro. Car. 340.
[8] *R. v. Clayton* (20 Car. II) 2 Keb. 409.

one hand that there was no statute which created the offence as such, and, on the other hand, that if common barratry were a Common Law crime, it became such only comparatively late in our history. In fact, the term began life with no technical meaning, and, as has been shewn, acquired none till the Tudor period. We find scarcely a word about barratry in the Year Books. Perhaps this is because the barrator could be laid by the heels as a maintainer or conspirator. There was law enough in theory to deal with these. How miserably it failed in practice has been shewn *ad nauseam* elsewhere.

Later judicial opinion is that while common barratry is a Common Law offence, yet it is right to conclude *contra formam statuti*[1], and in the last instance of it the experiment was tried—whether successfully or not, we are not told—of dropping this conclusion[2]. The older commentators in general have views similar to the judicial opinion[3]. Since the rules appended to the Indictments Act, 1915, make the technical conclusion needless in any indictment, the point is of no practical importance[4].

§ 6. *The offence in modern times.* The definition which has been quoted from the *Case of Barretry*[5] is reproduced in a condensed form by Blackstone as "the offence of frequently exciting and stirring up suits and quarrels between his majesty's subjects, either at law or otherwise"[6]. Text-books of the present day repeat this[7], or adhere to the full definition in the *Case of Barretry*[8]. Any definition can be little more than a museum label, for the law on this topic is in an almost fossil condition. The last recorded case occurred a generation ago[9], and no other case appears to have been reported during the 19th century. The abolition of the offence was recommended

---

[1] *R.* v. *Bracy* (8 Will. III) 12 Mod. 99. *Obiter per curiam.*

[2] Arch. (ed. 22) 1026–7, citing *R.* v. *Bellgrave* (1889) and indictment therein.

[3] 2 Hale P.C. 191. 1 Hawk. P.C. ch. 81, sect. 10. 2 Chitty, *Cr. Law*, 232 note.

[4] 5 and 6 Geo. V c. 90.

[5] *Ante* sect. 1.     [6] IV. 133.

[7] St. Dig. Cr. Law Art. 156. He criticizes the definition as "so vague as to be quite absurd." *Ibid.* App. Note III. Arch. (ed. 1918) 1146.

[8] Russ. (ed. 1909) I. 585.

[9] *R.* v. *Bellgrave* (1889) Arch. (ed. 22) 1026. A prosecution for stirring up a series of fraudulent actions against a railway company.

in the Fifth Report of the Criminal Law Commissioners. The details given in the following sections must be regarded as relating to an offence which is practically obsolete.

§ 7. The definition implies that the offender must be described as a "common" barrator. A man cannot be a barrator in respect of one act only[1]. Nor, as has been indicated, can similar terms be used for "common barrator" in an indictment[2], for that is the only description which the law recognizes and understands[3]. The crime is a well-recognized exception to the rule that the description of a person accused in an indictment as being a "common" offender without specifying particular examples makes the indictment too general[4]. When this became the settled rule is not clear[5], but it was recognized in Charles II's reign[6]. Nor does the accused suffer any injustice from this; for by a practice equally well established, the prosecutor must supply him with a note of the particulars of the charge, otherwise the trial will not proceed[7]. The accused can, it seems, move for a rule to have such particulars delivered to him, and the prosecutor cannot give evidence of any particular not included in the notice[8], except possibly to aggravate the punishment[9].

§ 8. It has been said that, if a man prosecute an infinite number of suits which are his own, he is not a barrator; for, if they are false, the defendants get their costs against him, and the contrary rule would include amongst barrators those who have some cause for suing[10]. But this rule has been doubted[11],

---

[1] *Case of Barretry* (30 Eliz.) 8 Rep. 36. 1 Hawk. P.C. ch. 81, sect. 5.

[2] *Ante* sect. 4, *sub fin.* and cases there cited. See too *Cornwall's Case* (33 and 34 Eliz.) Moore, 302.

[3] *R.* v. *Ledginham* (20 Car. II) 1 Mod. 288. The case is reported under three different names in three other reports (2 Keb. 697; 1 Lev. 299; T. Raym. 193, 205).

[4] *Per* HOLT C.J. and six other judges in *R.* v. *Baynes* (5 Anne) 2 Salk. 681.

[5] BULLER J. in *J'Anson* v. *Stuart* (1787) 1 T.R. at p. 754.

[6] *R.* v. *Ledginham* (*ubi sup.*).

[7] *R.* v. *Grove* (6 W. and M.) 5 Mod. 18. HEATH J. in *R.* v. *Wylie* (1804) 1 B. and P. (N.R.) at p. 95. Recognized as an exceptional practice by the Lord Chancellor in *Clark* v. *Periam* (1742) 2 Atk. at p. 340.

[8] *Obiter* by all the Court in *Goddard* v. *Smith* (3 Anne) 6 Mod. 261. In *R.* v. *Ward* (13 Will. III) 12 Mod. 516, notice of the particulars was adjudged ill, because it was left with the accused's servant.

[9] *Iveson* v. *Moore* (11 Will. III) 1 Ld. Raym. at p. 490.

[10] 1 Roll. Abr. 355.      [11] 1 Hawk. P.C. ch. 81, sect. 3.

and it proceeds upon the double fallacy that a defendant is sufficiently compensated for vexatious litigation by getting his costs, and that the law would ever classify as a barrator a plaintiff who has any reasonable ground for litigation. However, the rule, if it exist, need trouble no defendant at the present day. If the proceedings instituted against him are criminal or in general of the kind redressible by an action for malicious prosecution, he has that remedy, and if they amount to a criminal conspiracy, he can indict for that offence. As to civil proceedings, the Vexatious Actions Act, 1896, provides that if any person has habitually and persistently instituted vexatious legal proceedings without reasonable ground, in any Court, against the same person or different persons, the High Court may, on the Attorney-General's application, order that no legal proceedings shall be instituted by that person in any Court, unless he obtain the leave of a judge of the High Court, and satisfy him that such legal proceeding is not an abuse of process[1].

§ 9. It has also been said that an attorney is in no danger of being judged guilty of barratry for maintaining another in a groundless action to the commencement of which he was in no way privy. In the case cited for this, the defendant, a barrister, was indicted for barratry. One, G, had been arrested at C's suit in an action for £4000, and was brought before a judge to give bail to the action. The defendant was then present, and solicited the suit, when in fact C was indebted to G in £200, and G owed C nothing. The Chief Justice was first of opinion that this might be maintenance, but not barratry, unless it appeared that the defendant knew that C had no cause of action after it was brought. If a man's design in making an arrest be not to recover his own right, but only to ruin and oppress his neighbour, that is barratry; so is the loan of money to promote suits. Here the defendant had entertained C in his house and brought several actions in his name where nothing was due, and he had therefore committed barratry. But if an action be first brought, and then prosecuted by another, it is not barratry, though there is no cause of action. The defendant was found guilty[2].

---

[1] 59 and 60 Vict. c. 51, sect. 1.
[2] R. v. —— (1 and 2 Jac. II) 3 Mod. 97.

Misconduct of this kind could now be remedied more expeditiously in the case of an attorney by making him pay the defendant's costs[1], or by taking disciplinary proceedings under the Solicitors Acts to strike him off the Rolls. And similarly steps could be taken to get a barrister disbarred.

It has been held that an agreement between *A*, a certificated conveyancer, and *B* an attorney, that in case *A* should introduce to *B* any professional business for which *B* would have a claim for costs, *B* would pay *A* a commission, is not such an agreement as would subject the parties to the penalties of common barratry[2].

§ 10. According to a meagre report, an indictment of a *feme covert* as a common barrator was quashed[3]. The decision has been criticized[4] and seems unintelligible unless it were one in which the presumption of marital coercion was raised.

§ 11. Upon the whole, it appears that it is unnecessary to allege in the indictment that the offence was committed at any particular place. An exception to an indictment on this ground was rejected in *R.* v. *Clayton*[5], and the Court seems to have ignored an opinion to the contrary in *Man's Case*[6]. Modern writers on criminal law favour the view that the place need not be specified. Its justification is that barratry consists in the repetition of several acts which may well have happened in several places[7].

§ 12. One or two other points as to the indictment have, since the Indictments Act, 1915, become of purely historical interest. An indictment was held insufficient for concluding "against the peace of our lord the king, or against the form of the statute"[8], and one was quashed which did not conclude

---

[1] R.S.C. 1883, Order LXV. r. 1.
[2] *Scott* v. *Miller* (1859) 28 L.J. (N.S.) Ch. 584.
[3] *Anon.* (16 Jac. I) 2 Roll. 39.
[4] 1 Hawk. P.C. ch. 81, sect. 5. Russ. 1. 585. Chitty, *Cr. Law*, 232 a.
[5] (20 Car. II) 2 Keb. 409.
[6] (3 Car. I) Godbolt, 383. 2 Hale P.C. 180 approves *Man's Case*, without rejecting the practice of naming no vill. In *R.* v. *Wells* (13 Jac. I) 1 Roll. 295, COKE C.J.K.B. implies that the place should be stated.
[7] 1 Hawk. P.C. ch. 81, sect. 11. Russ. 1. 586. In 2 Chitty, *Cr. Law*, 232, no reference to place is made in the form of indictment there given. Cf. Arch. (ed. 22) 1027.
[8] *Palfrey's Case* (17 Jac. I) Cro. Jac. 527.

"against the peace" though "against the form of the statute" preceded this[1]. More modern indictments concluded "to the common nuisance of the liege subjects of our lord the King"[2].

It may be added here that there is some doubt as to whether *procendedo* applies to an indictment for barratry[3].

§ 13. Common barratry is a misdemeanour punishable by fine, imprisonment, and binding over to good behaviour[4]. A distinction has been drawn between ordinary persons who incur no further penalties, and those of any profession relating to the law, who, it is said, ought to suffer the additional punishment of being disabled from practice for the future[5]. And in *Alwin's Case*[6], an attorney, proved to have been guilty of false practice and barratry, was ordered to be put out of the roll of attornies, to be fined £50, to be turned over the bar, and to stand committed. And turned over the West end of the bar he accordingly was. But something worse than this awaits, in theory at least, attornies or solicitors who, after being convicted of common barratry, act in their professional capacity in any Court of law or equity. A statute empowers the judge of the Court, where the action is brought, to examine the matter in a summary way in open Court, and to sentence the offender to seven years transportation (now penal servitude)[7]. This law, says Stephen, would be utterly intolerable if it had not been long forgotten. I should suppose that there is no other enactment in the whole statute book which authorises any judge to sentence a man to seven years penal servitude after a summary inquiry conducted by himself in his own way[8].

The statute is unrepealed, but the jurisdiction of the Law Society over its members is a better safeguard against the malpractices of solicitors than the savage punishment of a statute passed at a time when abuses of the kind were not uncommon.

---

[1] *Periam's Case* (6 Car. I) 2 Roll. Abr. 82, pl. 5. *R.* v. *Urlyn* (17 Car. II) Saund. 308, exemplifies a verdict held good in spite of surplusage in the conclusion.

[2] 2 Chitty, *Cr. Law*, 232. Arch. (ed. 22) 1027.

[3] *Upham's Case* (14 and 15 Car. II) 1 Lev. 93.

[4] 1 Hawk. P.C. ch. 81, sect. 14. Bl. IV. 133 omits the binding over to good behaviour.

[5] 1 Hawk. P.C. *ubi sup.*      [6] (1655) Style, 483.

[7] 12 Geo. I c. 29, sect. 4.      [8] Dig. Cr. Law. App. Note III.

§ 14. In spite of 34 Ed. III c. 1, which is still in force and which enables those assigned to keep the peace to punish barrators, doubts have arisen as to whether common barratry is triable at Quarter Sessions. The judges of Henry VII's reign had no hesitation in saying that the Statute empowered Justices of the Peace to arrest and imprison every common barrator till he found surety for his good behaviour[1]. And from *Barnes* v. *Constantine*[2] it may be inferred that Justices of the Peace have not only authority to restrain barrators, but that they can do so without any special commission of oyer and terminer, for all the judges except one acceded to the defendant's demand for oyer of the record, though it made no reference to any such special commission[3]. On the other hand, it was held in an anonymous case of James I's reign that barratry is an offence of a mixed nature of which the Justices at Sessions of the Peace have no cognizance by virtue of their commission of the peace[4]; and in *R. v. Nurse* a verdict of guilty was reversed for the reason, among others, that it was tried by the Justices of oyer and terminer instead of those of gaol delivery[5]. Since 5 and 6 Vict. c. 38, sect. 1, there should be little doubt that the offence is triable at Quarter Sessions. That statute enumerates the crimes which are not triable at Quarter Sessions, and common barratry is not included in the list.

§ 15. In the same category as common barratry Blackstone puts "an offence of equal malignity and audaciousness; that of suing another in the name of a fictitious plaintiff; either one not in being at all, or who is ignorant of the suit." This offence, he says, if committed in any of the King's superior Courts, is punishable as a high contempt at their discretion; in Courts of a lower degree, the punishment is fixed by 8 Eliz. c. 2[6]. Sect. 4 of this statute provides that if any person shall maliciously cause any other person to be arrested or attached to answer in

---

[1] *Anon.* (13 Hen. VII) Keilwey, 41.

[2] (2 Jac. I) Cro. Jac. 32; Yelv. 46.

[3] *R. v. Clayton* (20 Car. II) 2 Keb. 409, is indirect evidence that it is triable at Quarter Sessions, but by what commission is not stated.

[4] (17 Jac. I) 2 Roll. 151.

[5] (19 Car. II) Siderf. 348. 2 Keb. 292. 1 Hawk. P.C. ch. 81, sect. 8 and Russ. 1. 586 reflect the doubt. Arch. (ed. 1918) 1146 states that Quarter Sessions have jurisdiction.          [6] IV. 134.

the Courts named in the Act, at the suit or in the name of a person where none such is known, the person causing the arrest or attachment shall be imprisoned for six months, pay treble the costs and damages of the person arrested, and shall also forfeit £10 to the person in whose name the arrest or attachment was procured. Sect. 5 gives an action for the recovery of these penalties, costs and damages. These provisions are still in force, except that as to treble costs which was repealed by 5 and 6 Vict. c. 97[1].

It does not clearly appear that 8 Eliz. c. 2, sect. 4 is, as Blackstone states, limited to inferior Courts; but the whole statute is such a specimen of diffuse and slovenly drafting that it is patient of that construction[2].

The offence is also maintenance, and an action upon the case has been held to lie for it[3]; and it would usually involve perjury[4].

---

[1] Sect. 2. The Public Authorities Protection Act, 1893 (56 and 57 Vict. c. 61), sect. 2 repeals this sect. as to any proceeding.to which the Public Authorities Protection Act applies.

[2] Of course, the superior Courts have, at Common Law, the power of punishing a contempt of this kind. *Waterhouse* v. *Saltmarsh* (17 Jac. I) Hob. 263; and in the very year in which 8 Eliz. c. 2 passed, one of them fined a man for such a contempt. *Worlay* v. *Harrison* (8 Eliz.) Dyer, 249 a. Inferior Courts can commit only for contempt perpetrated *in facie curiae*. Oswald, *Contempts* (ed. 1910), 11.

[3] *Thurston* v. *Ummons* (15 Car. I) March, 147.

[4] Russ. I. 586. There it is treated under the head, "Frivolous Arrests."

# INDEX

Jurors (*contd.*)
challenge, 178
conspiracy, 61, 69, 70–71, 108
conspirators excluded, 100
entertainment, 182
evidence to, 184–189
expenses, 172–174
fire, 184
illness, 180, 184
indecision of, 189–190, 196
knowledge, 188–189
maintenance, 137
misconduct, 175–199
absence, 176–177, 178–180, 184, 187
affidavit of, 192–193
bias, 190–193
bribery, 175–176
casting lots, 189–190, 192
conspiracy, 69, 70–71
contempt, a, 176, 177, 178–180, 182 sqq.
corruption, 7, 14, 15, 107
default, 176–177
departure, 178–180, 184, 187
drinking, 181–184
eating, 181–184
entertainment, 182
evidence, as to, 192, 193
evidence, reception of, 184–189
false presentment, 14
imposing on Court, 189–190
indecision, 189–190, 196
maintenance, 137
oath, false, 193
perjury, 99
personation of, 193
physic, 184
proof of, 192–193
refreshment, 181–184
refusal
to be sworn, 177–178
to give verdict, 180–181
separation, 179–180
smoking, 179
talking with, 179, 186–188
treating, 183–184
verdict, after, 193
false, 193–199
improper, 176, 189–190, 192
perverse, 197–199
punishment for, 195–199
refusal to give, 180–181
personation of, 193
physic, 184
procurers of, 95
punishment for verdict, 195–199
refreshment, 173, 174, 178, 179, 181–184

Jurors (*contd.*)
separation, 179–180, 184, 187
special, 173
talking with, 186–188
threats against, 174–175
verdict. *See* Verdict (*also* "misconduct" *supra*)
witness, as, 71, 172, 188–189, 195
Jury, trial by
writ *de odio*, 17 sqq.
Justices of Peace
conspiracy
defence to, 78–80
guilty of, 154
to check, 103
special sessions for livery, etc., 158
unprincipled, 107

Kelyng, 198
Kinship
appeals, in false, 12
defence to
conspiracy, 73*n.*, 77
embracery, 172
maintenance, 134, 148

Lancashire, false charges in, 106
Lawyers
defence to
champerty, 148
conspiracy, etc. *See* Advice
embracery, 172
maintenance, 148
retainer allowed, 158
Legal advice. *See* Advice
Leges Henrici Primi, 4
Leicester, Earl of, 166
*Lex*, 33
Lilleshall, Abbot of, 4
Lincolnshire, conspiracies in, 95*n.*
Livery, 1, 52, 60, 140, 156–157, 158, 161
London, complaints of citizens of, 27, 94

Magna Carta, 20
Maintenance, 65*n.*, 90*n.*, 100*n.*, 103, 104, 131–160
aiding malefactors, 134, 155*n.*
apprentice. *See* Apprentice
attorney. *See* Attorney
bailiffs, 52, 60
barratry, 200, 202, 204, 206
civil remedy, 151
clergy, 154–155
combination for, 113
Common Law, at? 138–150
commonest, when, 161
Commons, complaint of, 140

Maintenance (*contd.*)
  complaint of, 165
  confederacy, 97
  conspiracy, 95, 146
  Council, by, 154
  counsel. *See* Counsel
  criminal proceedings, of, 136
  *curialis*, 131, 135–136, 167
  De Conspiratoribus Ordinatio, 26
  definition, 131, 136
  election petition, 133–134
  embracery, 162, 167, 168, 169, 174
  Exchequer officials, 154n.
  excommunication for, 102–103
  fictitious plaintiff, 212
  general, 131, 136–138
  heretics, of, 134
  history, 131–160
  judges. *See* Judges
  jurors. *See* Jurors
  justices. *See* Justices of Peace
  kin, of, 134, 148
  King, by, 154
  legal advice, 148
  livery, 156–157
  lords, 151–152
  meaning, 135, 140, 144n.
  Middlesex, in, 155
  neighbours, 148
  Northumberland, in, 155
  officials. *See* Officials
  Ordinance of Conspirators, 60
  origin, 138–150
  pardon of, 105
  pending plea, of, 133
  pleaders. *See* Pleaders
  rebels, of, 134
  remedies
    failure of, 154–157
    *temp.* Ed. I, 150
    *temp.* Rich. II, 150–154
  *ruralis*, 131, 132–135, 150
  special, 131, 136–138
  Statute of Conspirators, 22, 23, 24,
    25, 40, 51, 52
  statutes of, 142 sqq.
  stewards. *See* Stewards
  tenants, 134
  term of pleading, 135
Malice
  in appeals, 9, 10
  in conspiracy, 66
Malicious prosecution, 118, 208. *See
  also* Case
*Manutenentia*, 131
  *curialis*, 135–136, 167
  *ruralis*, 132–135, 150
Married woman. *See* Wife
Ministers. *See* Officers

Mirrour, The
  conspiracy, 29, 30, 94
  *de odio*, writ, 19
  false appeals, 7
Misconduct of jurors. *See* Jurors
Misdemeanour
  false indictments of, 53, 54n.

New trial, 173, 179, 180, 182 sqq.
Norfolk, champerty in, 155
Northumberland
  maintenance in, 155
Nul tiel record, 90

*Odio et atia*, writ de, 15–22
Officials, royal
  abuse of procedure, 99
  champerty, 24–25, 144–145, 147
  conspiracy, defence to, 80–81
  maintenance, 24–25, 132, 142–146
  offences of, 151–153
*Officina brevium*, 36, 39
Outlawry, 30, 106

Palgrave, 99n., 104n.
Pardon, of conspirators, etc., 105
Perjury, 212
Perrers, Alice, 155
Place, of conspiracy, 89–90
Pleaders, 22
  champerty, 148
  maintenance, 146
Pleas
  appeals, to, 16
  Common, 92
  Crown, of the, 92
  meaning, 41
Presentment, 13n., 14
Procedure
  civil and criminal, 92–93
  conspiracy, in writ of, 89–91
Procurement
  conspiracy, in writ of, 81–83
Prosecutions, repeated, 207–208
Provers, 6, 7

"Quarrels," 40, 51, 103, 143, 200, 202
*Quia multi per malitiam*, Statute, 6
*Querelae*, 40

Registrum Brevium, 29n., 34
  champerty, 141n., 141–142, 144
  conspiracy, 31 sqq., 66, 81, 82
  *decies tantum*, 164n.
  maintenance, 152–154
  organic nature of, 35
Richard II, feeble rule of, 165
Rokell, John, 165n.
Roman Law, 93, 156

Printed in the United States
149113LV00003B/42/A